INTO THE HEART
OF THE MAFIA

Also by David Lane

Berlusconi's Shadow: Crime, Justice and the Pursuit of Power

INTO THE
HEART
OF THE
MAFIA

A Journey Through the Italian South

DAVID LANE

Thomas Dunne Books
St. Martin's Press
New York

THOMAS DUNNE BOOKS.
An imprint of St. Martin's Press.

INTO THE HEART OF THE MAFIA. Copyright © 2009 by David Lane. All rights reserved. Printed in the United States of America. For information, address St. Martin's Press, 175 Fifth Avenue, New York, N.Y. 10010.

www.stmartins.com

Library of Congress Cataloging-in-Publication Data

Lane, David (David Colin)
    Into the heart of the mafia / David Lane. — 1st U.S. ed.
        p. cm.
    Includes bibliographical references and index.
    ISBN 978-0-312-61434-8
    1. Mafia—Italy—History. I. Title.
HV6453.I83M354332 2010
364.1'60945—dc22

                                                    2010002344

First published in Great Britain by Profile Books Ltd

First U.S. Edition: June 2010

10   9   8   7   6   5   4   3   2   1

For my wife Franca and in memory of her parents Michele and Angelina
three fine southerners

CONTENTS

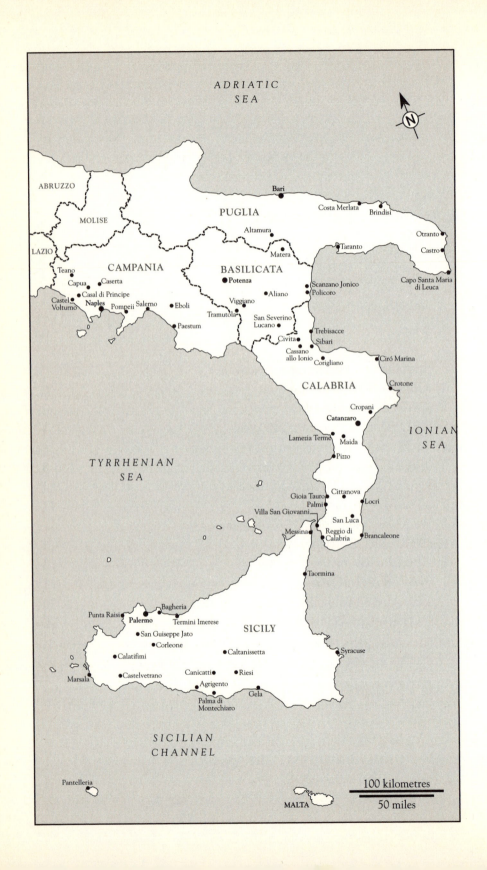

ADRIATIC
SEA

N

ABRUZZO

MOLISE

PUGLIA

Bari

Costa Merlata

Brindisi

LAZIO

Altamura

Otranto

Castro

CAMPANIA

Teano

BASILICATA

Matera

Taranto

Capo Santa Maria
di Leuca

Capua

Caserta

Potenza

Scanzano Jonico

Casal di Principe

Viggiano

Aliano

Policoro

Castel
Volturno

Naples

Pompeii

Salerno

Eboli

Tramutola

Viggiano

San Severino
Lucano

Trebisacce

Paestum

Civita

Sibari

Cassano
allo Ionio

Corigliano

Ciró Marina

CALABRIA

Crotone

Cropani

Catanzaro

TYRRHENIAN
SEA

Lamezia Terme

Maida

IONIAN
SEA

Pizzo

Gioia Tauro

Cittanova

Palmi

Locri

Villa San Giovanni

San Luca

Messina

Reggio di
Calabria

Brancaleone

Taormina

Bagheria

Punta Raisi

Palermo

Termini Imerese

SICILY

San Guiseppe Jato

Corleone

Caltanissetta

Syracuse

Calatifimi

Canicatti

Riesi

Marsala

Castelvetrano

Agrigento

Gela

Palma di
Montechiaro

SICILIAN
CHANNEL

Pantelleria

100 kilometres

50 miles

MALTA

INTRODUCTION

Mysteries and Mafiosi

THIS IS A BOOK about Italy's home-bred Mafias: Sicily's Cosa Nostra; the Camorra in Naples and Campania, the region around it; Calabria's 'Ndrangheta; and the Sacra Corona Unita in the Apulian heel. It is a book about crime: murder and mafia wars; extortioners and their victims; the trafficking of arms, drugs and people; and the crooked politicians and businessmen whose complicity helps the Mafia thrive.

The Mafia is the thread, from Gela on Sicily's southern coast, through Corleone, across the Strait of Messina, where ferries ply between Scylla and Charybdis, northwards past Calabria's citrus orchards and olive groves and beyond Naples, the city to see and die. But this is also the story of dedicated magistrates and policemen who struggle against the odds to enforce the law and see justice done in parts of Italy where law and justice are often private matters. It is the story of young people who form cooperatives to work land confiscated from the Mafia and ordinary Italians who want the Mafia beaten. It is the story of a journey through the Mezzogiorno, of discovering its contrasts and contradictions, from the ruins of Magna Græcia and Baroque palaces to the relics of doomed industrial ventures and ugly developments along the coast. And it is the story of the good and the evil in the South.

My Italian travels began in the spring of 1972 when I moved to Rome on a six-month assignment at the Cassa per il Mezzogiorno, the development agency for the South, and stayed for ever. Perhaps there was a reason that a young foreigner, an ingenuous newcomer to the seductive Bel Paese, as Italians often call their country, was allowed to read the files of hundreds of engineering projects that took electricity and water to towns and villages, and joined them with roads and railways. Caught up in discovering the tourist's Italy and exploring Rome, the Eternal City, I was incurious about the firms involved and the powerful politicians who wrote to the agency supporting projects or soliciting payments to those firms.

When my interests shifted, I would see roads leading from nowhere to nowhere else, a huge viaduct built in fields and half-completed hospitals where construction had halted long ago, and learn that the Mafia had a hand in public works throughout the South. Indeed, for me, my full sighting of the Mafia only came many years later, although I wonder now if I did not brush against it much sooner, and get closer than I did in the Cassa's drab offices in Rome.

––––––––––

Few of the tables, set with white linen and tasteful chinaware, were taken at around eight thirty on that morning early in 1978. The restaurant was quiet, an occasional clink of cup on saucer and rustle of newspaper pages being turned. It was not a week when models strutted along Milan's catwalks, drawing crowds of buyers, journalists, gawkers and other fashion-followers. Unhurried, waiters lavished attention on a smartly-dressed businessman sitting on the other side of the room. A regular guest perhaps, but how the waiters served him said that he was somebody who counted more than most.

Like Rome six years before, Milan was a city to be discovered, its museums and churches to be visited, its hotels to be experienced. Since then I have stayed at around thirty different places in the Lombard capital: luxury hotels and modest ones, five-star and two-star, the smart and the scruffy, some in the financial district, others near the old trade fair and San Siro, and a small hotel, which for some reason Italians describe as meublè, in the fashionable heart of Italy's fashion capital. Yet after staying occasionally between the beginning of 1978 and summer of the following year, I have never returned to the Hotel Splendido where the enigmatic man also stayed.

At number four Viale Andrea Doria, the Splendido is a hundred yards from Milan's central station, one of dozens of anonymous hotels that pack whole streets in that dismal district of transients, but one of the smartest, boasting four stars and the Rendez-Vous, a restaurant that the Touring Club Italiano nowadays calls elegant. I was eating breakfast there that morning because of an appointment with a client. The consultancy firm for whom I worked had an assignment with a company whose offices were about ten minutes' walk from the hotel. The company's owner used the Splendido, was the person I had to meet and, as I would soon learn, was the man at the table on the far side of the restaurant whom the waiters treated with such respect.

Twenty-five years later I came across the hotel again, towards the end of a book – the story of the work and death of Giorgio Ambrosoli, the Milanese lawyer responsible for liquidating the Banca Privata Italiana, a bank owned by Michele Sindona, a Sicilian financier. Hotel Splendido: the name sprang from the page.

Using a false American passport bearing the name Robert McGovern, William Arico had arrived at Milan's Malpensa inter-continental airport on the morning of 8 July 1979 and, after renting a car, had driven to his usual hotel. This was his tenth visit to Milan and the Hotel Splendido since September of the previous year and those visits had often coincided with threats against Ambrosoli or other acts of intimidation. And that visit would be Arico's last. Almost certainly when he stayed there during the second half of June, Arico had used his time to decide where and how he would murder Ambrosoli. He returned in July to do the job. Just before midnight on 11 July Arico, a hit man hired by Sindona, murdered Ambrosoli as he returned home after dinner with friends. On the following day the lawyer had been due to give evidence in the Milan court to American prosecutors who, pursuing their case against Sindona, had also arrived in the city on 8 July.

I am curious about the businessman, an Italian-American, and trawl distant memories to recall the hotel, the man and his firm, with its offices in Milan and a factory south of Rome, where generous government grants enticed firms to invest. Memory says that he was also involved in a business in Sicily.

And I remember later hearing talk that he was linked to the *lista dei 500*, a list of five hundred people for whom Sindona had provided channels for illegally exporting capital, but there were also facts. A judgement of a court of appeal in a murder case contains an intriguing line, not much but enough to set the imagination running. The court said that the name of the businessman 'appeared in several companies connected to Sindona'.

In how many companies was he involved? The court named two in which he and Sindona had been partners, but were there others in which, in some way, they were together? Was the company in Milan one of them, or the company in Sicily? How much did the businessman, long since dead, know about Sindona? Did he have doubts about Sindona? Had he been a front for Sindona? And if he had been a front, had he subsequently broken with Sindona? But how is it possible to break off business affairs with a man tied to the Mafia, as Sindona was? The Splendido was convenient for reaching the company's offices but why did he not stay at the nearby five-star Excelsior Gallia or four-star Anderson, or one of the three five-star hotels in the much nicer Piazza della Repubblica, not far away?

By early 1978 Sindona's crimes in Italy had been known for more than three years. A ministerial decree in September 1974 had thrown a line to Italians whose deposits had sunk with Sindona's bank. In the middle of October the court in Milan ordered the bank to be wound up, appointed Ambrosoli as the liquidator and issued a warrant for Sindona's arrest alleging he had falsified company statements and illegally distributed profits before his bank collapsed. Ten days later magistrates signed a second arrest warrant alleging fraudulent bankruptcy, but Sindona had fled to America.

The Sicilian financier had enjoyed support at the highest level of Italian politics. And few Italian politicians have risen higher than Giulio Andreotti, seven-times prime minister and nominated senator for life in 1991, who in December 1973 at a dinner in New York's Saint Regis hotel had described Sindona as the saviour of the lira. During the 1970s and through to the spring of 1980, Andreotti enjoyed friendly and direct relations with leading members of Cosa Nostra and had knowingly and deliberately cultivated a stable relationship with *mafiosi*. Andreotti's trial for aiding and abetting the Mafia ended in Italy's supreme court in October 2004 with a judgement that found he had been involved in criminal association until the spring of 1980, but the crime was time-barred. Insufficient proof brought him acquittal for the period after that. Such was Sindona's protector, a person whom many Italians still call a statesman.

But Sindona, extradited from America, convicted of commissioning Ambrosoli's murder and himself murdered in March 1986, in Voghera prison by a cup of coffee laced with poison, had other powerful allies. Some were in the Vatican where he had woven a web of financial relationships with the Istituto Opere di Religione (IOR), the Vatican's bank. Headed by an American prelate, Paul Marcinkus, the IOR would find its reputation blackened further following the collapse of the Banco Ambrosiano in June 1982 and the mysterious murder of its chairman, Roberto Calvi, whose body was found hanging under Blackfriars Bridge in London. Was it a coincidence, I wonder, that the businessman's offices in Rome, where I called to collect documents, were owned by the Amministrazione del Patrimonio della Sede Apostolica, the body that administers the property of the Holy See?

How many hands had Sindona shaken to seal his deals? And how many businessmen, like the one at whose company I worked, would never be indicted or found guilty of wrongdoing, and would perhaps later regret their connections with Sindona? But which businessmen and politicians had eagerly clasped Sindona's hand while knowing about his shady affairs? Giovanna Terranova, the widow of a magistrate murdered by the Mafia in Palermo in 1979, remembered her disgust at shaking 'hands that weren't clean' when people at her husband's funeral offered their meaningless muttered words of sympathy. '*Condoglianze, Signora*, a fine person, how terrible,' such men, members of Palermo society, would have murmured, secretly pleased that the magistrate was dead.

Tramping through Sicily's Greek ruins or Roman Pompeii, or sweltering on the beach in Taormina or on the Amalfi coast, tourists do not ask about the Mafia or imagine how close it might be. They do not wonder which young men are the Mafia's emissaries extorting protection money, or who the victims are, or if the middle-aged man given everyone's respect is a mafia boss. 'Here you can feel the 'Ndrangheta's presence, touch it with your hands,' Emilio Sirianni, a prosecutor in Calabria told me as we talked in the late afternoon on the terrace of his holiday home near Brancaleone, on the region's southern coast. Constant, oppressive, menacing, palpable – a mafia presence that Sirianni, himself a Calabrese, can feel; but outsiders cannot feel what locals do.

My questions began long after I arrived in Rome. I had followed with horror the bloody trail of death that mafia wars left throughout the South, with fascination the maxi-trial of hundreds of *mafiosi* in Palermo's bunker court that began early in 1986 and ended just before Christmas of the following year, and been shocked by the murders of the anti-Mafia magistrates Giovanni Falcone and Paolo Borsellino and their escorts in Palermo in 1992. I had written about Calvi and his bank ten years before. Yet six years passed after those terrible months in the summer of 1992 before I would write about the Mafia. In the *Financial Times* of 16 December 1998, almost twenty-seven years after I stepped off the aircraft that had taken me to Rome, were my first words on the Mafia – *Organised Crime: in fear of mob rule* – now a fading pink cutting on my desk.

It was then that I met Gian Carlo Caselli, a white-haired magistrate from Turin who had asked, after the murders of Falcone and Borsellino, to be transferred to Palermo to head the prosecution service in the Sicilian capital. Interviewing Caselli involved running a gauntlet of checks, even within the high security of Palermo's court building, passing a platoon of armed policemen in civilian clothes on guard outside his office before being ushered by one of them through an armour-plated door. That is what fighting the Mafia means for those who lead the fight.

Caselli had brought the prosecution against Andreotti that proved the elderly politician had been friendly with Cosa Nostra, and the magistrate would later feel the vengeance and spite of Italy's rightwing politicians. And Caselli's signature was on a request for indictment in October 1996 that led to the trial of Marcello Dell'Utri, a close friend and associate of Silvio Berlusconi, the media magnate who set up his own populist political party and won power in 1994, in 2001 and again in 2008. Dell'Utri was found guilty of complicity with the Mafia in December 2004 and sentenced to nine years in prison (against which he would appeal), giving Italy's right-wing politicians more cause to want revenge.

Italy needs a radical change in culture, an enormous moral and political commitment, and the job will be long. 'We must start with schoolchildren, showing them that there is no honour in the Onorata Società,' Caselli told me. While he was in Palermo, Caselli put the idea into practice by visiting schools, although Italians knew of him mostly through Andreotti's trial and his efforts against the Mafia.

For Caselli, the transfer from Turin meant sacrificing personal freedom, a life always shadowed by bodyguards, travelling in armour-plated cars whenever on the move and a spartan barracks as home. Once a mafia target, forever a mafia target. Caselli had bodyguards at a book fair in Turin, his home city, in May 2005 and later that year when we walked together in the centre of Bari, a city in the heel of the Italian boot far from Palermo. And those bodyguards would be on watch for years ahead, even in towns like Carpi, an apparently safe, quiet backwater of Emilia in northern Italy. They are with him everywhere at every moment. As much as some rightwing politicians might wish Caselli dead, with the blood of magistrates and other public servants on its hands Rome cannot allow Caselli to be murdered too.

During the seven years that Caselli worked in the Sicilian capital, from the beginning of 1993 to the end of 1999, his team would investigate nine thousand people suspected of being in or connected with the Mafia and win indictments against more than three thousand. Even so, that would leave the war far from won. 'Cosa Nostra has been hit but it is still effective, dangerous and well organised,' Caselli told me in 1998. The years that followed confirmed the prosecutor's grim assessment.

'For decades, businessmen denied the Mafia's existence. But firms had agreements with the Mafia and with politicians. Those that did not collude were badly handicapped,' Fabio Cascio, the bright young chairman of the small-companies association in Palermo told me when I was preparing the article for the *Financial Times*.

Cascio showed me a community project on the eastern edge of Palermo that employed forty young people considered at risk to delinquency. It was in the heart of Brancaccio, a desolate district of densely packed high-rise apartment blocks, shabby workshops and commercial storage buildings, a district notorious for being under Cosa Nostra's firm control. The four-star San Paolo Palace hotel across the road from the project was empty at the time, confiscated by the court in Palermo because its owner was a front for the Graviano brothers, Brancaccio's bosses. One of the first Sicilian associations of Forza Italia, Berlusconi's political party whose creation had been Dell'Utri's work, was inaugurated there.

Before visiting Brancaccio I had called on Cascio in his offices at Centralgas in Carini, on the other side of Palermo, a few miles from where Falcone met his death, his car blown up by explosives placed in a drainage channel under the autostrada to Punta Raisi airport. An up-and-coming figure in Sicilian business circles, Cascio would be elected chairman of the industrialists' association in the province of Palermo in June 2005. Outlining his programme, he said that the industrialists wanted security and legality. Cascio's predecessor spoke about the importance to the association of having a young and dynamic leadership, 'the perfect expression of the needs of Palermo's business community'.

Six months later Cascio would be in the news again, his companies seized by Palermo's court in a measure that also suspended him from company duties. He was under investigation for fraud and money laundering. Sitting on the boards of Cascio's companies was Francesco Paolo Bontate, son of Stefano Bontate, the bloody boss of the Santa Maria di Gesù family who was gunned down in 1981, one of hundreds of dead in a mafia war. Bontate had been arrested in October 2003 and was convicted of drugs trafficking at the beginning of June 2005.

And Bontate's two cousins, both called Giovanni Teresi and both from families with mafia ties, were also directors of Cascio's companies. Cascio spoke tough words against Cosa Nostra but sat in boardrooms with men whose families had connections with it that were indisputable and known to all. 'A disquieting case,' said Elio Collova, the judicial administrator of Centralgas to whom the court decree had entrusted Cascio's business. In October 2008, however, prosecutors would not seek Cascio's indictment but would ask the judge at a preliminary hearing to close the investigations. Even so, Cascio remained suspended from company duties and his companies continued to be confiscated, though he was appealing against this ruling.

———

Who and what should be believed in the Italian South where so much is hidden or disguised and gestures often take the place of words? Uncertainties and suspicions colour my experiences there. Have I shaken the hands of people with ties to the Mafia? Yes. Have I had suspicions? Often. The certainties are misgivings and doubts. What special power did a businessman have that he, with me by his side, would be taken through a side entrance of the airport in Catania, dodging check-in queues and security controls, and board a flight for Rome untroubled by the usual routines of air travel and other travellers? Why did a businessman in Calabria turn icy and threatening when I asked about the 'Ndrangheta? And why did a teacher in the south of Sicily tell me that the winemaker whose cellars we had just visited was once an arms dealer, had been remanded in custody for more than a year on suspicion of involvement with the Mafia and continued to be harried by the police?

However, these were matters for the future when I met Caselli and Cascio at the end of 1998. Thanks to Silvio Berlusconi, I started to understand more about the Mafia just over two years later. The foundations of my journey through the South began to be laid in February 2001 when *The Economist* called to involve me in a special report on Berlusconi's business empire. The report's publication would be pegged to parliamentary elections in which Berlusconi, heading a rightwing coalition that included a post-fascist party, was trying to return to office after six years away from the levers of power. Research soon moved the report in a new direction, from a straightforward business story to something very different. From Milan, where Berlusconi's businesses are based, the trail led south to Sicily where Dell'Utri was on trial and where Dell'Utri and Berlusconi were under investigation in connection with the murders of Falcone and Borsellino. In May 2002 Giovanbattista Tona, a judge in Caltanissetta, ruled that these investigation should be closed and that the two founders of Forza Italia were not accomplices in those terrible murders ten years before. People connected with the Mafia had been in contact with companies in the Fininvest group (the holding company for Berlusconi's business empire) and these proven relations, said Tona, 'lent plausibility to depositions, made by various mafia witnesses who were cooperating with the authorities, that Berlusconi and Dell'Utri were considered easily contactable by the criminal organisation'. But Berlusconi and Dell'Utri were not involved in the murders of Falcone and Borsellino.

Before I left Rome for Palermo on one of my trips, my wife, concerned about the project, warned: '*fascisti e mafiosi*'. At a meeting in London, the editor asked about risks. Legal risk? Definitely, and a writ arrived after the report appeared, Berlusconi's face on the magazine's cover, the words *Why Silvio Berlusconi is unfit to lead Italy* splashed above. Physical risk? It is hard to imagine an uglier combination than fascism and the Mafia, but physical danger never materialised and the risk probably never existed. A different

Italy unfolded when I began writing about Berlusconi. Apart from interviewing Caselli I had met nobody in the magistracy, never been in a court and knew nothing about crime, but writing about Berlusconi would change that.

During one visit to Palermo I bought a book to read on an evening flight to Milan: *L'Eredità Scomoda* (The Uncomfortable Inheritance) by Caselli and Antonio Ingroia, an assistant prosecutor in the Dell'Utri case, whom I would get to know. Ingroia's first job in the magistracy, in 1989, was as Borsellino's assistant in Marsala, and he would transfer to Palermo in April 1992, shortly before Falcone's murder, to work again with Borsellino on anti-Mafia investigations. The book describes the drama of being a prosecutor in Palermo following the two magistrates' murders.

The book that Caselli and Ingroia had written was a gripping and moving read on that late-evening flight. The inheritance about which the two magistrates wrote and about which they would tell me more was one of tragedy but also of hope, that those awful murders in 1992 would put political backbone into the war against the Mafia. Alas, those hopes would soon be bitterly dashed. 'I tell myself that Falcone and Borsellino were right to say that the Mafia could be beaten … if only that were truly wanted,' said Caselli.

Italy was at a moral crossroads in 1992. Falcone and Borsellino were murdered soon after magistrates in Milan began blowing the flimsy covering off the widespread and deep-rooted corruption that polluted the city's political and business life. Milan was called *tangentopoli* (bribesville), but corruption was everywhere. Mafia and corruption, a pairing as nasty as *fascisti* and *mafiosi* and another that shows the Bel Paese's ugly side. But Italians stopped at those crossroads, forgot the killings in Palermo and the greed and dirt of *tangentopoli*, turned their backs on moral renewal and put Berlusconi into power.

Even before reporting on Berlusconi for *The Economist* I had begun to visit Sicily regularly, though not to write about the Mafia. That changed in 2001 and when I travelled there in the spring of 2002 I was to write about progress in dealing with the Mafia during the ten years that had passed since the two magistrates were killed. And I would write a book on corruption, Cosa Nostra and Berlusconi.

Yet there is more Mafia in the South than Sicily's Cosa Nostra, more to the South than the Mafia, and far more to the South than Sicily. I had been captivated by the evocative Greek ruins at Selinunte in Sicily's south-west corner, the columns of temples standing timeless above the Mediter-ranean Sea. I had swum on the first day of November in the warm clear waters of Vendicari in the southeast of the island, a curving bay of fine pale sand where a disused tunny cannery closes one end. I had met prosecutors and policemen, bankers and businessmen, professors and politicians. I had watched eagles soar above Lo Zingaro, a wild promontory in western Sicily, drunk the island's wines, eaten at the Sant'Andrea in Palermo's Vucciria market, and I wanted more.

1

———

GELA

Modern Tyranny

'GELA? Why do you want to go to Gela?' asked a friend in Palermo. 'It's the ugliest town in Sicily.' Perhaps it is, but it seemed the right place to begin, on Sicily's southern coast in the deep south of the Italian South, much nearer Tunis and Tripoli than Rome, in a town with the blackest reputation for everything in which the Mafia excels, such as extortion rackets, economic crime, political collusion and violent death.

The hotel where I had booked was then Gela's best but a local news-wire stringer warned me that it ranked low on comfort. I saw what he meant when I drove into the busy service station that shares the hotel's site, checked in and took the lift to my room. A dim corridor with stained carpeting and battered doors to rooms, some with chipped jambs that looked as if screwdrivers or chisels had been used for entry instead of keys, was uninviting and the room matched the corridor. However, the hotel was convenient, an easy walk to everywhere I wanted to go.

Crossing the ring road and making my way up the hill towards the centre, past mean buildings, Gela appeared a place without charm. I had arranged to meet the mayor and waited on a bench in the square outside the town hall. Soon a dark blue Fiat drew to the kerb. A casually dressed man got out, turned his head right, looked back down the square from where the car had come, then left towards the town hall's entrance and the neighbouring seventeenth-century church of Saint Francis of Assisi. The door on the car's other side opened, a second man appeared and also looked carefully around. But on that Sunday afternoon, like most Sunday afternoons, Gela's centre was a sleepy place with few passers-by, none suspicious or a cause of concern for the two men.

Had there been onlookers, they may not have seen the third man in the car. But many people in Gela would have known that their mayor, Rosario Crocetta, was a passenger; that the car was armour plated; that its thick, dark windows were bullet proof; and that the two men who had got out of the car before him were armed policemen in plain clothes. Crocetta was given bodyguards in July 2003, a few months after the regional administrative court in Palermo declared him the winner of the election that had been held in Gela in May 2002. I walked a few steps and said hello to Crocetta, a thickset man of indeterminate middle age with wavy black hair whom I remembered vaguely, having met him a few years before. 'Let's go for a coffee,' he said, taking me by the arm and leading me to the Bar Siracusa across the square.

Ten minutes later, sitting behind his desk, Crocetta began telling me about himself, the town and the Mafia that threatened him as soon as the court gave the ruling that installed him as mayor. In an interview with Italy's state broadcasting company he had said that his priority would be to fight crime. 'The Mafia didn't like that,' Crocetta told me. A large crowd had gathered in the piazza in Gela to celebrate the court's ruling when Crocetta's lawyer told him about a telephone call he had received from a person so powerful and confident of being above the law that he did not hide his identity. Crocetta should change tack or he would be dead within a week, the caller threatened. 'I went to the town hall next day and issued my first ordinance. From that moment, all bids for public tenders would be adjudicated in the presence of the police,' Crocetta recalled, 'and then I went to the police to tell them of the threat.'

Crocetta's election had itself been part of his campaign against the Mafia. Even in his own party on the radical left, the Comunisti Italiani, and among its allies, nobody thought that Crocetta could win the election. One year earlier Silvio Berlusconi's rightwing coalition had made a clean sweep in Sicily, taking all of the sixty-one first-past-the-post seats that were contested in a parliamentary election. When his opponent was declared the winner by just over one hundred votes, Crocetta's supporters were not surprised. 'Everyone thought my bid to be mayor was a lost cause.'

But Crocetta suspected that the rightwing candidate had won thanks to ballot rigging and took the matter to the regional administrative court. 'Something very strange happened in the second round of voting. The votes simply didn't tally with those of the first round. The Mafia had organised a campaign to prevent my election,' Crocetta explained to me. He refused to accept defeat and asked the court to examine the ballot papers handed in at thirty of the town's one hundred and eighty polling stations; the check showed him leading his rival by more than five hundred votes rather than lagging. By marking ballot papers, the Mafia controlled about fifteen hundred votes in Gela and was able to ensure that voters had voted the way it wanted.

A homosexual, Crocetta would cut an unusual figure anywhere on Italy's political stage. In the conservative south of Sicily, where a culture of *padre-padrone* (father-boss) still lingers widely, the figure is even more unusual. Going against the run of public opinion, perhaps it was no surprise that he captured the votes of many of Gela's young people but, surprisingly, Crocetta's biggest supporters were pensioners. He beat his rival because he was different, a politician outside the normal scheme of things and the usual party lines, and because he got enough voters to believe in his vision of the town with a future better than its past. And he was successful again in May 2007, winning two-thirds of the vote when he sought re-election.

'I am an Aquarius,' Crocetta confided to me, eyes twinkling through his thin-rimmed spectacles. According to those who believe that one's birth-star determines who one is, being an Aquarius means being friendly and compassionate but also unpredictable, with an aversion to convention. That sounds much like Crocetta.

Born in February 1951 in the centre of Gela, less than two hundred yards from the town hall, he grew up in the outskirts where his working-class family moved after being given an apartment in a development of social housing. Taught by Salesian fathers, Crocetta's first steps in politics were not in the ranks of the establishment, with the Christian Democrats, but with a grass-roots socialist Christian movement. It was a brief experience and by the age of twenty-one Crocetta had shifted left, to the junior section of the Communist Party. Four years later he was a card-carrying member of the party itself and within two years a member of Gela's town council. 'But I didn't agree with the other councillors and resigned after three months,' Crocetta told me. A long absence from active politics followed and a long period of work abroad.

Away from Gela during mafia wars in the 1980s, Crocetta was there on a terrible evening of slaughter in November 1990 when eight young men were murdered in two amusement arcades. 'Something had to be done. The Mafia had to be tackled one way or another. It had become the central issue here, the root of the town's economic and social failure.'

Crocetta and a small group of like-minded people set up a school and called it Preferisco Vivere (I Prefer to Live). 'Our efforts were of some use and we were able to keep some youngsters out of the Mafia's hands.' Run by teachers who gave their services free, the school took in teenagers who had dropped out of state schools in the town. Preferisco Vivere was a place for difficult kids with whom establishing relationships was hard. 'Normal schools don't allow smoking in class, but that was not an issue for us,' said Crocetta. Those teenagers in Gela had more important things on their minds than cigarettes and smoking; matters of life or death, like getting a heroin fix, planning a killing or thinking about the murders they had been involved in.

'It was at this school that I began to understand what the Mafia really is. Before then I thought that educating Gela's youngsters, offering them alternatives to lives of crime, was enough. But beating the Mafia needs more than education and showing young people different values,' said Crocetta. He told me about Alessandro, a sixteen-year-old shepherd who could not read or write when he arrived at the school. Alessandro was a member of a family of the Stidda, the Mafia whose clans control areas of southern Sicily, the equivalent in the south of the island of Cosa Nostra in the west. 'Alessandro was bright and learnt quickly. One day I asked him why he didn't change the way he lived. The reason was simple. He told me that human remains found a few months earlier had belonged to a young man who'd wanted to break free from the Mafia. The young man had been buried alive in a pit of lime. Had Alessandro tried to make a new life for himself that would also have been his fate.'

Once a member, always a member. Resignation is not a choice for those who might want to leave; the Mafia is not a gentlemen's club. 'It's the most ruthless of criminal organisations. It holds its members in total oppression, in a complete negation of freedom. What a terrible awareness for a sixteen-year-old of what the future held for him,' Crocetta reflected. It was then that he decided to return to politics and to campaign against the tyranny of the Mafia.

Gela has suffered tyranny before. The first records go far back in antiquity with the Greeks who began arriving in Sicily in the eighth century BC, a wave of colonisation which ended towards the close of the century with the arrival of Greeks from Rhodes and Crete in Gela, where they established a settlement in what would be the eastern part of the modern town. Tyrants would make their appearance during the sixth century BC. Classical scholars record that Phalaris, who seized power in Agrigento, a town established in 581BC by Greeks from Gela as they spread west along the coast, was given the honour of being Sicily's first tyrant. According to legend, he was a monster whose tastes included eating new-born infants.

Tyranny arrived in Gela itself in 506BC with Cleander, whose brother Hippocrates assumed power when he was murdered. Cleander and Hippocrates were responsible for the defensive walls on the northern side of the hilltop town and for building up an army, particularly its cavalry, to lay the foundations for Gela's expansion in eastern Sicily. Hippocrates's success was due in large measure to Gelon, the cavalry's commander, who seized power when Hippocrates died in 491BC. Forging an alliance with Agrigento, Gelon turned Gela's attention eastwards again, towards Syracuse and its port. Syracuse capitulated in 485BC, Gelon transferred his capital there from Gela and within ten years he became the most powerful figure in the Greek world.

Some modern-day Sicilians say the tyrants were simply the leaders of their times who in their own ways of government interpreted the aspirations and interests of the urban and rural plebs. Moses Finley, one of the great classical scholars of the twentieth century, was harsher. He thought that adjectives like brutal and despotic were inadequate to describe the rapidity with which tyrants founded and destroyed whole cities and the frequency with which they transplanted tens of thousands of people. In 282BC, for example, the people of Gela were forcibly moved by the tyrant of Agrigento to what would be the town of Licata, about twenty miles along the coast towards Agrigento. Gela was destroyed but it was already in decline.

About thirty years before this enforced migration, the tyrant of Syracuse had ordered the massacre of around four thousand of Gela's inhabitants. The bloodletting was typical of the time and place; many people said much the same when ferocious mafia wars left hundreds dead in the town during the 1980s and 1990s.

Crocetta had suggested that I talk to Paolo Caffà, a left-leaning civil lawyer who had been a member of the town's council for many years, and I was able to arrange a meeting. 'Agrigento was a colony of Gela. Syracuse was conquered by Gela. Yet tourists travel from one to the other without even stopping here. They just pass Gela by,' he told me. And so I discovered. Few tourists call at the town's museum with its large, well-presented collection of archaeological finds; apart from a handful of staff, it was empty when I went there. In their cars and coaches, travellers from Agrigento to Syracuse keep travelling around Gela's ring road and through the urban sprawl on the town's northern outskirts. With little left of the glory that the ancient Greeks gave Gela, the modern town is a place that many have been to but few have visited.

Yet standing on a narrow plateau, overlooking the Mediterranean to the south and rising steeply out of a broad plain that spreads inland to the north, Gela ought to have become a magnet for tourists. It enjoys an enviable position. The fascist dictator Benito Mussolini had swum there, in the clean, clear sea, in August 1937 and later spent the evening dancing with 'young ladies of good Gela families'. Even today it is not hard to imagine how it was then and what it might have been now had the town developed differently. A long esplanade overlooks a broad sandy beach, large areas invaded by rough grass and rushes, and directly below the town hall a white pavilion standing on the beach, its roof blackened and one wing collapsed, tells of different, better times. Was it here, I wondered as I walked past, that the Duce swam and danced?

Thanks to the depredations of modern man, Gela does not draw visitors. It offers grim evidence of man's violence towards his fellows and also towards his surroundings. Planning abuse has been the rule; thousands of homes were built without permits and the old town centre destroyed as the authorities granted licences for the demolition of houses and palaces. A director of the museum complained that almost all that was old has been lost and what remains is ruined. Blocks of apartments sprung up everywhere with no concern for appearance as well as no regard for permits, the narrow streets of mid- and late-twentieth-century back-to-backs enjoying little light and no greenery to soften the desolation. Most are inhabited, many remain unfinished. 'Few people think that external plastering is necessary,' said Caffà. And so I found when I explored the warren of streets between the centre and my hotel; streets so narrow that two cars fit tightly, homes whose living rooms open directly onto narrow pavements, some living rooms turned into garages, the daily wash decorating balconies that almost touch, imposing cheek-by-jowl living on those who live there.

One of my calls in Gela was on the Confederazione Generale Italiana del Lavoro (CGIL), Italy's large, left-leaning trade union, and I walked to the western end of the town's main street to reach its offices. There I talked to Emanuele Scicolone, its secretary, finding him to be yet another local willing to speak about his town and its problems: 'For the many young-sters who live in social housing's concrete boxes, or in the decaying homes typical of districts built without permits, the street is the only training ground for life. Here they often bump up against the criminal organisa-tions that preach their myth of immediate and easy success, and gospel of violence.' Teenagers are not alone in thinking that Gela, a town of about eighty thousand, is short on attractions. In 1990, when the government in Rome decided that Gela should have its own law court it was put in a small category of hardship posts where magistrates – judges and prosecutors – enjoy benefits not granted to colleagues who work in the many easier, less isolated and better provided Italian towns and cities.

At the eastern, smarter, end of the Corso Vittorio Emanuele, past the large parish church and the shops selling fashionable eyewear, perfumes and jewellery that are found in all large towns, next to the museum with the acropolis just beyond, the Hotel Venezia stands shut, not for renovation but for good. The faded blue paintwork and the crumbling pillars on the top-floor terrace suggest that if there ever was a golden age it ended long ago. Rusting gates, slightly ajar, lead to an overgrown garden, where I could imagine that guests once enjoyed *aperitivi* before dinner or *digestivi* after. Like the Hotel Excelsior that I had noticed when walking to the centre, another closed and shabby remnant of a distant past, perhaps the Hotel Venezia had been built expecting that visitors would give the town more than passing attention and stay overnight.

Greek emigrants, voyagers and adventurers from the East, had first settled where the hotel now stands. And it was on this acropolis that a Doric temple was built after Gelon's victory over the Carthaginians in 480BC. Just one worn column of the temple remains, eroded by the weather and corroded by pollution. Behind it loom the chimneys of an electricity power station and the pipework of an oil refinery, so close that they too seem part of the archaeological gardens.

Scicolone worked in one of the chemical plants near the refinery during the 1970s and 1980s. 'Enormous damage was done,' he told me, 'when factories dumped mercury and other poisonous chemicals untreated into the sea and ships cleaned their tanks and discharged toxic waste offshore.' The reason for the refinery and power station, and the petrochemical plants that sprouted up near them, was the discovery in 1956 of oil behind the town, under the plain where pumps still nod slowly. At the end of 1959, ENI, the state-owned energy and chemicals corporation, started to exploit those oil reserves, building a large refinery and petrochemical plant on the Piano del Signore, the Lord's Plain. Oil refining and petrochemicals production began in 1962 and changed Gela and that part of Sicily dramatically; the refinery alone covers well over one thousand acres and dominates the eastern edge of the plain. The town was one of many in southern Italy to feel the effects of the government's efforts to push the Mezzogiorno's economy into the twentieth century but, alas, successive administrations in Rome took little account of the environmental costs.

About twelve thousand workers were employed in building the refinery and nearby plants in the early 1960s. Some trained to become skilled tradesmen and joined the three-thousand-strong army of welders, metalworkers, plumbers and electricians who helped build the refinery, but few found employment when ENI's refinery was completed and most had to emigrate. However, the state corporation continued to provide work directly for about five and a half thousand and another three thousand indirectly in the second half of the 1970s.

Scicolone thinks the refinery merely offered a mirage of industrialisation and led agriculture to be abandoned and local society to fracture. 'There was no real development at Gela, just the building of a refinery and base chemicals plants with nothing further downstream. State corporations treated Gela as colonisers treated Africa,' he complained to me. Even so,

ENI still employed just over two thousand workers at the refinery, satellite firms dependent on ENI gave work to one thousand seven hundred and the salaries they paid each month were essential for Gela's fragile economy. However, some local leaders, including Paolo Caffà, call the refinery a cathedral in the desert, accuse the industrial complex of being dangerous to health and want it closed. 'At least twenty years would be needed to clean up the damage it has caused and this would provide jobs for ten thousand people,' Caffà told me. He noted that the incidence of cancer in Gela is unusually high, something that a young prosecutor with whom I spoke was investigating, along with the level of infantile deformities in the town.

So there were suspicions that the oil refinery and the chemical factories were the cause of serious health problems for people in Gela. There were also suspicions that the refinery and the chemical factories were infected by the Mafia. Construction of the petrochemical area had sucked labour into Gela from its hinterland, expanding its population five-fold, and with that immigration came the Mafia. 'You know, Gela was not a mafia town, not like Riesi. The Mafia arrived here with the refinery and the chemical plants,' Scicolone told me. 'I began to report mafia infiltration of tenders in 1998. The absence of legality has been an obstacle to progress here and the situation will not improve until there is a clean-out.'

Rosario Crocetta began voicing his concerns loudly as soon as he became mayor. 'Work put out to tender at the refinery is in the Mafia's hands and I continue to say so to every conference I address and on every possible occasion,' Crocetta told a conference on legality organised by the CGIL. Simply to claim, as the refinery's managers did, that contracts were subject to competitive bidding was just not enough. The town's authorities had tried, by introducing strict bidding procedures and by evaluating bids in the presence of the police, to prevent mafia infiltration into the work it contracted out but there was outside interference all the same.

'If I were aware that most of those who work in my business and who hold positions of responsibility were subject to Cosa Nostra, how could I pretend that this did not matter?' Crocetta asked. The few firms who reported illegalities stood no chance of winning contracts at the refinery. 'Tenders should be handled differently because honest firms are excluded from work in the petrochemical plant if Cosa Nostra always wins. We must tolerate this no longer; it is not just a question for the company but for the whole area.'

Some details of what had been happening in the refinery and chemical plants on the Piano del Signore became public in April 2006 when a judge in Caltanissetta, the capital of the province, issued an order that put five men and a woman from Gela into custody. The judge found that there was evidence of mafia association and ordered that they should be kept in isolation. Subsequently, the court accepted plea bargains that allowed shorter prison sentences than might otherwise have been imposed had their case gone to trial. For at least thirty years a consortium of firms had been winning contracts in the refinery because of a system that was a cocktail of legal and illegal connections and support. Jobs were not allocated according to ability but simply to strengthen the system and provide salaries for the members of mafia families.

Two *mafiosi* serving sentences in Caltanissetta's prison were part of the group that ran and profited from the consortium, said the judge. One had been the regent of Gela's Emmanuello clan, the other was called Nele u Ragiuniere, Nele the bookkeeper. Bugs and telephone taps had allowed investigators to gather evidence against the six people whose arrest the judge ordered. The woman who was arrested was the wife of one of those in jail and, said the judge, had been a conduit between the men in the prison and their associates on the outside.

The Mafia's grip on Gela's economy had affected other parts of life there, including local politics. Crocetta would never forget an election campaign during which political meetings were held at the plant. Workers were taken on before election day and fired immediately after. 'During my first week as mayor, the owner of a small firm sent me a message that I should not poke my nose into tenders at the *petrolchimico*. How work was allocated was not open to discussion; tenders were a matter over which one could die.'

Dirty business in the petrochemical area was the biggest concern, but criminal behaviour was everywhere. In August 2004, when a judge ordered the arrest of twelve men suspected of rigging public tenders, loan sharking and extortion, the warrant showed the difficult conditions in which Crocetta worked as mayor. He had had good reason to ask the police to be present when envelopes containing bids for contracts from Gela's town council were opened. The mechanisms for rigging tenders were well oiled, virtually automatic and went back years. Money was given to some firms to encourage them not to bid and the discounts offered on the base prices at which tenders were set were fixed before bids were made. In one case, involving maintenance in one part of the town, forty firms responded to a call for bids, of whom thirty-seven offered discounts of twenty-seven per cent. 'It is impossible to imagine that almost all the forty firms that took part hit by accident on the same figure of twenty-seven per cent, with variations of just fractions of a percentage point,' the judge observed.

Gela's administration, its politics and firms were closely intertwined. Telephone conversations that the police overheard revealed a web of relationships involving town employees and the potential to influence decisions made by the town's authorities. One of the men arrested as a result of the warrant was both a town employee, whom Crocetta had transferred to a different post, and a provincial councillor who had exploited those positions both within the town hall and in political circles. His son, a town councillor, who was also arrested, had been involved in businesses his father controlled.

Obtaining evidence that those arrested had been engaged in loan sharking had not been easy. Victims were reluctant witnesses, not least because loan sharking and extortion, accompanied by threats of violence, go hand-in-hand. Investigations allowed the identification of some of the loan sharks' victims, despite the fact that none of them, for understandable reasons, had ever laid complaints or provided information about their position as victims. They were businessmen whose firms were in difficulty and who were unable to obtain credit from the banks. By borrowing from private sources, they faced massive interest rates of between ten and fifteen per cent a month, and interest was added monthly to the original loan. The victims found their finances worsened sharply once the loan sharks had become involved and they were then forced to hand over property, businesses and stocks of the goods in which they dealt.

Fear was the loan sharks' lever. One of the victims, from a town near Gela, fled from Sicily to escape the threats. Another victim was taken by car into the countryside behind Gela. And the investigators overheard the driver of the car tell a third victim about that trip: 'We went into the rough scrub where there is an old house from where you cannot get away. I told him that I was going to kill him.' When he signed the arrest warrant, the judge noted the seriousness of the intimidation to which the victims had been subjected and the sheer terror that this had caused them.

During their investigations the authorities found evidence that the band of loan sharks was close to Gela's top mafia families. They also found a link to a Lithuanian whom they suspected of criminal ties. 'We work like a team from Corleone,' the Lithuanian told an Italian friend in Gela, a conversation that a bug in a Mercedes car picked up. 'What a disgusting town. We even have gay mayors,' said the Italian. Crocetta was a problem. 'He always tells the newspapers that Gela is *mafioso*; that he's against the Mafia; that everyone in Gela is *mafioso*; and that he's clean,' he told his Lithuanian companion. Some people thought that the conversation was an attempt to hire a team of foreign killers to deal with the mayor. After Lithuanians were found reconnoitring the area near his home, Crocetta was sure that he was the target. 'Mafia density is high in Lithuania and Gela businessmen with links to the Stidda go there.'

Certainly the mayor was a threat to those in the town who made their living from crime. 'Either you accept the Mafia's rules or you challenge them. That is the choice. The Mafia can only be beaten when its interests are hit, when its economic roots are attacked.' And attacking the Mafia's economic roots is what the authorities have tried to do. At the end of 2004, when Caltanissetta's anti-Mafia team, whose responsibilities include Gela, found that a small bank in the town had been infiltrated by the Mafia, they quickly took control of the bank, installed a special commissioner and arrested the managers. They had placed bugs and could overhear the employees' agitated conversations. One of the employees thought that they should meet late at night away from the bank. Another asked, 'Are we the only bank with this kind of client? Don't other banks have them? Aren't there other banks more *mafiose* than us?'

In one way or another money has always been the Mafia's driving interest. According to one legend, money was invented in Lydia, in what today is Anatolia in Turkey. It became part of life in Gela when large-value coins were minted there in the reign of the tyrant Hippocrates, but Gela was not the first Greek settlement in Sicily to make its own coins. That honour belonged around 540BC to Naxos, near Taormina, the first Greek colony on the island whose port provided a landfall for vessels arriving from Greece and a centre for trade; some historians believe that Naxos minted coins to facilitate commercial transactions and the payment of port dues.

Gela may not have led the way in minting money, but it became famous in June 1956 when workers at the site of the town's old railway station came across eight hundred and forty-eight silver coins, the biggest hoard of ancient Greek coinage ever discovered. Almost two thousand five hundred years before those workers of the mid-twentieth century made their discovery, the place where the find was made had been a sanctuary outside the town which, given the coins' different origins, might have served as a kind of state bank. The coins had been minted not only in Gela but in Syracuse, Zancle (now Messina), Athens and Macedonia.

The silver coins of the Tesoretto di Gela, as the hoard is called, weighed more than twenty pounds. Some were soon stolen and the museum suffered a second theft in 1976, but about two-thirds of the coins were recovered. More than five hundred were put on display in Gela's museum. In the bright light of their cabinets, the shiny relics recall a distant past when the naked lancers on galloping horses, stamped on many of them, were images of the fearsome cavalry that helped make Gela powerful. In modern times the Mafia, with its terrible power, would impose its rule on Gela and subject the town's people to its own brutal brand of tyranny.

Yet Gela is far from alone in suffering the Mafia's tyranny. Throughout all the Mezzogiorno, in greater or lesser degree, people suffer the different forms of violence to which the Mafia turns its hand. Leaving Gela, I drove north across the Piano del Signore, past the nodding pumps drawing up oil, towards another town with a black name: Riesi, the town that Scicolone had described as a mafia town. After about twenty-five miles of drab, dry countryside, shades of brown unrelieved by other colour, it appeared ahead of me on the left, a large, tight cluster of buildings sitting on a low hill close to the road which swept around its northern edge.

I had asked Nicolò Marino, an experienced anti-Mafia prosecutor whose patch includes Gela and its hinterland, about Riesi when I met him in Caltanissetta, in the law court where the killers of the magistrates Falcone and Borsellino had been tried in the late 1990s. 'Riesi is a very difficult town. Despite being small, it enjoys great importance as a mafia strong-hold. Don't forget it was the home-town of the notorious boss Giuseppe Di Cristina.' Di Cristina was gunned down in 1978 in Palermo, murdered by the rising Corleonesi, a foretaste of the bloody mafia war that would erupt three years later.

Arrest and custody warrants for forty-two people mainly from Riesi, issued by Giovanbattista Tona, a judge in Caltanissetta, at the end of 2005, and for another three from the town in July 2006, showed that the authorities continue to be concerned about mafia activity there. And murder continues to be the Mafia's way of imposing its rule. Acting on Marino's instructions, just after midnight on an April night in 2006, police took Giuseppe Tardanico from his cell in Caltanissetta's jail and drove him back to Riesi where he would show them those places where mafia arms were hidden. On the way, Tardanico pointed out a construction site where a murder victim had been buried in his car beneath a building.

Telephone taps used in Marino's investigations confirmed that the Mafia's interest in politics and politicians in Riesi has remained undiminished in the thirty years since Di Cristina and his family determined who should represent the town's people. Riesi, along with Gela, was one of twenty-one southern towns whose councils were dissolved because of mafia infiltration in 1992. By the time Riesi's council was dissolved yet again, in January 2006, the town's population had fallen from over fifteen thousand to less than twelve thousand because of the Mafia's deadening hand, the opportunities it stifles and the hopes it kills.

About twenty minutes after passing Riesi I drove into Campobello di Licata, a town of a similar size to Riesi. Like Riesi, its council was also dissolved in 2006, following the arrest of its mayor on suspicion of complicity with the Mafia. I had been there before, invited by him to speak in the civic centre in November 2005. The vivid murals on the town hall that I stopped to admire again and the Valle Divina Commedia, where massive pieces of travertine have been brightly painted with scenes from Dante, are works of Silvio Benedetto, an Italian-Argentinian painter. Campobello di Licata's long-serving, left-leaning mayor had nonetheless made a difference, giving a nondescript town colourful works of which it can be proud.

Continuing west, skirting Naro and Favara, I travelled through countryside typical of that part of southern Sicily – stands of eucalyptus, clumps of grotesquely formed prickly pears with their curious bat-like leaves and a fruit in the autumn whose colour ranges from yellow to a deep crimson-brown, vast sweeps of vineyards and groves of spindly almond trees whose blossom is a wonderful sight in the early spring, though the glorious sea of white-pink flowers once spread much wider, before landowners grubbed up the trees to plant acre upon acre of table-grape.

I had decided to cut across country to Corleone and turned left in the direction of Agrigento where the road from Favara joins the main road to Caltanissetta. A small book lay on top of the maps scattered over the passenger seat, *Il Giudice Ragazzino*, a sad and disturbing work, and a bitter indictment of governmental indifference to the Mafia and its power. It tells how a young judge, Rosario Livatino, met a tragic, violent end as he was travelling from Canicattì where he lived with his parents to work in the law court in Agrigento, one morning in late September 1990, on the same stretch of road along which I was driving.

I first met Nando dalla Chiesa, the author of *Il Giudice Ragazzino*, in 2002. Three years later he sat beside me in a bookshop in Palermo, offered kind words about the book I had written on Cosa Nostra, corruption and Silvio Berlusconi, and spoke with feeling about the Mafia and the hard struggle against it. He is the son of the Carabinieri general who was gunned down by *mafiosi* in the Sicilian capital in 1982, his small saloon car offering no protection. Nor indeed did the purply-red Ford Fiesta protect Livatino when he was attacked on the road to Agrigento. Undulating, with peaks and hills, some steep, others gentle, broken by rocky outcrops, the countryside probably looked then much as I saw it now, arid and unwelcoming. There, alone, about three miles from Agrigento, a loyal servant of the Italian state died, trapped by killers who had suddenly appeared, in a car and on a motorcycle.

Hit in the shoulder, Livatino was able to draw to the roadside, clamber over the guard rail and try to escape down the valley where I was looking, seeing what he saw in the desperate, fleeting moments as his end approached. The killers followed, hit him again, and when he had fallen shot him in the head to make sure he was dead. A simple marble obelisk now stands there by the road. I read the inscription. 'To Rosario Livatino. Magistrate. Martyr for Justice.' Occasionally a car or lorry passed.

2

———

CORLEONE

Lawful Harvest

FOR ITALIANS, the town of Corleone, deep in western Sicily, about forty miles south of Palermo, was already notorious in 1969 when Mario Puzo's book *The Godfather* appeared. Corleone meant Mafia. It was, after all, the birthplace of Luciano Liggio, the most ruthless of killers who even murdered his own *padrino* and whose word was law around Corleone and well beyond for decades until his capture in 1974. Puzo's book stayed on the best-seller list for over a year, sold more than twenty million copies, made a fortune for the author and ensured that Corleone (literally, lionheart) would become known outside Italy's borders as well as within.

Two years after *The Godfather*'s publication came Francis Ford Coppola's box-office hit and Oscar-winning film, with Marlon Brando starring as the mafia boss Vito Corleone, the book's central character, attracting unsought global recognition for the Sicilian town and tying its name still more tightly to the Mafia. The film won Academy Awards as best picture, for Marlon Brando and for the screenplay, but some cinema buffs wondered about its artistic merits. It ran for about three hours, and its sequel, *The Godfather Part Two*, for even longer, leading one critic to say, 'Like star, like film, the keynote is inflation. *The Godfather* was made from a big best-seller, a lot of money was spent on it, and it runs over three hours. Therefore it's important.' Another critic remarked, 'The immorality lies in his presentation of murderers as delightful family men.'

Indeed, speaking on CNN's television programme *Larry King Live* in 1996, Puzo described *The Godfather* as more a novel about a family than a book about crime. 'I always wish I'd written it better,' Puzo admitted. He had written it to make money rather than for the kind of critical approval that had greeted his first two novels. 'Until I was forty-eight years old, I was very poor. I never took a vacation … I just worked and so money became very important.' Born in 1920 in Hell's Kitchen, a part of central Manhattan once known for its tenements, abattoirs and factories, he grew up in one of New York's poorest and roughest districts. Italians were among the different waves of immigrants who passed through there, bringing the dialects, traditions and customs of the regions they had left behind and holding on to them when they settled in their new country.

The seventh of eight children of immigrants from the Campania region, Puzo learnt about poverty at first hand. In a family like his, and in those New York surroundings, his knowledge of Italy and Italians would have been almost as intimate as if he had been brought up in the noisy, chaotic, narrow backstreets of any large southern Italian city. He would have seen how Italians managed relationships, and would have understood the networks of power linking them and how to interpret expressions and gestures. Some people thought that Puzo had connections to the Mafia but the depiction of intrigue and violence in his book came from research, he told King, not from his own involvement with the Mob.

When Puzo decided to call the central character of *The Godfather* Vito Corleone he may have picked the surname by chance, although by dipping into Norman Lewis's book *The Honoured Society* he would have learnt that Corleone was a town on which the Mafia had a firm grip and that the *mafiosi* there were among the most ferocious. 'In this world one occasionally stumbles upon a place which, in its physical presence and the atmosphere it distils, manages somehow to match its reputation for sinister happenings. Such a town is Corleone,' wrote Lewis in 1964. He reckoned that the rate of death by violence in the town, one hundred and fifty-three murders between 1944 and 1948, was probably the highest in the world.

Un pezzo della Sicilia fra storia, arte, cultura, divertimento e legalità – a piece of Sicily made of history, art, culture, pleasure and legality. So claimed a colourful hoarding promoting Corleone that greeted me, decades after Lewis's damning verdict on the town, as I waited for my luggage at the carousels in Palermo's airport at Punta Raisi on several visits to the city. The airport is called Aeroporto Falcone-Borsellino in memory of the two anti-Mafia magistrates, Giovanni Falcone and Paolo Borsellino, murdered in 1992 in a campaign of terror masterminded by Salvatore Riina, like Liggio a son of Corleone. Born in 1930, and tied to him until Liggio's arrest in 1974, Riina was the driving force behind a ferocious mafia war in Palermo in the early 1980s that ended in victory for the Corleonesi. In an assault aimed at bringing the state to terms, Riina targeted ordinary Italians as well as magistrates and policemen. The car bomb that exploded in the centre of Florence in May 1993, and those that followed in Milan and Rome two months later showed that he was not averse to indiscriminate killing, although plans that included scattering infected syringes on the beaches of popular resorts and poisoning food in supermarkets were not put into effect. Riina was captured in January 1993 after twenty-three years on the run.

A town of about twelve thousand inhabitants, Corleone still struggles to shake off the reputation that its past, Mario Puzo's book and the film have given it. Yet the small town is also the birthplace of two saints, San Leoluca who protects people against earthquakes and San Bernardo who stood up for agricultural labourers, and it boasts a pair of noted artists. But a handful of artists, minor saints and other religious figures does not change the widely held view of Corleone as simply Cosa Nostra. What other small town, indeed what other town, has a mafia museum? Called Il Centro Internazionale di Documentazione sulla Mafia e sul Movimento Antimafia (International Centre of Documentation Regarding the Mafia and Anti-Mafia Movement), it was inaugurated by Italy's president Carlo Azeglio Ciampi in December 2000, at the same time as a United Nations conference on transnational organised crime was underway in Palermo.

Ciampi would have been driven past the large piazza near the northern edge of town, where the blue coaches of the Azienda Siciliana Trasporti pick up passengers for Palermo, and drop them off, and where they depart for towns like Prizzi and San Giuseppe Jato. Windows streaming with condensation in winter, these coaches arrive at Palermo's railway station early in the morning, packed with students and the carless of Corleone and of places in between, many of the young on their way to university lectures, the old often to their business with bureaucracy. And they make the return trip in the early afternoon. After parking my car near Corleone's bus stops, across the road from a small public garden that like many in southern villages some call the *villa*, I set off towards the centre. The town had changed little since I first travelled through; it was grey, lacking appeal then and was grey and without appeal now. During that visit several years before, I had needed to receive a fax from London and found a small shop where I could do so and where a silent old crone charged me steeply for the service. That had been my first taste of the town.

When I reached the small raised square outside the town hall I sat and waited until Gino Felicetti joined me and took me across the road to the museum where he worked. After pointing out the plaque that Ciampi had unveiled in a courtyard, he showed me the vast archive, yard upon yard of shelves filled with dusty, fading box files of court papers from the maxi-trial of over three hundred *mafiosi* that took place in Palermo between February 1986 and December 1987. The maxi-trial was the trial that gave Falcone public prominence and left the Mafia eager for revenge.

Felicetti's parents had emigrated to England in the early 1960s and he was born in Bristol in 1965. 'My father was a bespoke tailor and both he and my mother thought that work would be easier to find there than here in Sicily, and that children would have more opportunities.' He returned regularly to Corleone and in 1989 remained to teach English, a job to which many young English-speaking people turn when they want to remain in Italy. After almost ten years of commuting between Corleone and the language school in Palermo he moved back to England, but the opportunity at the mafia museum lured him once more to Corleone.

'You know, returning here again hasn't really worked out. I've been screwed by coming back,' he told me when I telephoned a while after we met in Corleone. Political infighting in Corleone meant he had not received money that had been due for months and he planned to return to England. 'It's rather a disappointment as working in the mafia museum is something worthwhile, a personal mission.' Felicetti's story is typical of the Mezzogiorno, the story of generation after generation compelled to seek work abroad and of hopes of opportunities in Italy dashed by maladministration or worse.

If Corleone is proud of its Roman milestone and other archaeological pieces displayed in the town museum, it is shy about its mafia museum, an attraction that it seems reluctant to acknowledge. Even so, Felicetti told me as we walked among the museum's box files, three or four coachloads of American tourists arrive every week, making a stop on their trips from Palermo, eager to absorb the atmosphere and learn about the Mafia in *The Godfather*'s own town. What they find is less threatening than the oppressive, suspicious place about which Lewis wrote in the early 1960s but like most towns in southern Italy whose shop windows are evidence of modest local incomes Corleone remains a poor community of dull colours and scruffy streets. The average GDP per head in the province of Palermo is around one half of that in many northern Italian provinces.

After saying goodbye to Felicetti I explored the town, where few people were around. The man who served me a cappuccino was less reticent than an almost wordless local behind a bar who had eyed me balefully on my first visit to Corleone, but his was a cold greeting all the same. He may have been thinking that outsiders only ever speak ill of the town or write of its black past, so why make them welcome.

Corleone offers little to tourists looking for mementoes or gifts. But who needs mementoes? To visit is enough: Corleone, Marlon Brando, *The Godfather* ... the Mafia. When their coaches round the bend and the town on its rocky outcrop comes into view excited anticipation ripples through the groups of American visitors. Yet as they file up the main street to the museum, a warehouse of records of a violent past, many of those tourists are probably unaware that Cosa Nostra is much more than celluloid fiction, that it is far from finished and that its grim hold over the town persists.

'The challenge here is the Mafia's nefarious presence,' admitted Nicolò Nicolosi, a soft-spoken, bespectacled politician who served as mayor from 2001 to 2006, and who sought me out after learning that I had spoken with Felicetti. 'Some people want to change Corleone's name to Cor di Leone, to improve its image with the outside world. But the important thing is to change its people's habits, to change the town's destiny. They need to recognise that it is possible to change, and to change what the future holds for them.' Not from Corleone itself, Nicolosi is a local man all the same, born in 1942 in the small town of Bisacquino, about fifteen miles to the south. An able political navigator who served from 2001 to 2006 in the lower house of the national parliament in Rome, on the government benches during Silvio

Berlusconi's rightwing administration, Nicolosi cut his teeth in the youth movement of the Christian Democrat Party.

This party dominated Sicilian politics from the end of the second world war until the end of the 1980s, so it is not surprising that the first politician to gain the dubious distinction of being found guilty of association with the Mafia happened to be a Christian Democrat. And perhaps no surprise either that this politician, Vito Ciancimino, came from Corleone. Perhaps Mario Puzo took the Godfather's first name from this infamous figure whose father had emigrated to New York in 1910 before returning to open a barber's shop in his home town. Vito Ciancimino was elected to Palermo's city council in 1956 but remained officially resident in Corleone for another seven years. He was briefly Palermo's mayor in 1970 but won his notoriety as head of public works, a position from which he was able to do favours for his *mafiosi* associates and cause enormous damage to the city. While Ciancimino held office, the city suffered what would later be called the sack of Palermo when citrus groves were grubbed up, and beaux arts villas and their gardens destroyed, to be replaced by high-rise blocks.

Nicolosi's long career in politics also included time on Palermo's city council from 1978 to 1984, during which he too headed public works for a period, and from 1986 until 2001 he was a member of the Sicilian parliament. Talking with Corleone's mayor was too good an opportunity to miss. 'How can the many and close links between Cosa Nostra and politics be cut?' I asked. Looking me straight in the eye, he replied firmly, 'Politicians who are touched by the Mafia should be put aside.' He was convincing when he spoke but politicians are skilled at sincerity – that goes with the job – and a sceptical ear helps in the South whoever the speaker is.

Certainly Nicolosi made a controversial decision when he was elected mayor, appointing a lawyer who represented the family of Salvatore Riina to be Corleone's head of tourism and culture. Some people thought that the town's first citizen had a duty to be openly and uncompromisingly anti-Mafia, and there also appeared to be a question of incompatibility. Under Nicolosi's predecessor, the town of Corleone had always been a civil co-plaintiff in cases where Riina and members of his family were defendants. This meant that the town's new head of culture and tourism would be opposing the town itself in the law courts. The uproar subsided as the Riinas' lawyer soon resigned, but for Sicilians, who measure words and actions carefully, able to say much while speaking little, a message had been sent about who might be interlocutors of Nicolosi's administration.

'A black past and a grey present, what does the future offer?' I asked. 'We put our hope in our youth,' Nicolosi replied. But many of Corleone's young people have left the town, and they continue to leave, drawn by prospects of brighter, less troubled futures elsewhere. One small group that has stayed calls itself the Cooperativa Lavoro e Non Solo (literally, not only work cooperative), an agricultural concern. 'We are known as the *cooperativa dei matti*, the cooperative of crazies,' Calogero Parisi, the cooperative's chairman, told me with a wry smile, 'because three of our nine members are socially disadvantaged, being either paranoid or schizophrenic.'

Some thought that mental illness affected the six other partners as well as those under treatment. Madness perhaps, but a certain courage is needed to break with local conventions and defy mafia bosses. Cooperativa Lavoro e Non Solo works land once owned by *mafiosi*, confiscated by the courts, taken into state ownership and then assigned to the cooperative for cultivation. Willingness to work land that had belonged to Liggio, Riina, members of their families and fronts for them, as well as to lesser-known *mafiosi*, is a measure of high unemployment, however, as well as of refusal to submit to the Mafia and commitment to change society for the better. Other young Corleonesi asked Parisi if they might join.

Cooperativa Lavoro e Non Solo was assigned its first land at the beginning of 2000, about twenty-six acres for arable cultivation near Corleone that had been confiscated from a member of Liggio's family. Two years later an even larger area of arable land in Corleone was handed over to Parisi's cooperative. And a further two years on, in May 2004, the cooperative was offered the chance to diversify by taking over twenty acres of vineyards in the town of Monreale, just south of Palermo. 'Following their confiscation, the vineyards had been handed to another cooperative but the authorities revoked the assignment after the police said there was a risk of mafia infiltration,' explained Parisi. The vineyards had lain abandoned until Cooperativa Lavoro e Non Solo took them over but it would suffer a bad setback when, after three years' work, *mafiosi* nipped most of the buds that were growing on the vines.

By then the cooperative had already moved further afield, accepting almost fifty acres of vineyards and arable land near Canicattì and presenting

Parisi and his partners with new challenges. One was the distance of about sixty miles, along poor roads across the middle of Sicily, through the broad sweep of rolling hills that Coppola vividly captured in his film of The Godfather.

Far more challenging, however, was the Mafia's presence in Canicattì and the surrounding area. At the end of 2002 the Consiglio Superiore della Magistratura (CSM, the Italian magistracy's governing body) held a two-day seminar for magistrates in Palermo; the subject was the evolution of organised crime and the effectiveness of counter-measures. One of the speakers was Anna Maria Palma, a senior anti-Mafia prosecutor with special responsibility for Agrigento province, who described Canicattì as a centre of particular economic wealth where the Mafia 'appears to have total control over the ground'. A little more than a year later, after investigations that included telephone taps and the shadowing of suspects, she was behind the arrest of forty-three people, including Canicattì's mayor. Two and a half months after the mayor's arrest a special commissioner, a vice-prefect at the home affairs ministry in Rome, was appointed to run the town and he decided that Corleone's Cooperativa Lavoro e Non Solo should be offered the opportunity to cultivate those fifty acres, land previously assigned by the arrested mayor to relations of the *mafioso* from whom it had been confiscated.

Under a law enacted in March 1996, real estate confiscated from *mafiosi* becomes and remains an asset of the state, even though its transfer to the local authorities gives the mayor of the city or town where the property is located the job of deciding what should be done with it. Local authorities are allowed to administer such property directly or to assign it rent free to official bodies or to voluntary associations, cooperatives, therapeutic communities or centres for treating drug addicts. The law prefers that local authorities assign such properties to other organisations rather than administer them directly.

Successive governments in Rome put forward legislation to tackle the Mafia, and laws were passed in 1956, 1962 and 1965, albeit to little effect. Italy had to wait until September 1982 for parliament to take serious action; it arrived in the shape of a law called the Legge Rognoni-La Torre, which takes its name partly from that of the home affairs minister at the time, Virgilio Rognoni. The second name on the 1982 law is that of Pio La Torre, the leader of the Communist Party in Sicily, whom the Mafia had gunned down just over four months before the law was approved. Rognoni would later keep up his efforts as head of the magistracy's governing body during Silvio Berlusconi's administration from 2001 to 2006, when legality itself seemed under attack from the government.

Luigi Croce, whom I would meet in Messina, where he had moved from the Sicilian capital, would tell me about La Torre's murder. He was the prosecutor on duty in Palermo on the day at the end of April in 1982 that La Torre died. From Messina at Sicily's northeastern tip, Croce had been a magistrate for seventeen years and was accustomed to the brutal reality of daily life in the city that had become his home. As the duty prosecutor he took the call that arrived in the late morning to report a shooting in Corso Pisani near the Cuba, an historic monument, the last remaining pavilion of a park laid out in the twelfth century, on the road to Monreale just outside Palermo's centre. The call merely said that people were injured and that Croce should get there at once. Pio La Torre's murder was the one that the prosecutor would always remember out of many with which he had dealt or would later deal.

Riding motorcycles, masked and armed with handguns and machine-pistols, the killers had ambushed La Torre as he was on his way to party headquarters. He died at once under a hail of bullets from the gunmen's weapons, but a colleague who was driving the car in which La Torre was travelling was able to draw his pistol and fire a few shots before he too was dead. By the time Croce had covered the mile and a half that separated the law court from the crime scene, many of La Torre's party colleagues and friends had arrived and were milling around, distraught and uncomprehending. 'The scene was truly terrible. Pio La Torre's body was splayed out in the car, his feet sticking from an open door.'

What lay behind the crime and who had commissioned it were far from clear at the time. During the late 1970s and early 1980s, leftwing extremists pursued a murderous campaign in which their targets included leftwing figures. Could the Red Brigades, the Front Line or one of the other terrorist groups have killed La Torre? Some people thought so but others suspected that deviant secret services, either Italian or American, might have been responsible as La Torre had also spoken out strongly against a decision to allow the installation of American cruise missiles at Comiso in southeast

Sicily, opposing the militarisation this would bring. In taking charge of the case, Croce could not afford to disregard any possible motive for the crime. However, the murder of La Torre, who had written a few months before about how the Mafia had raised its visibility with a dramatic sequence of political killings that had already hit a peak with that of the Sicilian region's president, Pier Santi Mattarella, turned out to be a mafia affair.

The Mafia was worried less by La Torre's words than by what he did in parliament where, because of his knowledge of how the Mafia operated and his determination that the state should fight it, legislation was in hand to write the crime of association with the Mafia into the penal code; it would become known as Articolo 416bis. As well as defining this new crime, the Rognoni-La Torre law struck at mafia assets, modifying the 1965 law that had clearly proved inadequate. Parliamentary inertia, encouraged by southern politicians who owed their jobs to the Mafia, blocked the bill and not even La Torre's murder speeded up its passage. The trigger for action and for the bill's approval was the killing in September 1982 of General Carlo Alberto dalla Chiesa, who had arrived in Palermo as the city's prefect immediately after La Torre's murder.

The Rognoni-La Torre law gives magistrates and the police wide powers to investigate the origins and ownership of assets in mafia cases and makes the seizure of such assets easier, the burden of proof lying with defendants rather than the prosecutors.

Capturing *mafiosi*, winning convictions and imprisoning them is only part of the battle against the Mafia. Another part, less obvious but crucial, is to separate *mafiosi*, their families and their fronts from the illicit wealth they have accumulated. Over the years I have come to know several *amministratori giudiziari*, court-appointed administrators of seized mafia assets like Elio Collova, a Palermo accountant, and Gaetano Cappellano Seminara, a lawyer in the city, who are responsible for the two of the largest seizures ever ordered. Both said that the man I should speak to was Cesare Vincenti, the presiding judge of the section of Palermo's court that deals with the seizure and confiscation of mafia assets in western Sicily. And I would later call on Vincenti in Palermo.

Armed police stood outside his office in the court building overlooking Piazza della Memoria, a square built as a memorial to those judges and prosecutors murdered by the Mafia. Vincenti had had police protection for a decade, from the time he was a prosecutor in the Sicilian capital's appeal court and inevitably involved in important mafia trials. However, Vincenti's work during the mid and late 1990s was not his first experience of the Mafia. He had been a judge in the criminal court in Agrigento in the 1970s and had transferred to Palermo's court soon after the enactment of the Rognoni-La Torre law to deal with the first cases of seizure and confiscation. Vincenti wrote the judgement that seized Vito Ciancimino's assets.

'It is a very effective weapon for attacking the Mafia's economic power and the law has attracted a lot of attention from the authorities in other countries.' But Vincenti was worried about proposals that threatened to limit the courts' control over mafia assets by creating a role for the civil service from the moment those assets were seized. 'The risk of "political" appointments must not be ignored as such appointments would increase the threat of mafia infiltration into the management of the assets.'

Figures supported Vincenti's satisfaction with how the Rognoni-La Torre law had sliced into the mafia economy. Between 1993 and 2004 the court in Palermo had seized assets conservatively valued at about two and a half billion euros and confiscated assets worth more than one and a half billion euros. Despite closing dozens of cases dealing with the seizure or confiscation of assets every year, the arrival of new cases meant that the court had well over a hundred outstanding cases in hand. And other courts throughout the Mezzogiorno could also point to the large volume of assets taken from the Mafia and to the heavy workloads they faced. Many cases involved agricultural assets, and from this came the need to find people to work the land.

For well over a century people in southern Italy have deserted the countryside, emigrating first to the United States and, when its doors closed and after the second world war, to Italy's industrial cities in the north, to Latin America, Australia, Canada and northern Europe, so the readiness of cooperatives like Lavoro e Non Solo to cultivate the land is a step back against time. I asked Parisi, the cooperative's chairman, to tell me his best memory of what had already been a remarkable experience. 'The finest moment was in September 2001 when our tractor entered the first field to begin ploughing,' he said, his face lighting up at the memory of that day.

Land was a burning issue in the South for centuries and while walking around Corleone I noticed a plaque on a wall in a side street that is a reminder of a particularly inflamed period when the town was the centre of unrest. Bernardino Verro, a Socialist mayor, was murdered there, in that anonymous side street, by the Mafia on 3 November 1915. He was not only the mayor and a political leader, the plaque told me, but also an agricultural worker who had fought for workers' rights and the brotherhood of man.

'Bernardino Verro was an historic figure and represents Corleone's other face. Everybody knows about Liggio, Ciancimino, Riina and Bernardo Provenzano, the bosses of Sicily's most ferocious Mafia, but few remember that Corleone was also a centre of a struggle for agricultural workers' rights and for democracy,' said Dino Paternostro, secretary of the town's Camera del Lavoro, the local branch of the Confederazione Generale Italiana del Lavoro (CGIL) trade union. I sat in his scantily furnished office, listening as he told me about himself, his family and the other side to the town. Until he went to work in Germany in the 1960s, returning home once a year to see his family, Paternostro's father had been an agricultural worker, a wielder of scythe and hoe, and had also been involved in a struggle for the land.

'Verro posed a serious threat to the region's landowners when he set up his agricultural workers' movement in 1892. The *fascio dei lavoratori*, sheaf of workers, strong when they stand together but weak when alone, would become one of Sicily's best organised grass-roots bodies,' Paternostro told me. The organisation met in Corleone in July 1893 to draw up a list of demands to improve the conditions of agricultural workers. Strikes followed, the movement was broken by government edict, and the leaders arrested and tried by military courts. After an amnesty and release from jail, Verro established another workers' movement. This was also banned and he fled to America to escape arrest, but the political climate in Rome was changing and he would return to Corleone and enter politics.

Verro had been on his way home, walking up the hill from the town hall, as I had done, when killers shot him, pumping four bullets into his head while he lay bleeding on the ground. Twenty-two men were later sent for trial but less than three weeks after proceedings began the prosecutor, probably a victim of the Mafia's well-known skills of persuasion, said he was convinced the defendants were innocent and closed his case.

In abeyance during fascism, the threat to landowners would be revived by laws promulgated in the autumn of 1944 that allowed labourers who joined together in cooperatives to take over uncultivated land or land that was badly managed. These laws also laid down new rules to govern the sharing of crops between owners and those who worked the land, but they encountered determined opposition from landowners, and the landowners had the support of *mafiosi*. The struggle to put those laws into effect would give Corleone another working-class anti-Mafia hero and martyr. At the time the laws were enacted Placido Rizzotto, a thirty-year-old from Corleone, was with the partisans, fighting the Germans and the forces of the fascist Salò Republic that Mussolini established on the shores of Lake Garda after Italy signed an armistice with Anglo-American forces in September 1943. When Rizzotto discarded his Italian army uniform, he joined the resistance movement in the mountains of northeast Italy, where it borders Austria and Slovenia.

Returning to Sicily in 1945, Rizzotto took with him the memories of his part in the fight for democracy and soon became involved in the agricultural workers' efforts to implement the laws on land reform. One of Dino Paternostro's predecessors, as secretary of Corleone's Camera del Lavoro Rizzotto helped organise its first direct action in the autumn of 1946, the occupation of pieces of land identified as suitable for takeover by agricultural workers. Formerly feudal land run by *gabelloti* and *campieri* (estate managers and guards) and belonging to the Mafia were the first tracts targeted, and on 23 October, travelling by foot or on mules from Corleone, the workers moved onto them. Wanting a map for the Rocche di Rao district that shows those areas of the countryside just north of Corleone where the *lotta contadina* (agricultural workers' struggle) got underway, I found that the best available is one prepared by Italy's military geographic institute in 1930, and still on sale almost eighty years later.

A surge of satisfaction may have raised the spirits of those poor agricultural workers as they stepped onto the Mafia's fields north of Corleone, but they quickly learnt that their struggle would be hard and bloody, exchanging fire that October day in 1946 with *mafiosi* near a hill called Sant'Oliva. Carabinieri military police intervened but instead of enforcing the laws on land reform they arrested four agricultural workers. No *mafioso* was apprehended and that evening *mafiosi* fired shots at the home of one of the *contadini*'s leaders. What happened in Corleone was far from an isolated event. Confrontations took place elsewhere in the Mezzogiorno and numerous trade union leaders and agricultural workers died trying to get the laws put into effect.

Probably no event in the *lotta contadina* would be remembered more often or more clearly than the *festa* on May Day of 1947 at Portella della Ginestra. A broad pasture lying between bare mountains, at about two thousand five hundred feet above sea level, Portella della Ginestra is around twelve miles to the north of Corleone as the crow flies but far more along the roads that twist between the hills and fields in that part of Sicily. It lies on the country road from Piana degli Albanesi to San Giuseppe Jato, a town with a reputation like Corleone, but the site draws visitors as I found when I went there and mingled with a coachload of leftwing pensioners and several groups who had arrived by car. In a field beside the road a group of large rocks forms a memorial. Carved on one of those rocks, and painted in red, are the words telling the story of what happened: 'To break the *contadini*'s fight for land reform, the bullets of the Mafia and the landowners were fired here on the men, women and children of Piana, San Cipirrello and San Giuseppe who were celebrating Labour Day and the victory of 20 April'. Eleven people died when a large band of *mafiosi* deployed higher up the hill opened fire with arms that included automatic weapons; police later found around eight hundred spent shells in the area.

Less than a year later, Placido Rizzotto himself would be dead. On 10 March 1948 he left the trade union's offices in Corleone at around eight in the evening with two colleagues, stopped to chat in front of a bar and was joined by another man who, acting on Luciano Liggio's instructions, lured him away after his colleagues left. At around ten o'clock Rizzotto started to walk for the last time down Corleone's main street, the Via Bentivegna, towards the public gardens and a square whose name would be changed about half a century later to Piazza Falcone e Borsellino. What then happened would never be known, but it seems likely that Rizzotto was forced at gunpoint to go with kidnappers who would soon become his murderers. In the days that followed, his parents and colleagues searched desperately but unsuccessfully for him.

A body thought to be Rizzotto's was found in December of the following year in a deep fissure in the side of Mount Casale, about five miles of rough countryside north of Corleone. Mount Casale is one of the lower peaks leading to Rocca Busambra, a menacing cliff rising to about five thousand feet and looming above Ficuzza, where a palatial hunting lodge was built for the Bourbon king Ferdinand III of Sicily in 1803. Wanting to learn more about the area, I drove past the palace and along an asphalted road that turned to track after a couple of miles. I would have done better not to have believed the map as I passed an anxious hour without seeing another soul on the deeply rutted track, a lurching, bone-shaking ride through the woods of scrub oak beneath the Rocca Busambra, experiencing the kind of terrain over which the king had hunted and Rizzotto's killers had taken him.

That the body was found was due largely to the determination of a young captain in the Carabinieri who had recently been posted to Corleone. He was Carlo Alberto dalla Chiesa, the man who would be murdered by Cosa Nostra in Palermo in September 1982, soon after he had taken up the post of prefect in the city. The fissure was evidently a tomb for mafia victims; along with the remains that were believed to be Rizzotto's were two other human skeletons. A carabiniere was lowered on a rope about one hundred and forty feet down the gap in the earth and was able to see the remains with a torch.

Well over half a century after Rizzotto's murder, mysteries still fog that fateful evening in March 1948. One involves a shepherd boy who was reported as having witnessed the killing in the Feudo Malvello where he was tending his father's flock. Admitted to Corleone's hospital in shock, he died soon after. The hospital was headed by the local mafia boss, a doctor and the godfather of Liggio, who would organise his own *padrino*'s murder in an ambush on the main road into Corleone in August 1958. And mystery surrounds the investigations and the trials of people accused of Rizzotto's murder. Despite the efforts of his family, trade unionists and dalla Chiesa, the Italian justice system was unable to find anyone guilty of the crime and in 1961, thirteen years after the murder, the supreme court confirmed the acquittals passed on numerous defendants in lower courts.

Long after the *lotta contadina* had been forgotten by most Italians, Placido Rizzotto would be remembered in 2001 by thirteen young people in San Giuseppe Jato when they decided to give the name of the murdered trade union activist to their newly born farming cooperative. Like the Cooperativa Lavoro e Non Solo in Corleone, Cooperativa Placido Rizzotto Libera Terra cultivates land confiscated from the Mafia. Five years after being set up, the cooperative was working about five hundred acres of land, more than three hundred of them given over to cereals, pulses and melons and the rest split between vineyards and pasture. In addition to the work of its own members, the cooperative needed to hire as many as ten day-labourers during busy periods of the year.

I had travelled from Corleone, past Portella della Ginestra, to reach the cooperative and a sign near the entrance to it, a cluster of farm buildings in a valley at the end of a track, told me that the property lies on the Sentiero della Legalità, the path of legality. Some locals still call the buildings the Casa Coglitore, after the baroness who once owned them. She sold them to her estate manager and from him the property ended up in the hands of the Brusca family of San Giuseppe Jato, allies of the Corleonesi; Giovanni Brusca was the killer who set off the explosive charge that murdered Giovanni Falcone, his magistrate wife and three members of their escort. Parts of the land assigned to the cooperative also belonged the Bruscas, other parts to Corleonesi like Salvatore Riina.

Gianluca Faraone, the cooperative's chairman, was doing university research in agronomy when he became involved. 'I was looking for something more than books and theory, something that would involve me directly in the society in which I live. As soon as I saw the notice about land being assigned to young people's cooperatives, I knew that this was what I wanted to do.' We sat in a large room that serves as a dining room for the cooperative and visitors who stay in the rooms that it lets; packets and bottles of its products stood on a table by the wall, evidence of what the cooperative had achieved.

Faraone's father was an official in the CGIL trade union. Politics was always discussed at home when he was a boy – the American missile base at Comiso, against which Pio La Torre campaigned, was one of the big local issues that Faraone remembers – and a supportive family buttressed his enthusiasm for a venture that faced serious difficulties from the beginning. Cosa Nostra was a constant worry, not least because the cooperative had directly impinged on the territory of the bloodiest part of that bloody organisation. 'There were problems as soon as we started. Taking possession of the land was one as some of the land we were assigned was hard to identify, and some was still cultivated by the family or friends of the people from whom it had been confiscated. The business was risky. No agricultural labourers in the area wanted to work for us when we began. They were scared.' And nobody would hire the cooperative a threshing machine for the first harvest in July 2002. The Carabinieri stepped in, however, found one and oversaw the work.

There were many setbacks. Flocks of sheep were deliberately driven across cultivated land and there were cases of arson. Moreover, the cooperative faced severe financial difficulties from the outset. None of its partners was paid during the first year and five years later, although the situation had improved, monthly pay ranged from just five hundred and fifty to eleven hundred euros. 'Our own labour was our investment in the business,' said Faraone. Borrowing start-up capital to buy seed and machinery was impossible as none of the partners had assets or earnings, and they could not borrow against the land because the land was not theirs to offer in guarantee. Not until 2005 would a commercial bank be willing to lend, and even then the loan it granted had to be repaid within the year.

Fortunately, Italy's strong, left-leaning cooperative movement came to the rescue with a donation to repair farm machinery, and a large Bologna-based consumer cooperative became an institutional partner and paid fifty thousand euros for its share. Establishing the relationship with the retail cooperative was crucial in another sense also, as it provides the Cooperativa Placido Rizzotto Libera Terra with a vital outlet for some of the lentils and chickpeas harvested each year and the pasta produced from the durum wheat grown on the land it works.

The cooperative decided that the pasta would be made in Corleone, in a small *pastificio* close to Piazza Falcone e Borsellino. 'We thought of sending the wheat to the Abruzzo or the Marches, regions with a tradition of making top-quality pasta, but believed that the right choice was a *pastificio* here, to involve others in the fight against the Mafia, to show that Corleone also means what Placido Rizzotto fought for and not only Mafia.' On the packets of pasta are the words 'from land freed from the Mafia', and those same words appear on the bottles of white wine made from catarratto, a Sicilian grape variety, and on the bags of durum-wheat flour produced by the Cooperativa Lavoro e Non Solo.

Boxes holding bottles of extra-virgin olive oil produced by the Casa dei Giovani in Castelvetrano, about forty miles southwest of Corleone, carry the words 'from land in Sicily returned to the legality of the state'. Like the products of Cooperativa Lavoro e Non Solo and Cooperativa Placido

Rizzotto Libera Terra, the products from Castelvetrano, grown on land confiscated from various *mafiosi*, including the Corleonese boss of bosses Bernardo Provenzano, are sold through a voluntary organisation called Libera based near Turin in northwest Italy. As with the two cooperatives, money is always a problem but the Casa dei Giovani, established to help drug addicts, former prisoners and prisoners on parole, by Padre Salvatore Lo Bue, a priest from Bagheria near Palermo, received some financial help from the Compagnia San Paolo, a philanthropic foundation in Turin.

The Casa dei Giovani sounded interesting, so I decided to make a detour to see what it was doing. I drove south after leaving San Cipirello, passing through Santa Margherita di Belice and Montevago, destroyed by earthquakes in January 1968, Montevago's gaunt ruins giving proof, if any is needed, of an earthquake's terrible power. Appropriately, I met Padre Lo Bue in a bar across the road from Castelvetrano's prison where some of his lads had been guests.

Like the two cooperatives, the Casa dei Giovani has encountered many difficulties. Farming several parcels of land spread over a wide area is one of them. And an ever-present concern is the fact that the land the young people work was once owned by powerful mafia figures. I watched as a small group worked in a vineyard in sight of the former owner, under house arrest after serving part of his jail sentence, not the easiest kind of neighbourly relationship.

By paying its young people seven hundred and fifty euros a month, giving them board and lodging, and keeping them off the streets, the Casa dei Giovani undermines Cosa Nostra's influence and it has been warned that it is unwelcome, its buildings and farm machinery set on fire, hundreds of olive trees cut down and livestock stolen. But the Mafia also operates indirectly and its insidious influence affects the Sicilian bureaucracy. 'Red tape caused us enormous damage. For three years we had to pay an outside contractor to press our olives and bottle the oil. Council employees said they had no time to prepare the certificates we needed to use our own equipment. Hidden hands were definitely holding back those certificates,' Padre Lo Bue told me bitterly.

Farming is a demanding physical activity and the young people have to work hard, but that is far better than one alternative. 'I have been in three prisons and nothing is worse than prison,' grimaced Antonio, a short, lively, muscular fellow who tried to get me talking about William Blake. 'This is the first time that I have earned money honestly and I have been able to buy a car.' Karim, another former prisoner who has been trained to look after livestock, sends his savings home to his mother in Casablanca.

The priest has no illusions about what lies ahead for his young charges, who stay at the farm for two years at the most. 'Many addicts fall back into drugs; finding work is very hard and not everyone is interested in farming.'

And Padre Lo Bue has no illusions about what to expect from politicians. They do not often speak against the Mafia; when they do, it is because they think they can win votes by doing so, and they rarely follow up their words with action. Padre Lo Bue expected nothing by way of real help from the visit of a senior minister at the inauguration of a farm renovated to provide accommodation for green tourism and buildings where livestock would be kept. But such events can be useful. 'They give us a higher profile and make local politicians and authorities think we enjoy powerful support,' he said.

Alas, there are few projects aimed at combating the Mafia or offering an alternative to it, like the cooperatives and the Casa dei Giovani, and those few struggle to survive. Perhaps in northern Italy such ventures would enjoy some official encouragement and backing. Certainly, civic spirit is missing in the South and what support the young people in the cooperatives and Padre Lo Bue have received has come mostly come from the north of the country.

Teenagers from Tuscany go to Sicily to work on the cooperatives' farms during their summer holidays. Luigi Ciotti, a priest from Turin, is a driving force behind Libera and an anti-Mafia 'caravan' that travels around Italy spreading the anti-Mafia message. Gian Carlo Caselli, the Turinese prosecutor who had asked to be transferred to Palermo to head the prosecution service when Falcone and Borsellino were murdered, actively supported Libera and the cooperatives after returning to Turin. I met a coachload of Genoese members of the cooperative movement on a visit to a former mafia vineyard who told me that, if they could, they always bought products grown by the young people's cooperatives. Yet, taking the lead from their politicians, Italians have been largely indifferent.

'You know, the biggest price paid in the struggle against Cosa Nostra has been paid by Sicilians themselves,' Paternostro remarked as we sat talking in his office. Certainly Corleone already had its own long list of murder victims before the Corleonesi became the experts in murdering elsewhere. Pio La Torre, the Sicilian whose name was on the law that helps confiscate part of the wealth the Mafia has accumulated, was well known in Corleone long before dying a national figure in Palermo. La Torre went there after Rizzotto was murdered to do the job in the Camera del Lavoro that Rizzotto had done and Paternostro would do later.

Not long after I talked with Paternostro in Corleone, Cosa Nostra showed that the CGIL trade union there continued to be an irritant by setting fire to his car. Across all the Mezzogiorno, arson is a favourite form of intimidation, of sending warnings to bring people into line. 'Cars burn easily but burn best if their windows are broken first and petrol splashed inside. Yet however it burns, seeing your own car in flames doesn't leave you unmoved,' he told me when we met up later in Rome. 'When you see the terror in your children's eyes you wonder why you stay in Sicily.'

For him, the renewed interest in Placido Rizzotto shows that some people refuse to stay under the Mafia's thumb, an expression of pride. 'But living with the name of Corleone is a heavy burden, having that name in your passport marks you out.' In fact, for most Italians and for Americans on their bus tours from Palermo, Corleone still means Mafia.

3

_____

PALERMO

Questions of Health

I LAST SAW GIUSEPPE CIURO, a non-commissioned officer of the Guardia di Finanza, Italy's financial police, in September 2003, when we had a long and pleasant lunch at Gigi Mangia, a small, discreet restaurant in a pleasant pedestrian precinct in the centre of Palermo. A journalist who covers crime in the city and in central and western Sicily, mainly Mafia, was with us at a table at the back of the restaurant. The bill settled, we left the restaurant and said goodbye near the flower seller at the end of the street. Embrace, left cheek against left cheek, right against right. 'Ciao, a presto, ci vediamo.' See you soon, we said to each other, but that was the last time I saw the chipper and chatty Pippo Ciuro.

Usually we ate the good local food at Le Tre Sorelle, a simple trattoria with tablecloths of green-check cotton and a brown-tiled floor a few yards from the top of the Capo street market, the bustling, grubby stretch of Via Porta Carini whose stalls are packed with brightly coloured fruit and vegetables brought from the countryside around the city, and with bulky swordfish, pulsating octopuses and other fish freshly pulled from the sea. When I visit Palermo I often call at Luigi Ciafrone's small shop, its shelves piled with packets of scorching Sicilian chilli powder, pistachios from Bronte, lentils from Pantelleria, dried figs from Monreale and dozens of other types of spice, nut, dried fruit and legume. Palermo's law court stands just round the corner, which is how I came to know the market and Le Tre Sorelle, and where I first met Pippo Ciuro in February 2001.

For about ten years he had been the right-hand man of Antonio Ingroia, an experienced anti-Mafia magistrate involved in some of the most delicate and complicated investigations and prosecutions handled in Palermo, and had shared an office with him. Ciuro helped ferret out details of the money that financed the beginnings of the business empire of Silvio Berlusconi, the media tycoon who turned to politics. Those investigations provided part of evidence in the trial that would end with the conviction for complicity with the Mafia of Marcello Dell'Utri. Ciuro's work resulted in a report of over five hundred pages and I was hoping to obtain a copy when I was let through the armoured door from the corridor into Ingroia's office.

Ciuro was a friendly source of information for journalists seeking leads and copies of documents but I did not want anything when we met in September 2003. I had telephoned him from England at the end of June to ask about Giovanni Del Santo, a Sicilian bookkeeper associated with companies in Berlusconi's empire in the late 1970s. It was a fine summer's day and I was sitting in the gardens of Rochester cathedral when I punched his number on my mobile telephone. 'Ciao Pippo. How's life in Palermo?' And after the usual exchange of greetings, I arrived at the reason for my call. 'Was Del Santo a mafioso?' The question was met with an intake of breath, silence and then 'Buon'anima', an invocation that Del Santo's soul should rest in peace.

When we met a few months after that telephone call in June 2003, we left the law court together, through the main door and past the ranks of old Fiats and Lancias, some with blue lamps on their roofs, all with extra steel in their bodywork and windows of armoured glass, defence against bullets but not explosives, as everybody learnt when Giovanni Falcone, his wife and bodyguards were murdered in May 1992. The names of Falcone, his magistrate wife Francesca Morvillo and their friend Paolo Borsellino, killed two months later, are engraved on a monumental grey stone wall that curves around the Piazza della Memoria behind the law court.

In the late 1970s when he was tackling bankruptcy cases, before he became involved in mafia investigations and tied by the restrictions that go with that work, Falcone might often have walked down the ramp from the law court's door, as Ciuro and I did, out of the gate where carabinieri stand, turned the corner and gone past the Le Tre Sorelle with its narrow balconies from where one can see the beginning of the Capo market and the small vans loaded with strong-tasting *broccolo siciliano*, dark green cone-like cauliflower. The Massimo opera house with its khaki-coloured stone, columns, palm trees and the large statues of lions guarding the ceremonial steps to its entrance is not far, perhaps three hundred yards, and Gigi Mangia only five minutes' walk from there. Over lunch Ciuro spoke little about his work with Ingroia or developments in the various mafia trials that were underway but talked mainly about his hopes and ambitions as a young man. Perhaps Ciuro talked about the past because he knew that his future held little.

My mobile telephone rang late in the morning of 5 November 2003 as I left the offices of an investment bank in Milan with an executive of the public relations firm that worked for it, and she watched as I listened. 'Rather a shock?' she asked as I closed the telephone. It definitely was. 'They've arrested your friend in Palermo,' the caller had told me. I wondered which friend. It was Ciuro, who had been as cosy with Cosa Nostra's friends as he had with journalists. As much as any, the case of Ciuro and the people with whom he was involved shows Cosa Nostra's ability to infiltrate institutions and suborn public servants.

With his desk in Ingroia's high-security office, Ciuro was well placed to spy. Aiming to discover what progress had been made in investigations, he lied to a non-commissioned officer of the Carabinieri, saying that Ingroia had asked him to coordinate a working group for the search for Bernardo Provenzano, Cosa Nostra's *capo dei capi*, the boss of bosses for whom the police had been looking for decades. Avoiding the use of his own password to make inquiries, which could have been traced, Ciuro asked other people who worked for anti-Mafia magistrates to dig into the computer system.

Now that Ingroia no longer shared his office, it seemed larger when I called on him three years later to ask about that difficult period in 2003. 'I had been let into the investigations into Ciuro long before he was arrested and was told to keep up appearances but to make sure he didn't get hold of confidential information.' In fact, the investigations began in December 2002. Having a suspected mole working at a desk across the room must have been stressful and made for a tense relationship, I suggested. 'Knowing my colleagues' suspicions, it was very hard to pretend that everything was normal. We had worked together for many years and I imagine that Ciuro guessed something was up.'

Short, with the type of closely trimmed beard that many Italians culti-vate, and a keen supporter of Milan's Inter football club, Ingroia is bubbly, confiding, confident and full of energy. During a late dinner one evening in Palermo I asked about his recent trips away from the city. He had begun that day with a morning flight at seven o'clock, having had three hours' sleep, and the day before had been the same. Would he be resting tomorrow? 'No, I will be at the football stadium. There is no way that I would miss Inter against Palermo.' He would be supporting the visiting team but that had been a loyalty of many years and was known to everyone. Ciuro's treachery on the other hand had been a bitter blow to him.

In April 2005 when he sentenced Ciuro, then aged forty-seven, to four years and eight months in prison for illicitly accessing information systems and aiding and abetting others to avoid investigations, a sentence confirmed by the appeal court eighteen months later, the judge described Ciuro's crimes as extremely serious. The damage done by Ciuro had greatly harmed the image of the justice system. People who knew him wondered why he had betrayed the trust that Ingroia and others had placed in him. I certainly did.

On the day that Ciuro was arrested, police also arrested Michele Aiello, a prominent businessman whose indictment anti-Mafia prosecutors in Palermo would request in September 2004, and Giorgio Riolo, a skilled technician in the Carabinieri, an expert in telephone-tapping technology and concealed listening devices. Ciuro and the carabiniere had been close to Aiello for many years and had accepted gifts from him. At the end of June 2003, Ciuro had suggested to Aiello that they should set up a secret network of mobile telephones to be used by them, the carabiniere and a small group of people they trusted, but that this network should never be used to call or take calls from other fixed or mobile telephones. Such precautions were not enough, and a slip by Ciuro's wife led to the network's discovery at the end of August. However, he had long been a target for anti-Mafia investigators, his telephone calls were being tapped and he probably suspected this when I telephoned him from England to ask if Del Santo was a *mafioso*.

Yet Ciuro was a minor figure in the authorities' struggle against Cosa Nostra. In Aiello, to whom Ciuro was overheard saying '*per te la vita*' (for you, my life), the anti-Mafia team in Palermo was dealing with a much more important figure. The authorities knew he had had many contacts with one of Cosa Nostra's leaders in Bagheria, a town about ten miles east of Palermo that prosecutors had long considered Provenzano's stronghold.

Aiello had taken over his family's construction business when his father died in 1992 and a *mafioso*, who began cooperating with the authorities in the mid-1990s, had told magistrates that the business had mafia ties. And after he was arrested in April 2002, Antonino Giuffrè, Provenzano's number two, began to talk about Aiello's relations with his boss and Bagheria's mafia family. Some of the messages that the police found on Giuffrè when they caught him dealt with Aiello's construction business which was responsible for a large number of minor access roads in the Sicilian countryside.

But Aiello's economic success arrived with his diversification into health services. According to the magistrates, this turned him from a modest businessman in the profitable but limited sector of rural road-building into a billionaire leader in one of the most important sectors of the Sicilian economy. Investigations by the Carabinieri found that Aiello had been the island's biggest taxpayer in the years before his arrest.

Aiello's move into private healthcare began in 1996 with two businesses in Bagheria, Diagnostica per Immagini-Villa Santa Teresa and Alta Tecnologia Medicale, diagnostic and radiotherapy clinics fitted with cutting-edge equipment for diagnosing and treating cancer. For Aiello, tackling tumours would be a massive money earner and the businesses' turnover rapidly grew from a few billion lire a year to many tens of billions. Profits soared, but building clinics in the vanguard of technology does not come cheaply and, soon after Aiello's healthcare business got underway, there were rumours that it owed something to Provenzano's funds.

The clinics' revenues, and their profits, came mainly from the regional government which had given such encouragement to the private sector that it had signed agreements with around one thousand seven hundred private healthcare facilities on the island, compared to only seventy such agreements by the regional authorities in Lombardy, Italy's biggest and wealthiest region. Spending of six and a half billion euros on healthcare absorbed more than one half of the Sicilian region's annual budget, attracted Cosa Nostra and triggered suspicions about Aiello's business.

Sicily's health services are one of the island's many contradictions. They provide care and cure for the sick while are themselves infected and need treatment. Indeed, Cosa Nostra has long been able to count on doctors for assistance. One boss was with his doctor when police arrested him in January 2001. However, the ties between the Mafia and the medical profession go beyond the treatment that doctors give sick *mafiosi*. 'Doctors have an important place in Italian society, particularly in the South. They provide a social, political and economic reference point. There is a close economic link between people in the health services and politicians, between the health business and local politics, and the Mafia goes where the money is. Medicine and the Mafia are inextricably entwined,' Maurizio De Lucia, an anti-Mafia magistrate in Palermo explained to me.

Those criminal connections may amount to more than just corruption in the undergrowth of power and some doctors have been *mafiosi*, fully initiated into the organisation rather than merely outsiders willing to help. Michele Navarra, the boss of Corleone, was one. 'Giuseppe Guttadauro, the *capomandamento* of Brancaccio, is a top-ranking *mafioso* and the typical mafia doctor,' De Lucia told me. Convicted of being a member of Cosa Nostra and sentenced to nine years' imprisonment, Guttadauro had returned to head his district when he was released from jail at the beginning of 2001. It was business as usual for him as he met people who counted in Sicilian politics and schemed on behalf of Cosa Nostra's preferred candidates. Investigators were, however, listening through the bugs they had planted in his apartment in Palermo, near the city's smart Via della Libertà, a broad tree-lined avenue of elegant shops.

I have often walked along Via della Libertà, glancing at the expensive Louis Vuitton bags, the watches and jewellery in Cartier and the elegant accessories in Hermès. It is a world away from the grim squalor of the closely packed, high-rise cement residential blocks in the Brancaccio district on the eastern edge of the city. 'This is one of the poorest parts of Palermo, a place of enormous poverty, but the Mafia has always considered it its own,' Padre Mario, Brancaccio's parish priest told me. Padre Mario had moved to Brancaccio after his predecessor, Giuseppe (Pino) Puglisi, was gunned down by a mafia killer in September 1993 outside his house, a few hundred yards from the church.

One of those who visited Guttadauro's apartment was Domenico Miceli, a young cancer surgeon who worked in the city's Policlinico hospital and whose enthusiasm for politics had led to his election to the city council in 1993. In December 2001, when the mayor chose the new heads of city departments after elections, Miceli was one of them, though he would resign after Guttadauro's arrest in December 2002. Almost five years after his appointment to run one of the city's departments, following a trial in which De Lucia was a prosecutor, Miceli was sentenced to eight years' imprisonment for complicity with the Mafia. After he heard the sentence, against which his appeal would begin in April 2008, his face whitened, he turned to kiss his wife and left the court without a word. Miceli was a protégé of Salvatore (Totò) Cuffaro, the Sicilian region's chairman, another doctor and a specialist in radiology, who would stand trial for helping *mafiosi*. The prosecution said that Miceli had been a go-between for Guttadauro and the region's chairman.

Another man from the medical profession would be involved in investigations and trials that would show how Cosa Nostra had penetrated Palermo's professional and social fabric. Salvatore Aragona had been convicted of association with the Mafia when he worked at the Ospedale Civico as he had provided false medical records showing that a mafia boss was being operated on when, in fact, the boss in question was busy murdering a rival. Arrested again, in June 2003 like Miceli, Aragona decided to cooperate and, plea-bargaining a six-month prison sentence, admitted that he had been a go-between for Guttadauro and Cuffaro.

While the authorities had uncovered a lot about Cosa Nostra and its links with politicians and other figures in Sicilian public life, they would have found out much more had their listening devices, which suddenly stopped working on 15 June 2001 when Guttadauro was tipped off about the investigations, not been betrayed by officers who worked inside the anti-Mafia service.

The end of that rich period of revelations was a blow for De Lucia and his colleagues. 'It is impossible to understate the enormous damage that the revealing of secret information did to our opportunities of following – through the conversations between Guttadauro and other *uomini d'onore*, including those from other districts – developments in Cosa Nostra, the strategies behind their operational decisions, the relationships at the top of the organisation and those between *uomini d'onore* in jail and their fellows who were still free.'

The person who revealed that Guttadauro's apartment was bugged was the very person who had installed the devices, Giorgio Riolo, the member of the Carabinieri who was arrested at the same time as Ciuro and Aiello. For more than a decade he had served in the special branch, and was expert at placing and using video and voice interception devices. The prosecutors discovered that this key figure in the Carabinieri had enjoyed a steady and trusting relationship with Cuffaro, for whom he had undertaken electronic sweeps to ensure that the politician's various offices and home were not bugged. Over a period of several years he had kept Aiello informed about what the Carabinieri's special branch and other police forces were doing in their search for Bernardo Provenzano and the progress of their investigations into various mafia families, particularly those of Bagheria.

Provenzano himself was always concerned about the possibility that his helpers were being bugged or observed by hidden cameras. In a note to one of them, he urged, '... look around to see whether they have been able to install one or more video cameras, nearby or distant, tell others to look carefully and not to talk inside or near cars, nor at home or near home, and not to talk loudly ... Thanks to Jesus Christ Our Lord.'

By June 2003, the month that I telephoned Pippo Ciuro from England, Bernardo Provenzano, Italy's most wanted man, had been on the run for forty years. With their most recent photograph of the person who had eluded them since 1963 showing a man in his late twenties, the authorities could base their hunt only on a rough identikit image that simply guessed at how Provenzano had aged. 'We do not know what he looks like and he may easily have been stopped by the police and slipped unrecognised through their fingers,' the anti-Mafia magistrate Maurizio De Lucia would admit to me more than two years later.

Even so, moving around was not without risks for the *mafioso*, especially when he was away from his Sicilian stronghold, and of course some means of travel were riskier than others. Flying was out of the question; documents come under scrutiny at check-in counters and departure gates, terminal buildings are under tight surveillance and heavily patrolled, and what makes other passengers stare and what they may be thinking is always unknown. Travel by road was less risky and the dangers were more easily managed. So a tiring journey of more than a thousand miles, across northern Sicily, over the Messina Strait and up the Italian peninsula from its southern tip to the border with France and along the Riviera almost as far as the city of Marseille faced Provenzano when he left, early in the summer of 2003, for the French clinics where he would receive treatment for prostate cancer.

Arranging an important surgical operation for a fugitive as notorious as Provenzano needed careful planning and his close helpers were busy preparing the trip at the end of May 2003. Nicola Mandalà, a boss of the mafia family that controls Villabate – a town east of Palermo, mid-way between the Sicilian capital and Bagheria where Provenzano was hiding – went to France in late May and early June to set things up. And as the police later established by tracing the movement of the cellular telephones that Mandalà used, he was there again, accompanying Provenzano, between the end of June and the middle of July and at the end of September as well as in November.

There had been rumours for many years that Provenzano had problems with his health; a *mafioso* who gave himself up to the police in 1993 told magistrates that Provenzano had prostate trouble. Clearly the need to deal with it had become pressing when he set off for France, arriving during a heatwave in La Ciotat, a pretty seaside resort mid-way between Toulon and Marseille. On 2 July, when Provenzano registered for a check-up at Clinique La Licorne, a modest white building overlooking a yacht marina and a casino called Les Flots Bleus, he gave his name as Gaspare Troia, a seventy-two-year-old pensioner from Villabate.

A French woman of Italian origins who was married to Salvatore Troia, the real Gaspare's son who had lived in La Ciotat for several years, accompanied Provenzano when he met his doctors. She acted as interpreter for the reserved Sicilian who could not understand French. Five days after the initial examination, Provenzano was admitted to the clinic, which would later change its name to Clinique de La Ciotat. Doctor Philippe Barnaud, whose name heads the list of urology specialists by the entrance, had signed a certificate for his urgent admission and his patient stayed four days while a biopsy was done on his troubled prostate. Unknowingly, Barnaud had found himself treating Italy's most wanted criminal. Discharged on 11 July, Provenzano began his return to Sicily the following day. The woman who claimed to be Provenzano's daughter-in-law returned to the clinic on 23 July to learn that the operation that was needed would be performed at the Clinique La Casamance on the outskirts of Aubagne, a town about ten miles east of Marseille.

Provenzano's trip to the south of France for medical treatment would not have aroused suspicions there. Many Italians had made similar journeys, particularly during the 1980s and 1990s, to the numerous hospitals and clinics in and around Marseille; a rehabilitation centre beneath the clinic in La Ciotat is called Notre Dame de Bon Voyage. I came to know Marseille well after my wife had orthopaedic surgery in a clinic there in 1990. From whatever direction Provenzano arrived on 3 October, to reach the clinic he would have been driven up the Boulevard des Farigoules, a one-way street of detached villas, lined with the plane trees typical of Provence, the stark ridge of the Chaine de l'Etoile to the north of Marseille, another Provençal feature looming across the valley.

Provenzano would travel up the Boulevard des Farigoules for further checks over the coming weeks before being admitted for surgery on 22 October, the day before Doctor Barnaud operated on the man whom he knew only as Gaspare Troia. He was discharged after eleven days and would return for checks before the long journey back to Sicily that would end at the Jolly hotel on the seafront near the centre of Palermo on 22 November.

Italian investigating magistrates and police forces were able to begin piecing together the story of the *mafioso*'s medical treatment thanks to a massive round-up of people suspected of ties to Cosa Nostra on 25 January 2005. Palermo's flying squad knew that Villabate's mafia family played a crucial part in Provenzano's postal service, collecting and delivering the *pizzini* (notes) through which he gave instructions, and that Nicola Mandalà was its boss. After the arrests, when Mandalà was brought in along with forty-four other suspects, police searched the home of his sister and found a document showing that a man called Gaspare Troia had undergone a medical check at the Clinique La Licorne in La Ciotat on 9 July 2003.

From there the trail led to France and, in March 2005, Pietro Grasso, the chief prosecutor in Palermo, wrote to the French authorities requesting assistance in those investigations. His letter was headed: 'Criminal proceedings against Bernardo Provenzano, born in Corleone 31 January 1933, wanted for the crimes of aggravated homicide and association with the

Mafia, under investigation in this case for association with the Mafia and complicity in aggravated extortion.'

As well as asking for copies of the medical records of Provenzano's treatment and details of telephone calls made on various numbers the authorities believed had been used by people they suspected of helping him, Grasso sought permission to question Doctor Barnaud and another doctor who had been involved in Provenzano's operation. Shown a photograph of the real Gaspare Troia, staff at the clinics said that he was not the man they had treated. And the real Gaspare Troia when questioned by police in Palermo said that he had not been operated on in France in 2003. Moreover, his blood group was different from that of the person on whom Doctor Barnaud had operated. The trail to Provenzano was warming up.

Immediately after the police swoop in January 2005, one of those arrested decided to cooperate with the authorities. Mario Cusimano belonged to the mafia family headed by Nicola Mandalà in Villabate, was close to the boss and told the investigating magistrates about Provenzano's recent period in hiding, particularly the organisational support provided by Villabate's mafia family during his medical treatment in 2003.

Help also came from Francesco Campanella, a senior employee in the town's branch of the Credito Siciliano bank. Campanella's home had been searched on the evening of 25 January and this had caused him and his wife enormous anxiety. 'She was unable to sleep for two months, so I sent her to her mother and then I followed as I could not sleep either.' His firearms permit was revoked in March and the next month he offered to cooperate with the authorities, but his confessions did not satisfy them and they sent him back to stew in the criminal cauldron of Villabate. On the evening of 16 September 2005 he again called on the Carabinieri to say that he wanted to cooperate with the authorities, this time expressing fear for his own life and for the lives of his family.

In league with Mandalà, Campanella had misappropriated large sums of money from the deposits of customers at his bank. The decisive factor in Campanella's decision to cooperate was the fear that enraged customers might take their revenge. 'I called my close family – my father, mother, brother and wife – telling them to meet at my father's home ... They had no idea and do not know the extent of the problem as I only confessed the most dramatic part, that concerning the bank. I left them in tears, got changed and went to the Carabinieri to turn myself in,' he told the investigating magistrates.

More than simply a bank employee, Campanella was an important cog in the political wheels that drove affairs in Villabate. He had been chairman of the town's council and was able to tell the authorities how the Mafia had infiltrated public works there. His position in local politics also provided the key to Provenzano's medical treatment in France. Campanella was the person who obtained the official stamp for the false identity card in the name of Gaspare Troia that had enabled the seventy-year-old Provenzano to travel to France and which was shown to staff at the clinic in La Ciotat.

The police operation that took Nicola Mandalà into custody and led to Campanella's decision to cooperate with the authorities was an important step towards capturing the boss of bosses himself. Francesco Pastoia, Mandalà's godfather and boss of Belmonte Mezzagno, a few miles inland from Villabate, was one of the key figures caught in the net. After the swoop Pietro Grasso described Pastoia's role as central to communications and the management of relations between mafia families in a huge area that extended far beyond his own district. A few days later, after prosecutors had shown him some documents, Pastoia committed suicide in his prison cell in northern Italy. The documents were evidence that Pastoia's conversations had been overheard and that he had committed the unpardonable offences of betraying mafia secrets and cheating the *capo dei capi*. His tomb would be desecrated and his coffin set on fire, a reminder of Cosa Nostra's rules.

The arrests in January 2005 stripped away the dense network of helpers that had allowed Provenzano to live safely in Bagheria, leaving little of the system of oaths, loyalties and duties that had protected him for so many years. Cosa Nostra's boss of bosses was forced to flee about thirty-five miles to the south, to his birthplace Corleone, where support still remained. From March the police concentrated on what Provenzano's family was doing. They placed tiny cameras around Corleone, even on the top of a street light in front of his wife's home, and put listening devices in the homes of all of the family's members. On the afternoon of 8 June 2005 they heard one of his brothers say, '*Iddu ancora quaè.*' (He is still here.) Provenzano's time on the run was running out.

In February 2006 police overheard the wife of Giuseppe Lo Bue, one of the suspects, complain about how during the preceding eight months he had given his family little time and how she worried where his extrafamiliar commitments might lead and about being left alone. 'This isn't a family. I am tired of seeing you only when you have a spare moment.' 'Listen to me, Mariangela,' he told his wife, 'I can stay for three or four years on my own and then we will be together again.' For the investigating magistrates and police who heard these words, he was talking about the length of the prison sentence that he would receive for helping Provenzano. Lo Bue, a partner of Provenzano's eldest son in an electrical goods business, was one hinge around which support for Provenzano turned.

There was a strange twist at the end of March 2006, when Provenzano's lawyer told a daily newspaper that the *capo mafioso* had been dead for years and dismissed the idea that Provenzano had undergone an operation in France in 2003.

Even so, the investigators' conviction that he was alive and that they were close remained unshaken. Indeed, within two weeks Provenzano was in custody, arrested in a shepherd's cottage on the Montagna dei Cavalli, in the countryside just south of Corleone. The police had caught the man who for decades had headed the list of Italy's most-wanted criminals simply by following packages containing food and freshly laundered clothes. Try as they might, even with a complex system of transfers, drop-offs and cut-outs, Provenzano's helpers in Corleone were unable to keep his hideout secret.

Police arrested Provenzano at twenty past eleven on the morning of 11 April 2006. The man once known as Binu 'u Tratturi, Bernie the Tractor, because of his readiness to run over people who got in his way and because no grass grew where he had passed, had eluded them for almost forty-three years. But he was more than a thug willing to eliminate those who opposed him or were threats, and his shrewdness came into play when Cosa Nostra suffered heavy setbacks as a result of the authorities' offensives in the aftermath of the murders of Falcone and Borsellino in 1992. Arrests and defections were huge shocks for Cosa Nostra but Provenzano was skilful, first at keeping the organisation together and then at getting it running again.

'Under Provenzano, Cosa Nostra has returned to its traditional modus operandi,' Antonio Ingroia, Borsellino's protégé, had explained to me at the beginning of 2002. There were no more bloody killings or violence against public servants. Cosa Nostra showed its capacity to adapt; it changed its structure, tightening the way that it recruited, and exploited its web of connections to graft itself still more firmly onto the political system.

Among the items the police found in the shepherd's simple home near Corleone were Bibles, a picture of Padre Pio and a hundred or so messages for directing Cosa Nostra, ready for delivery. The police also carried away a bag of medicines. Provenzano had certainly enjoyed the attention of local doctors while in hiding and there was speculation he may have been treated by a Sicilian doctor who was found dead in his home in a town north of Rome in February 2004. The parents of the doctor, a urologist who special-ised in prostate operations, said that he had looked after a patient in the south of France in October 2003 and believed that, unknowingly, he may have been recruited to assist Provenzano during his stay near Marseille.

Others may also have unwittingly helped the fugitive *mafioso*. In order to obtain medical treatment for Provenzano outside Italy, his helpers had presented a request, apparently signed by Gaspare Troia, to the local health unit in Villabate, part of Palermo's health authority like the unit in Bagh-eria, and this had issued the European Union's form authorising treatment in another member state. Just over a year after Provenzano's operation, the ministry of health in Rome received a bill for almost two thousand euros from the Caisse Primaire d'Assurance Maladie de Marseille, the French city's health fund, for the treatment given to Gaspare Troia.

Some people involved in the health services in and around Palermo may have been unaware of being exploited by Cosa Nostra but others helped willingly. 'From what we know, the doctors in France did an excellent job and returned Provenzano to good health, but he has certainly needed doctors and check-ups since his return to Sicily,' Maurizio De Lucia, the anti-Mafia magistrate, told me just two months before Provenzano was caught. But clearly he did not think that the French doctors had in any way been complicit.

And, of course, there was speculation that Aiello's clinics in Bagheria, so convenient for Provenzano, might have been used by the boss of bosses. I took the train there from Palermo, a fifteen-minute trip on a stopping service. Squeezed between the railway and the autostrada that links Palermo with Messina, it is a drab town but boasts a glorious past from the eight-eenth century when Palermo's nobility built palaces there, on the hillside overlooking the sea. The Villa Cattolica, which now houses a collection of works by Renato Guttuso, arguably Sicily's greatest twentieth-century painter, is one of them. The large lorry park nearby, used by Provenzano's messengers as a sorting office for their boss's mail, is a landmark of another kind.

I had travelled to Bagheria to talk to Andrea Dara, an accountant from Palermo who had been appointed judicial administrator to run the clinics soon after Aiello was arrested and his assets seized. I could see the Villa Santa Teresa from the station's platform but reaching it meant walking back towards Palermo, crossing a level crossing and then stepping out along the old main road from Palermo to Messina, a brisk twenty-minute walk. Was this where Provenzano laundered mafia money and where he was treated, I wondered as I stood on the road in front of the clinic, outside railings covered with bougainvillea. At the beginning of July 2003, probably from somewhere in the large car park inside the railings, a police observer had seen Giuseppe Ciuro make two brief calls on a mobile telephone before entering the clinic, raising the investigators' suspicions as those calls did not register on their intercept system.

I thought of Ciuro, paying for his treachery with a prison sentence. When the trial of Giorgio Riolo, the non-commissioned officer of the Carabinieri who had also betrayed secrets, ended in January 2008, he too would be found guilty and sentenced to seven years in prison. A radiologist would receive a prison sentence of four years and six months. However, most attention would be focused on the chairman of Sicily's regional government when the president of the court read its verdict and announced the sentences; Salvatore Cuffaro would be found guilty of helping *mafiosi* and sentenced to five years' imprisonment. Michele Aiello, the boss of Sicily's private health services, would face the longest time in prison, fourteen years for crimes that ranged from corruption to complicity with the Mafia. (They would appeal against the verdicts.) I was about to visit the Villa Santa Teresa, the capital of his criminal empire.

After climbing the ramp that Ciuro had climbed, past the palm bushes and through the large doors into the smart lobby, I asked for Dara, who had offered to show me the clinic when we met in Palermo. An earnest man in his early forties, he told me about the difficulties he had encountered when he began his work in Bagheria. Keeping everything running was his priority and there were those among the two hundred employees who realised that he represented their only chance of continuity. But Aiello had taken on people who had important patrons and the interests of these had been harmed. 'Some employees thought, and still think, that I am an intruder who should be opposed,' Dara remarked dryly.

'We had dozens of telephone calls from worried patients. Dealing with cancer is such a sensitive and urgent matter. It was vital not to interrupt their treatment. And don't forget that it would have been a huge boost for the Mafia if patients had been affected when the court ordered the seizure of Aiello's assets.'

As he showed me around late in the afternoon, after the bustle of the day's cases had ceased, leading me into the treatment rooms with their high-technology equipment, he explained how he had to tackle a serious financial situation. Palermo's health authority had been charged as much as two hundred thousand euros for a cycle of treatment under Aiello's management and the average amount that Aiello had charged the authority was sixty-five thousand euros. After Dara took over, those figures fell to a maximum of twenty-five thousand euros and an average of ten thousand euros, bringing them roughly into line with what clinics would receive for similar treatment in northern Italy. Medical consultants found their monthly earnings slashed from forty thousand to six thousand euros.

For Dara, running Aiello's businesses marries his professional skills to civic values. He had been affected by the murders of Falcone and Borsellino, describing them as servants of the state who died defending the state and the values that he holds. 'People who are on the side of the general good must put their abilities to work for it. Observing the law must be the starting point. An economic system without legality is a sick system and good results can be obtained even by working legally.'

The Villa Santa Teresa is the kind of place suitable for a boss of bosses, a world away from the shabby public hospitals with which Palermo's sick must usually make do, its equipment far ahead of theirs and with none of the large blue trailers packed with scrap metal parked outside or the garbage that greets visitors when they near Palermo's Ospedale Civico. Aubagne in southern France was fine for Provenzano's prostate operation, but afterwards? The Villa Santa Teresa in Bagheria, where well over half of the patients have prostate cancer and receive radiotherapy three or four times a week for a month, would have suited Provenzano perfectly, although there was no evidence that the *capo dei capi* was treated there. But, as Dara remarked, 'We have the right equipment for treating a condition like the one he suffered from.' And, of course, there never seems to have been a shortage of doctors willing to make their skills available to Cosa Nostra.

4

————

MESSINA

Earthquakes and Institutions

THE EVENING BEFORE I LEFT Palermo was like many spent there; dinner at the Sant'Andrea, hidden away down a narrow street off the Piazza San Domenico with its large Baroque church, and close to the Vucciria market, once brightly depicted in a painting by Renato Guttuso but now a dull and dirty remnant of what it was then.

I would travel east by train to Messina, on the single-track line that winds along the coast, through Brancaccio, Villabate and Bagheria. The hundred and fifty mile trip between the two cities takes almost three hours on the fastest train, but my journey would be longer as I would stop in Termini Imerese. It was on this stretch of track in February 1893 that Emanuele Notarbartolo di San Giovanni, an aristocratic politician, banker and former mayor of Palermo, was stabbed to death in a railway carriage and became the Mafia's first illustrious victim. His killers belonged to the mafia clan in Villabate and the man who commissioned the murder had business interests and close contacts with the Mafia in Caccamo, a town a few miles inland from Termini Imerese.

However, my curiosity about Termini Imerese lies in recent times, although illustrious victims of the Mafia are partly behind the interest. During earlier visits to Palermo, I had attended hearings in the trial of Marcello Dell'Utri, a difficult trial as Dell'Utri, a friend and associate of Silvio Berlusconi, stood accused of complicity with the Mafia. Leonardo

Guarnotta, the white-haired presiding judge who sentenced Dell'Utri to nine years' imprisonment in December 2004, had a personal story that I wanted to hear. He had been the fourth member of the original anti-Mafia team in Palermo, established early in 1984 with Falcone and Borsellino as the first of its investigating magistrates. (Giuseppe Di Lello was the third.) And Guarnotta would be the one who, by then on his own, wound up the maxi-trials in 1995, eleven years after the first real effort against Cosa Nostra was launched with the issue of arrest warrants for three hundred and sixty-six people.

After heading one of the criminal sections of Palermo's court, Guarnotta was appointed president of the court in Termini Imerese, and I made my way there from the station. There is none of the bustle of Palermo's busy law court in Termini Imerese's small, modern building, none of the tension that Guarnotta lived with during the 1980s and 1990s, the security less tight. Palermo is close, less than twenty-five miles, but his experiences seemed distant, a lifetime away, as Guarnotta relived them, his memories of the early years on the anti-Mafia team, of working side-by-side with the two magistrates that Cosa Nostra murdered in 1992 tinged with sadness. Bright sunlight streamed through the windows and warmed his office but there was a cold, dark vein to Guarnotta's words. 'I feel an emptiness, an awful sense of something missing. If only Giovanni and Paolo were here now.'

The three hundred and sixty-six arrest warrants were issued on 29 September 1984, Saint Michael's day. 'I called for Paolo at three o'clock in the afternoon and his wife Agnese asked what we would be doing and when we would get back. "Don't ask questions, Agnese. Just make the coffee," Paolo told her. We finished preparing the warrants at three o'clock in the morning.' Borsellino was light-hearted, an extrovert, cigarette always between his lips; Falcone was reserved in public, could even seem timid. 'But Giovanni opened up completely with his friends and close colleagues. "Leonardo, let's stop disturbing the state," he would call out with a laugh at around a quarter to nine in the evening,' Guarnotta remembered.

He was forty-three years old and had been a magistrate for eighteen of them when Antonino Caponnetto, who had taken over as head of the investigative office after Rocco Chinnici was murdered in July 1983, invited him early in the following year to become part of the anti-Mafia team. Three other magistrates would join later. 'I was very proud but apprehensive as well. I knew my life would change completely.' The team broke up after Caponnetto's departure and the arrival of a new head but Guarnotta remained, the only member to do so, despite opportunities elsewhere. 'I was the historic memory and I felt that Giovanni and Paolo had left me a moral bequest, entrusting me with completing the investigations and the maxi-trials. When I closed the door behind me for the last time there were about one and a half million documents in our files and I could remember the number and position of almost every one of them.'

Cosa Nostra had had him in their sights; one plan to kill him was unsuccessful because the car in which he and Caponnetto had intended to travel had been replaced at the last moment. More recently, after he had become a judge and was president of a court that was trying a friend of Salvatore Riina, the imprisoned boss, his elderly mother who lived in an old-people's home received a package containing a black dress, a message that she would soon need mourning clothes.

'Something in me died on that Saturday in May when Giovanni was murdered. What did I feel when I saw him lying dead in the mortuary, just a small wound visible and his face at peace? Anger, pain. For me, the scar reopens every year in May.' And the death of Borsellino, who was looking urgently for him the day before he was murdered, continues to trouble Guarnotta. 'What did he want to tell me? Was there a connection with his notebook that was never found?' he still wonders. There are many aspects of that intense part of his life that he prefers to keep to himself but another that he was willing to share with me. 'There was no jealousy. *Ci volevamo bene*, we loved each other.'

Breaking my journey in Termini Imerese to meet Guarnotta and hear his recollections had been an enriching experience. He had wanted to introduce me to a colleague but the young judge was in court trying a case; when I said goodbye, I hoped I would return.

I made my way back to the station and from the platform, as I waited for the train to Messina, gazed across the broad sweep of the gulf of Termini Imerese that curves from Cape Zafferano to Cefalù, the blues of the water shimmering under the late morning sun. There would be other fine views from the carriage as the train rattled slowly east. Cursed with the Mafia, Sicily is blessed by some wonderful scenery.

Called Zancle in ancient times, Messina's name is associated less with the Mafia than with earthquakes, particularly the one of Monday 28 December 1908, a catastrophic seismic shock that was reckoned Europe's worst ever. The epicentre was in the Strait of Messina, the two-mile stretch of water that separates Sicily from the mainland. Slight tremors began to be picked up at around eighteen minutes past five by an observatory about two hundred miles to the south, on the island of Malta, and these continued for a little less than three minutes until a massive shock wave drove the recording device to the edge of its scale. Worse arrived ninety seconds later and Messina and Reggio Calabria, across the strait, were devastated as shocks brought down buildings, disrupted water and energy supplies and destroyed roads and jetties.

Soon after six o'clock a tidal wave hit Malta, flooding streets and houses, beaching small boats but leaving undamaged Britain's Mediterranean fleet, which had assembled in Valletta's Grand Harbour for Christmas. One of the few ships away from the British base at the time was HMS *Sutley*, a cruiser that was off the Sicilian coast when the earthquake happened. After taking on emergency supplies and a medical team in Syracuse the warship proceeded overnight to Messina, navigating with difficulty since lighthouses had been put out of service. It arrived there around dawn on the day following the earthquake.

Other British warships were quickly underway and heading towards the disaster, but the first help arrived with sailors from Russian warships that had been on exercise and were at anchor off Augusta about fifteen miles north of Syracuse, in the direction of Messina. The well-organised Russians quickly set about searching for survivors among the rubble, treating the wounded and feeding the homeless. The *Sutley* arrived off Messina soon after the Russian warships and, like these, had in its complement many young men who were completing their training. Aiding Messina's stricken population would be a dramatic experience for hundreds of young Russian and British sailors.

The earthquake had caught people asleep. When dawn broke, the survivors saw the awful effects that the shock waves had wrought on their city. It had been razed, only two per cent of buildings were undamaged, the destruction was almost total and a huge number of injured and dead lay in the ruins.

How many people had died would never be known. One estimate put the number of people killed at two hundred thousand, almost eighty thousand of them in Messina itself, or more than one half of its inhabitants. Perhaps twenty thousand died in Reggio Calabria, whose fate, and that of the surrounding region, had been neglected in the efforts to help Messina. When more units of Britain's Mediterranean fleet arrived at Messina three days after the earthquake they saw that substantial Italian forces were at work and diverted to the mainland, where they provided the first help for the people of southern Calabria.

Right from the beginning, the disaster found Italy's own institutions wanting. Communications broke down, and for many hours the authorities in Rome failed to grasp the gravity of what had happened. Moreover, the rescue organisation fell far short of what was needed. France's military attaché noted in a despatch that the Italian troops who were sent to tackle the disaster lacked proper equipment and victuals, that the supplies France provided for the victims were used by the Italian rescuers, and that orders and counter-orders increased the chaos.

The British military attaché had harsh words for town officials, mayors and prefects, whom he described as wholly unreliable. Funds could not be placed in their hands and the goods meant for the victims of the earthquake were often misappropriated. Writing to the ambassador in Rome, the attaché observed that the impossibility of trusting the civil authorities was an enormous handicap for Italy.

Messina's institutions would come under fire ninety years later when another kind of earthquake struck the city. In February 1998, a fourteen-strong delegation of parliament's anti-Mafia commission swooped from Rome to find out about organised crime in and around Messina and the efficiency of the organisations that were supposed to tackle it. Rome's interest in the Sicilian city was sparked by the murder, in a typical mafia killing, on 15 January of Matteo Bottari, a professor in the medicine faculty of Messina university. 'Messina is alarming, both in its view of the legality that ought to characterise life in civil and democratic society and in the means that the state has employed in that society to combat illegality,' reported the commission. The city was calm on the surface but there were undercurrents of violence.

According to the commission, restoring legality and the certainty of democratic and juridical rights required the renewal of the state's principal functionaries in Messina, the representatives of the forces of law and order, the magistracy, education and administration. Some of Messina's citizens welcomed the commission, seeing it as providing hope for a better future, but others did not, claiming implausibly that Messina was a crime-free paradise. Bottari's murder shook the city, but many people were reluctant to face the truth.

Messina had been rebuilt after 1908's earthquake and the fascist regime in the 1920s and 1930s decided that the city should be an administrative and military centre. It was heavily bombed by British and American air forces in July and August 1943, rebuilt after the second world war and its economy bounced back. 'The city's industries did well during the 1950s and 1960s. We had a flourishing privately owned shipyard. Then, during the 1980s and 1990s, the private sector ran into difficulty and the public sector was cut; the military hospital was closed, the naval dockyard was closed and the naval command was shut down,' Antonio Saitta, Messina's deputy mayor and a law professor at the university, told me when I called at his chambers near the city centre.

As Messina declined towards the end of the twentieth century, the importance of its university to the local economy grew. Employing about six thousand academic and administrative staff, and teaching around forty thousand students, the university is Messina's biggest business and big business attracts the Mafia. Violence, or the threat of it, is rarely far away where mafia interests are at stake. The anti-Mafia commission listed in its report some of the outrageous incidents of the seven years before it began its inquiry: two professors were kneecapped; a medical student was murdered; an economics student was seriously injured; two bombs exploded (one in the economics faculty, the other in the law faculty); cars belonging to a professor in the faculty of medicine were torched; a legal institute was an arson target; and Professor Bottari was murdered.

The politicians in Rome were spurred into action by Bottari's murder but they should not have been surprised. More than twenty years before the killing that drew the anti-Mafia commission to Messina, its university had been infested with students from Calabria who had carried out serious acts of intimidation and vandalism. However, the details of most crimes never came to light and the authorities did not know how these students wielded their influence, how they managed their economic interests, intimidated teaching staff, or connived with them, to ensure that students on whose behalf they were acting passed their examinations.

In May 1976 the court in Messina had banned a group of Calabrian students from the city because they had committed crimes against people and property there. Some of the crimes had taken place in the *casa dello studente* (student house); two woundings in early 1974 were the result of a turf war for the control of the *casa dello studente* itself. One of the students was known as the 'Sten-gun man', because he used this weapon to fire intimidatory bursts and drill holes in cupboards and furnishings in the *casa dello studente* where he lived, simply for amusement.

According to the court, those students had been preparing the ground for a mafia band that would subsequently be established in 1984. The head of the student body, from Locri, a town on Calabria's Ionian coast notorious as a stronghold of the Calabrian Mafia, was killed by a shotgun blast as he returned home late one evening in December that year. A judicial report said that the motive for the murder was to be found in the world of organised crime with which the victim had links.

In June 2005, more than seven years after Italy's politicians woke up to the fact that Messina was infiltrated by the Mafia, the court there delivered its verdict on sixty-six defendants linked to the university whose trial had begun in February 2002. The crimes of which they were accused, committed between 1984 and 2001, ranged from mafia association to trading in university examinations and degrees, drug dealing, illegal possession of arms, receiving stolen goods and forgery. The court found thirty-three of them responsible for various crimes and handed down sentences of eighteen years in prison to the two of the accused who had been found guilty of the most serious offences and fourteen years to four others.

Evidence given in the trial showed that intimidation was widespread in the university, sometimes in the form of physical violence, at other times through threats, but that teaching staff were reluctant to report this. *Mafiosi* exerted continuous pressure to obtain favourable results in examinations. Staff were approached and asked to look kindly on certain candidates. Menacing late-night telephone calls were made to instil fear. Three men dressed in black entered the examination room after one student had been failed and sat staring at the examiner. A few months earlier, the student had appeared in the faculty's secretariat brandishing a pistol. Police found a pistol in the *casa dello studente* at the beginning of January 1999 and at the end of that year they stopped a student who was leaving the building with a sawn-off shotgun in a bag.

An area on which the anti-Mafia commission focused was the university's medicine faculty, not least because Matteo Bottari, the murdered professor, was a member of that faculty, the son-in-law of a former rector and one of the closest colleagues of the current rector at the time the crime was committed. The commission gave particular attention to the pharmacy and its information system where a tip-off in 1993 had brought to light an enormous waste of medicines and materials, and irregularities in purchasing at far above manufacturers' list prices.

A company called Sitel that had been awarded a contract in May 1989 to supply computer services to the pharmacy was later also contracted to purchase medicines and medical supplies on the pharmacy's behalf; it earned a commission of five per cent on the cost of those purchases. It is probably not surprising that the pharmacy and the stockrooms of the hospital were full of materials that sat on shelves beyond their use-by dates. Reporting in April 1998, the parliamentary commission noted, 'The point is that the more the hospital spent, the more Sitel earned.'

Neither was it a surprise that the prices paid were way above those on the manufacturers' lists. The hospital paid twenty-three per cent more for surgical sutures, sixty per cent more for disinfectants, sixty-five per cent more for one supplier's products and fifty-two per cent for another's, for example. Instead of raising the pharmacy's efficiency, the company profited from its inefficiency. According to the parliamentary commission, 'We consider that Sitel's business was simply that of perpetuating the state of serious disorganisation because it generated waste and its own resulting large commissions.'

Part of a large group comprising almost forty companies, operating mainly in health and pharmaceuticals, Sitel was one of a handful that provided consultancy and information technology. The anti-Mafia commission and Italy's financial police called the conglomerate Gruppo Cuzzocrea as it was headed by Dino Cuzzocrea who had negotiated the contract for the pharmacy's system and supplies with the university's rector. The rector had been close to the professor who would succeed him, Dino Cuzzocrea's brother Diego, who was indirectly a shareholder in Sitel. Only in February

1997 would Diego Cuzzocrea, then the rector of the university, give up that shareholding by transferring it to Dino. By then, however, Sitel was the centre of a judicial storm and the matter had become public knowledge.

The commission censured the rector's behaviour. As head of the university, Diego Cuzzocrea held a prestigious position in the local community and wielded influence in the city. Moreover, his family's business empire played an important role in Messina's economy. Among Sitel's contracts was one, obtained despite the fact that another firm had offered a lower price, to provide information services to the city council.

Where the examples set by public figures are morally dubious, corruption and malpractice become part of the way of life. And in southern Italy, morally dubious behaviour helps the Mafia to thrive. Far from being an untroubled city, the unsavoury truth was that Messina suffered from institutional sepsis and the Mafia benefited.

'Messina was not considered a mafia city but it was polluted by the Mafia, and it lies in a buffer zone where the influences of Palermo's Cosa Nostra, the Mafia from Catania and Calabria's 'Ndrangheta meet,' Luigi Croce, who became Messina's chief prosecutor following the parliamentary commission's inquiry, told me. Cosa Nostra started to invest heavily in Messina province in the 1970s and 1980s when the authorities began tackling its influence in western Sicily, mafia families of Palermo entrusting their business to a family in Barcellona Pozzo di Gotto, a town about twenty-five miles west of Messina. Blood would be shed occasionally but the Mafia usually ensured that the city and the surrounding area were left undisturbed.

This suited most people, including some in the city's court, as the parliament's anti-Mafia commission discovered. Rumours had circulated about some members of the magistracy in Messina and the commission found deep conflict, irreparable splits and such a serious breakdown within it as to cast doubts over the most basic expectations of the administration of justice. When they listened to magistrates, the commission heard what it described as 'an extraordinary number of denunciations, contestations and accusations' and concluded that the judiciary in the Messina district needed urgent, radical reform.

The animus infecting relations between colleagues was not the only matter that shocked the commission; the court in Messina was sinking under the weight of investigations that had ground to a halt. The prose-cutor-general in Messina's appeal court said that the large hall of Messina's prefecture, a room about eighty feet long, fifty feet wide and twenty-five feet high, would have been too small to hold all the files relating to investigations that had never been finished. There were magistrates who seemed to avoid trials that might have ended in acquittals in the belief that such trials would have brought about a fall in the magistracy's popularity.

Some magistrates sought popularity in the local community, many were busy fighting colleagues, one had socialised with a businessman of dubious reputation, two would be arrested and put on trial in Catania for being in cahoots with the Mafia. The brother of a judge in the town of Patti had been found guilty of murder by the court in Barcellona Pozzo di Gotto, raising serious questions of incompatibility. (Both towns are part of the judicial district covered by Messina's court.)

Yet another hint of incompatibility hung over Antonio Zumbo, the chief prosecutor when the parliamentary commission began its inquiry. As with many investigations, that into the contract for the university's pharmacy, where the suspected crimes included embezzlement and abuse of office, encountered lengthy delays. Dino Cuzzocrea, who was being investigated, was Zumbo's brother-in-law. Zumbo was never directly involved in the case, but as chief prosecutor he oversaw the investigations and could influence and control what was done. 'Given the relationship of his wife with Dino Cuzzocrea, one of the principal suspects, it would have been appropriate for him to have stepped aside,' reported the commission. About five weeks after the commission began its work, the Consiglio Superiore della Magistratura, the magistracy's governing body, opened an inquiry into Zumbo's suitability as Messina's chief prosecutor. He would become a judge in Italy's supreme court, a change of job that one member of the commission thought damaged the supreme court's image.

Angelo Giorgianni was another magistrate attached to Messina's court whose appointment was queried by the commission. Born in Polistena in the province of Reggio Calabria, Giorgianni had turned to politics, been elected to the senate in May 1996 and was considered a high-flyer. The forty-two-year-old, as he was when Romano Prodi formed his government, was appointed to a junior ministerial post at the ministry of home affairs, the ministry that controls the police and oversees anti-Mafia efforts. He would stay there less than two years, until 13 March 1998 when, in the aftermath of the anti-Mafia commission's visits to Messina, he lost the job.

As an assistant prosecutor in Messina, Giorgianni had socialised with a local businessman with a criminal record. Moreover, one of the most important *mafiosi* to give evidence about his former associates, a person known as Cosa Nostra's head of public works and the go-between for Palermo's Cosa Nostra in its dealings in Messina, said that the businessman was involved in their affairs. Others knew or had doubts. 'His years of investigating the public sector should have led him, particularly in his new role as a representative of the government, to keep his distance,' was the commission's verdict on Giorgianni.

However, the biggest shock to Messina's magistracy arrived in March 2000 with the arrest of Marcello Mondello and Giovanni Lembo. Mondello had retired from the magistracy as president of Messina's appeal court, after having coordinated the work of the judges who oversee cases during preliminary investigations. Lembo was an assistant prosecutor in Messina from 1987 until 1994, when he transferred to the national anti-Mafia body where he was responsible for cases in Messina. Accused of regular contacts with mafia bosses and with helping *mafiosi*, Mondello and Lembo were put on trial in Catania. One of the *mafiosi* who seemed to be closely associated with them was a leading businessman who had moved to Messina from Bagheria and was considered Cosa Nostra's man there. The businessman would later commit suicide, leaving a note to say that he did not wish to return to jail. The trial of Mondello and Lembo would end in January 2008 when the court found them guilty and sentenced Mondello to seven years in prison and Lembo to five years, against which they would appeal.

'The prosecution service was seen as a band of delinquents, a snake pit,' remarked Luigi Croce about the organisation that he was appointed to head soon after the commission's inquiry. Born in Messina, Croce had spent most of his career, thirty-three years of service by the time he moved back to his birthplace, as a magistrate in Palermo. 'It was not easy to take over here,' he told me, an understatement of what he faced. However, he had acquired the experience in the Sicilian capital to tackle the challenge in Messina. 'It was very difficult in Palermo in the years immediately before the terrible murders in 1992,' said Croce. Indeed the venomous climate of the court in the Sicilian capital had led it to be called the *palazzo dei veleni* (poison palace). Giovanni Falcone and Paolo Borsellino had worked in an atmosphere of suspicion, ill-will and intrigue after a new chief prosecutor arrived.

In Austria when Falcone died, Croce flew back to Palermo at once, but he was in Palermo when Borsellino was killed two months later. 'I was with Paolo at a colleague's home one evening, four or five days before his murder. He said that his moment was close, that explosives were arriving also for him. It was awful, terrible, the tension, the awareness that something ghastly was going to happen soon. We were all so distressed when he was killed. From that moment everything changed.'

The violent deaths of their two colleagues helped to unite Palermo's divided magistracy; they realised that they needed to work together and differently. Of course they had gone through a similar experience after the Mafia murdered the head of Palermo's investigative office in 1983, and it was then that Antonino Caponnetto, a chief prosecutor in Florence, transferred to Palermo. As Leonardo Guarnotta told me when I stopped in Termini Imerese on my way to Messina, team spirit collapsed after Caponnetto's departure at the beginning of 1988.

'We knew that we needed an outsider at the top, someone who had not been involved in what happened after Caponnetto left. However good a Palermo magistrate might have been, he would not have been able to make the changes that were needed,' recalled Croce about the prosecution service there in 1992. He would become the deputy of Gian Carlo Caselli, a senior prosecutor from Turin who, like Caponnetto almost ten years before him, volunteered to leave an easier post to take on the awesome challenge of leading the prosecutors in Palermo. Restoring confidence, bringing harmony and brightening the badly tarnished image of the magistracy in Messina was Croce's aim when he arrived in the city.

Although born in Messina, Croce is an outsider. Apart from three years in the late 1960s as a prosecutor in Agrigento in southern Sicily, he had worked only in the Sicilian capital before his move. 'A magistrate from Messina would have social relationships in and around the city but I didn't.' His arrival in the troubled department was greeted with suspicion by demoralised magistrates who did not know what to expect from him. However, he found that they welcomed the opportunity of rebuilding the department and he was helped by the arrival of nine young magistrates that took the number of prosecutors to twenty.

Croce's decision to keep clear of social engagements in the city showed his independence and helped him to be accepted. 'I'm completely detached from local society. My life is just home and work; I arrive at the law court at half past eight in the morning and return home at half past seven in the evening. I don't attend receptions, I don't go to dinner parties, I don't belong to clubs. The only public events that I attend are the annual *feste* of the Carabinieri, the police and the financial police. It's not an easy life.'

I had passed briefly through Messina some years before to learn about plans for a bridge over the strait to the mainland and spoken with the owner of the private-sector ferry service. This time I would stay for several days, meet more people and discover something of the city. A friend in Palermo had given me the name of a young judge who works in the court in Reggio Calabria but was born and lives in Messina. I could not have wished for a more pleasant or fitter guide than Daniele Cappuccio, who led me around at a cracking pace that befits the marathon runner he is, me panting behind, he bounding upwards as we climbed the two-hundred-feet high tower alongside the cathedral, one of the stops on the tour. Cappuccio would prefer the stairs to lifts when we met in Reggio Calabria's law court. 'It's quicker and healthier.'

How many people in an English city would have been so generous with their time to an Italian as Daniele Cappuccio was with his to me, a stranger? He showed me around his city, took me to dinner in a trattoria overlooking the water, on the flat promontory that forms Sicily's northeast point, and to lunch at an elegant cafe in Messina's smartest piazza. And he would help me find my way through Calabria, a region of which I then knew little. I had found similar disinterested generosity, a willingness to spend time with a stranger and talk about past events and the present, and themselves, elsewhere in Sicily, and would find it through much of the South. In Messina, Giovanni Marra, the elderly archbishop, passed an hour talking to me, propped up on cushions while recovering from a broken leg. It is often said that southerners know little about the value of time, less often about how much they value relations with others. I was fortunate in meeting Daniele Cappuccio, as I had been in meeting many Sicilians and would be in my encounters with people on the mainland.

Since 1944, the Irrera cafe, established in 1910, has stood in Piazza

Cairoli, smart shops now around it and in neighbouring streets. Like the dazzling displays of fruit in Palermo's markets, seen best in the evening under the harsh light of naked lamp-bulbs, the *frutta martorana* of marzipan strawberries, figs, mandarins, apricots and other fruits in the Irrera tempt the customer. Everywhere he or she looks, displays and cabinets of brightly coloured Sicilian cakes and confectionery – the island is famed for them – like the *cassata* filled with *ricotta* buttermilk curd and covered with green marzipan, the small, one-mouthful *cassatina*, almond *fior di mandorla* and *torroncini* nougat catch the eye and whet the appetite. It was here that Cappuccio brought me for a quick lunch and it is here that Messina's smart set meet for coffee or an *aperitivo*.

Yet something less attractive lies behind Messina's mask. The murder of Matteo Bottari, the university professor, and the revelations of parliament's anti-Mafia commission gave the city unwanted attention, but this did not trigger moral cleansing. As the court proceedings concerning a leading politician would show, Messina's citizens did not decide that the city's public figures should be morally above suspicion.

'I have a pile of documents a metre high on Giuseppe Buzzanca,' said Antonio Saitta, the deputy mayor, explaining the complexities of a case that interested him as both a politician and a law professor. The case began in August 1995 when Buzzanca, a politician belonging to the far-right Alleanza Nazionale, was chairman of the province of Messina. Buzzanca used the car and driver that went with his office for personal benefit, to travel with his wife from Messina to Bari to embark on a cruise ship and then from Bari to Messina on their return. On 5 June 2003, after a legal marathon of court hearings and judgements, Italy's supreme court confirmed a jail sentence of six months that had been given in December 2002.

Yet despite this – conviction in the courts of first instance and appeal for an offence that should have excluded him from office – Buzzanca stood in the city's elections as a candidate for mayor about a week before the supreme court's verdict. And he won and was declared the winner. A group of citizens who thought it was wrong that Buzzanca should be mayor took legal action to have the election nullified and were fought at every step by him. Eventually, almost six months later, a ruling of Messina's appeal court overturned his victory.

Far larger sums have been misappropriated from the public purse in Italy than that which Buzzanca's improper use of his official car cost the citizens of Messina. However, what some people found hard to accept was that although his misdeeds had been uncovered, Buzzanca nevertheless stood for office, won and stubbornly refused to stand down. Saitta, who became Messina's deputy mayor in 2005, took another view on the matter. Buzzanca's election said something about the city's moral health. 'According to those who elected him, misuse of public funds was not a serious matter. Voters completely ignored the ethics.' Saitta thought that the people of Messina had not learnt from the lessons that the revelations of 1998 should have taught them. 'Messina needs shaking up from top to bottom.'

Saitta was also concerned about a relaxation of moral rigour at the university. The man that Diego Cuzzocrea had followed as university rector, the father-in-law of the professor in the medicine faculty whose murder had sparked the interest in Messina, had headed the university for twelve years. Cuzzocrea would last just three years and be succeeded in 1998 by one of Italy's leading constitutional lawyers. His departure in 2004 to become a judge in Italy's constitutional court was followed, Saitta thought, by a decline in efforts to build a solid and durable ethical framework. 'We must be unyielding on civic values. Any relaxation in the Mezzogiorno is dangerous; experience shows that the battle for legality is never really won.'

Yet the Sicilian city once enjoyed a different name from that earned in the late 1990s and the early years of the twenty-first century. From the 1950s to the 1970s its cultural life flowered, notably in the visual arts and literature, but this would wither in the 1980s. One of those whose enthusiasm and energy helped Messina make a cultural mark was Salvatore Pugliatti, the university's rector for twenty years; another was Antonio Saitta, grandfather of the deputy mayor. Among their high-school friends was Salvatore Quasimodo, a poet who was awarded the Nobel Prize for literature in 1959. But the city would become known further afield, and by far more people, thanks to what would later be recognised as an event of geopolitical importance.

In June 1955, ten years after the end of a war that had devastated Europe, the foreign ministers of six of the continent's nations met in Messina in an attempt to forge their countries' economic integration. By 2008 those six had been joined by twenty-one others, so that the combined population of the twenty-seven countries amounted to about five hundred million. The

European Union was born in the Italian capital, with the Treaty of Rome in March 1957, but it was conceived in Messina almost two years earlier. Italy, France, Germany, Belgium, Netherlands and Luxembourg, the founder members of the European Economic Community, as it was then known, would be joined in 1972 by Britain, Denmark and Ireland. Most European nations would follow, but until Greece joined in 1979, followed by Spain in 1985, Italy was the community's only truly Mediterranean member and the island of Sicily, detached from the continental land mass, its most southerly extension.

Joining Sicily to the mainland has been a talking point for many years. Amid controversy, Italy's highways agency and the state railways joined forces in 1969 to seek proposals for a fixed crossing of the Strait of Messina and just over a decade later a company was established with the building of a bridge as its aim. Bettino Craxi, one of the prime ministers during the 1980s, breathed life into the idea and a feasibility study carried the project further, though Italy's ballooning public sector deficit would deflate enthusiasm. Financial constraints tightened during the 1990s, particularly during the second half of the decade when Italy was trying to squeeze the lira into Europe's single currency; for one of the three large original members of the EU to have been excluded would have been a major setback. The idea of a bridge between Calabria and Sicily then seemed to be abandoned.

However, work was going on behind the scenes, and when Silvio Berlusconi gained power in May 2001 the Messina crossing was high on his government's agenda. And controversy over the project grew more heated than ever, perhaps because it seemed close to being realised. For the project's opponents, Berlusconi posed a real threat. His rightwing government enjoyed a hefty majority, its parliamentary ranks packed with Sicilians and Calabresi, and Berlusconi, like any politician, was keen on big gestures and a lasting legacy. What better way to achieve both than an enormous bridge spanning the Strait of Messina?

Less than two years after the elections that took Berlusconi to power, the project grew in importance. Early in 2003 the state-controlled company responsible for its construction approved the preliminary design for a combined road and rail bridge as well as access roads and lines, and gave its blessing to an environmental impact study. Milestones were quickly passed. The environment ministry gave its approval, as did the government's economic planning committee; laws were passed, some money was found, agreements were signed and the European parliament decided that a bridge across the Strait of Messina was an important European project. And at the end of May 2005, when the deadline arrived for tendering for the job of general contractor, two Italian-led consortia lined up for it.

Meanwhile a heated debate raged between the bridge's supporters and its opponents. The bridge would boost the local economy by providing thousands of jobs for those building it, and by stimulating business and commerce in and around Messina and Reggio Calabria. And business throughout Sicily would benefit from a quicker link to the mainland. Some people thought that the bridge would be a huge tourist attraction and that visitors would arrive from all over the world to see it. The project that was unveiled was certainly striking; the biggest suspension bridge in the world would join Calabria to Sicily with a central span about two miles long supported by pillars more than one thousand feet high. The bridge would carry a double-track railway and a dual-carriageway road with two lanes in each direction.

Environmentalists were horrified. The strait would be irreparably damaged by the monstrous construction and the migratory path to Europe of birds of prey that winter in Africa would be threatened. The impact of the project would extend far beyond the bridge itself, in the construction of a huge network of roads and railway lines leading to it. Work on the railway would bring years of disruption to Messina and when the bridge was finished the city would be a long way from it, as would be Reggio Calabria. Some people worried that an earthquake would bring the bridge down. Critics said that the forecasts of traffic were grossly inflated to make the economics seem attractive, that the bridge would be a white elephant and would never pay for itself. Others said that if funds were available for infrastructure there were better ways of spending them in Sicily than on a bridge to Calabria.

Moreover, there is the Mafia. It is not that people are concerned that the bridge would help Cosa Nostra travel from Sicily to the mainland or the 'Ndrangheta to manage its affairs better in Messina; both have been able to get along well enough with the ferries between Messina and the Calabrian side. The source of concern is the bridge's construction itself. With costs initially put at around five billion euros, the bridge is an appetising project for *mafiosi* on both sides of the strait. Magistrates of the national anti-Mafia body noted that production and the supply of inert materials in Calabria and Sicily are controlled by mafia organisations. 'If it is true, for example, that 1.1 million tonnes of cement will be needed to build the bridge over the Strait of Messina, it is easy to imagine what the economic effect will be for mafia organisations.' Luigi Croce, the chief prosecutor in Messina, said that the construction of the bridge would be hell for the city and would mean much more work for his team. 'The bridge would make a lot of money for Cosa Nostra here and for the Mafia in Calabria.'

Berlusconi's hopes of laying the foundation stone seemed to die when he lost the parliamentary election in April 2006 but they were soon revived. The project will never lack supporters and was high on the list of promises in Berlusconi's manifesto for the election that returned him to power two years later. The Mafia will be ready for its share of the business when the first earth is moved.

5

REGGIO CALABRIA

Violent Death

I HAD ARRIVED at the Aeroporto dello Stretto before, shaken about in Alitalia's ageing MD80s as they made their way down. There is no congestion in the skies over Reggio Calabria, no stacking for incoming flights as the aircraft descend steeply above the Strait of Messina, Mount Etna in Sicily on the right, banking sharply left towards the Aspromonte mountains and then sharply left again towards Reggio Calabria's southern outskirts, to line up with the runway. Ten minutes' drive from the city's centre, its single-storey terminal handling the passengers from around twenty landings and take-offs each day, the small airport is a reminder of air travel in distant, less stressful times.

This time I arrived by coach, on a service from the centre of Messina directly to the airport, avoiding the trouble of getting to and from the terminals where ferries ply back and forth across the strait. After hiring a car at the airport, I turned right at the exit and then right once more onto the Via Ravagnese that takes traffic to the autostrada, almost at the southernmost point of mainland Italy's autostrada network. The next exit, heading away from the city towards the very toe of the Italian boot, leads to San Gregorio and to Croce Valanidi, a place that won notoriety in the late 1980s and early 1990s. The pace at the Aeroporto dello Stretto may suggest that time is not important but the area between the airport and Croce Valanidi, less than three miles long and a mile wide, was once notorious as somewhere that human life itself counts for little.

Before travelling to Calabria I had read the story of a bloody mafia war between families of the 'Ndrangheta, as the region's Mafia is known. This war had finished many years before, but the end of what the prosecutors called the Valanidi trial was recent, in a supreme-court judgement of 2003. The trial had been listed as 'Criminal Proceedings Against Giacomo Latella Plus 98', ninety-eight being the number of defendants on trial with him, the boss of the honoured society of Croce Valanidi. The trial and the appeals that followed provided a gruesome and detailed record of the brutality that had racked the area.

Blood was shed often in that part of Calabria. Fortunato and Lorenzo Turoni met their deaths around seven o'clock on a January evening in 1988 in a district called Saracinello, a continuation of the grimy and anonymous Via Ravagnese, inland from the autostrada. The body of Fortunato was found first, lying face-up between a wall and a small car, and Lorenzo, Fortunato's brother, who was just fourteen years old, was dead on arrival at the local hospital. The double murder was revenge for the killing of Pasquale Latella, boss of the family and brother of Giacomo, whose name headed the list of the accused in the Valanidi trial. Members of the mafia family had met after Latella's murder in November of the previous year and decided that it called for a quick settlement in blood if the family was to be shown as still a power to be reckoned with even after its leader's death.

Three of the opposing clan would be the targets, Latella's family decided, and they included Fortunato Turoni who, they thought, had driven the van from which the shots were fired that killed Pasquale. Turoni would be the first target for a four-man hit squad, a driver plus one man armed with a 12-gauge shotgun and two carrying pistols. They would wait in their car in a bergamot grove in Croce Valanidi for a tip-off from a *mafioso* watching a billiards hall that Turoni used. An earlier attempt had failed but on 13 January the hit squad was successful.

The killers needed only a few minutes to reach their target, driving downhill from the bergamot grove, along the Via Croce Valanidi that becomes Via Saracinello not far from the autostrada. As soon as they saw Turoni's car the driver stopped and the hooded killer sitting beside him got out and opened fire with a 7.63 calibre pistol. He was quickly joined by the two accomplices who had been sitting in the back. One used a .38 pistol and the other the shotgun, firing two or three shots from a distance of about ten yards that hit a fleeing figure, Fortunato Turoni's young brother, mistaken in the gloom of a winter evening for one of the other two of the opposing clan who had been chosen for retribution.

Making their getaway, the killers switched cars and the member of the clan who had tipped them off hid the car and the guns used in the attack. The switch took place near the Fiumara Valanidi, a seasonal river running from the mountains behind Reggio Calabria. I drove there. Squalid, unpleasant, sinister and probably unsafe at night, it is the kind of spot where the authors of thrillers and film directors have their murders happen or criminals meet. It is easy to imagine the Turoni brothers' killers, pulses still racing from the kill, arriving there on that dark January evening, jumping from the car they had used for the crime and into another that their accomplice had ready.

The sides of a track running along the river valley, deeply rutted by trucks that go to and from a concrete works, are strewn with waste. But beyond the worn tyres, broken refrigerators, dumped basins, heaps of brick and plaster, and stained mattresses there are orderly groves of dark green bergamot trees whose powerful fragrance when they flower between March and May, the *zagara*, masks even the strongest smells. For the Calabresi of Reggio Calabria, however, it was the pungent odour of gunpowder and smell of death that was familiar for many years.

This was not somewhere to linger. Only curiosity brings strangers to the track beside the Fiumara Valanidi and having noses poked into their affairs is not something that the locals like, so after taking photos I got into the car, drove to the main road at San Gregorio and turned right towards the city. Back along the Via Ravagnese, then past the airport to Viale Calabria where I made a small detour, turning left towards the sea, a short drab stretch to Via Aldo Moro, which like many places in the city has had its moment of notoriety.

Violent death, so frequent in and around Reggio Calabria that it ceased to shock, was what drew me to this most southern part of the Italian mainland where a murder committed in June 1988, and another that was a direct consequence, were two that stood out in the long list of killings. Around a quarter past ten in the morning Santo Nicolò was shot as soon as he stepped outside his workshop. The investigating magistrate who took charge of the scene of the crime was faced with an awful, stomach-turning sight. 'Nicolò's head had been smashed and most of the brain matter had come out,' was how the victim was later described. Photographs showed that his skull had been split in two and its top blown off.

An eyewitness said that nobody was near Nicolò when he was shot and police deduced that the weapon was a high-precision, high-calibre rifle fired at long range. They thought that there had been two shots; one had struck Nicolò and another had ricocheted off a car's roof and then dug itself into a shutter. The police subsequently found what they believed was the spot from where those shots had come, the terrace of a low building near the sea.

However, members of Nicolò's clan were faster at working out what kind of weapon had been used and searching the area than the police. With another of Nicolò's close associates, the eyewitness to the murder went looking and, on the beach, hidden beneath a boat, found a .30-calibre carbine fitted with a telescopic sight. The use of this weapon, a rifle for big-game hunting loaded with explosive rounds, was most unusual, according to the court. Fitted with a silencer, it would be employed again in exceptional circumstances, on the orders of Antonino Nicolò, who said it should be used to 'defend the honour of his dead brother' and to kill those he held responsible for his murder, the Libri family, allies of the Latellas. And it was. Shortly after leaving Via Aldo Moro and returning to Viale Calabria, I drove past the place where Pasquale Libri died.

Libri probably felt safe as he took his morning's exercise in the yard of the prison in Reggio Calabria on Sunday 18 September 1988, but he was mistaken. A death sentence had been passed on him by the Nicolò family and his executioner, Giuseppe Lombardo, who admitted to the crime at a court hearing in May 1997, did not miss when he centred his target in the rifle's sight from far outside the prison and pulled the trigger. Lombardo was also the killer of the two members of the Libri clan involved in the murder of Santo Nicolò, but he failed in his attempt to shoot Domenico Libri as he left Reggio Calabria's court under a heavy escort of carabinieri. Luck favoured Domenico Libri that day; he survived because he had bent to tie a shoelace.

Outsiders find it difficult to understand the complex web of relationships that lie behind the wave of murders that swept through the southern outskirts of Reggio Calabria in the late 1980s and would lead to the Valanidi trial. The killing of Santo Nicolò led to other killings, but he and his clan had themselves been responsible for targeting the Latella family and their allies. Behind the bloodshed were issues of territory, money, power and blood relationships. Notorious, as the boss of a hit squad, the military arm of the Serraino clan, Santo Nicolò had committed crimes that included preparing and installing a bomb beneath the car of a member of an opposing clan. He knew that he would be targeted by families against whom he had organised attacks or to whom he was a threat, and whenever he left his workshop he travelled in an armour-plated vehicle.

Reggio Calabria's police and investigating magistrates were even busier than usual the day that Nicolò was killed. Around seven o'clock in the evening, the body of Francesco Alati was discovered, slumped on his right side across the passenger seat of his car near the Via Saracinello. His killer's claim that he 'had opened him up' was a fair description. On the ground beside the driver's door, among the fragments of the car's shattered window, the police found four 12-gauge cartridges; an autopsy revealed that the victim had been struck in the chest and belly by four or five shotgun rounds. Alati's wounds, in the words of the court, 'were so severe that they caused loops of his intestines to fall out'.

The investigators thought there was a connection between Alati's murder and Santo Nicolò's murder earlier in the day, since Alati was close to the Serraino family and his wife a relation of Nicolò. Alati was, however, only a minor figure in the murderous struggle between the clans and his death was easy to organise and risk-free for the killer. His role had been secondary; he was simply a passive member of one clan, and certainly not active in its hit squad's operations, but this was enough to ensure his death.

That members of the Alati and Serraino families called each other *compari*, an expression used between in-laws and between godparents and godchildren, was a sign of closeness. Moreover, the Alati family had given the body of Alessandro Serraino hospitality in their family chapel and this was significant. For the Serraino family's opponents, such kindness to the dead man's family confirmed the close ties between the Alatis and Serrainos, and at a time of violent conflict between clans closeness was 'sufficient to decide a person's fate'.

Its recent past may deter tourists but Reggio Calabria is unfortunate in another way; like Messina, it was destroyed by earthquakes in 1783 and 1908 and battered by bombers in 1943 so that almost nothing remains of the city that Edward Lear, an English writer and painter, visited in 1847 and described as one of the most beautiful places on earth. Lear found gardens of oranges, lemons and bergamot under the castle's walls and there were fig trees and bushes of prickly pears wherever he looked. Nowadays, as I discovered, there is little greenery to soften the concrete.

Helpful staff in the airport's tourist office had given me a handbook of hotels in the city and the surrounding province. I chose the two-star Mundial on the southern edge of the centre, on the other side of a seasonal river, the Torrente Calopinace, from the prison and within walking distance of everywhere I wanted to go. After checking in for two nights I looked around the centre and found a grid of dull streets.

The city's main attraction is its archaeological museum in Piazza De Nava, at the far end of the main street, a brisk twenty-minute walk from the hotel. When I arrived, I remembered a conversation I had had with Tonino Perna, a jovial professor of economics and sociology at Messina university, and something of a maverick, whom I had met when we were both involved in a conference in Riva del Garda, a town once part of the Austrian Empire and far from the Mezzogiorno and its problems. A Calabrese, Perna lives in Reggio Calabria and commutes across the strait, and he had told me over lunch in Messina of a terrible day, a heart-stopping and unforgettable experience for him, when two young men were shot dead in Piazza De Nava.

'The piazza is where Reggio's youngsters gather. As soon as my wife heard of the murders she called me as our two boys, then fifteen and eighteen years old, were there. They were unharmed but, standing about three yards from the victims, they had been in the front line. At times, I just wanted to escape from the city.' However, he stayed on and later became chairman of the Aspromonte National Park, the vast and impenetrable mountain area behind Reggio Calabria where the 'Ndrangheta hid many kidnap victims.

The city's few tourists usually head for Piazza De Nava, but certainly not because a couple of youngsters were gunned down there twenty years ago – Reggio Calabria has many such places that bring back bloody memories. They go to see the Riace Bronzes, the famous bronze statues of Greek warriors displayed on the museum's lower floor.

I stood before them, carried back in time, absorbed in the beauty that has survived the centuries, wondering if the ancient Greeks marvelled at them as I did. A group of schoolchildren giggled, nudging each other at what they had seen in a display cabinet, but nothing disturbed the stillness surrounding the two bronze warriors. They had been found in 1972 on the bed of the Ionian Sea about three hundred yards from the shore, some eighty miles northeast of Reggio Calabria. These masterpieces of Greek art are remarkable works that make a visit worthwhile, although few make the trip to see them; one is thought to have been made around 460BC and the other about thirty years later.

People in the city are probably as proud of their *lungomare*, a broad esplanade about a mile long that runs beside the Messina Strait, and it is a grand walk I discovered as I went back to my hotel and watched ships sailing through and ferries crossing between Sicily and the mainland. I had passed southwards over forty years before, standing watch on the open bridge of an elderly destroyer on passage to Malta after exercising with other warships west of the Gulf of Naples. The Messina Strait was magical then as we passed through, with the daylight fading and the lights onshore beginning to sparkle, and some of the magic remained as I walked along the esplanade.

'People in Reggio hated their city, were ashamed of it, but now there is some pride. Look at the *lungomare*,' Vittorio Mondello, the archbishop of Reggio Calabria told me the following day when I called on him in his office beside the cathedral. A Sicilian from Messina, he had been the bishop of Caltagirone in the southeast of the island from 1983 until his appointment in 1990 as the archbishop of Reggio Calabria, a diocese where he cares for over a quarter of a million souls in the most violent part of Italy's most soulless, brutal region.

Like many anti-Mafia magistrates, the archbishop thinks that conditions in Calabria are far worse than in Sicily. He blames centuries of history for how the Calabresi behave. 'Those in authority have rarely considered the people's wellbeing, only how they could exploit Calabria's resources for their own benefit. This has led to a certain way of life, created a mentality that we could call *mafiosità*.' His voice quietly rasping that last word, Vittorio Mondello seemed less a tender shepherd than one of those large white dogs that protect Italian flocks, growl threateningly and terrify those who step too near.

Writing about what was still a feudal society, a British aristocrat called Henry Swinburne, who travelled around Calabria on horseback in 1777, observed that Calabria's *baroni* usurped public land and left nothing for their vassals to cultivate. He thought that Calabria could have flourished if government had been more interested in the public good rather than private interests and if justice had been administered honestly and impartially. An Italian called Domenico Grimaldi who reported on the economy of the Neapolitan kingdom in 1780 wrote that the South, particularly Calabria, was forgotten and abandoned to its poverty by a nobility that usually lived in Naples and was indifferent to the miserable conditions in which the peasants lived.

'The *baroni* simply left the management of their land to *guardiani*, tough local estate guards who were often nothing but gangsters. There were no carabinieri and the *guardiani* administered their own justice. It was in this parallel state of private policing that the 'Ndrangheta was born,' Roberto Di Palma, an anti-Mafia magistrate in Reggio Calabria explained to me.

That the 'Ndrangheta is powerful a hundred and fifty years after Italian reunification owes much to the failure of the state. Reggio Calabria's archbishop noted that the perversity of those who govern still continues. 'Government employees who abuse their positions, who consider the public at their service, rather than them being at the public's service, are an example of *mafiosità*.' The Calabrian mentality needs changing because this way of thinking lacks civic values and Christian virtues and allows the Mafia space in the region's social, economic and political fabric. 'Creating a healthy mentality is the only way to beat the Mafia and the way to create a healthy mentality is to educate young people in the need to respect others.'

The widespread *mafiosità* that worries Archbishop Mondello is not necessarily criminal, but even so it is a mafia way of thinking, living and dealing with others. 'It is in this mentality that the Mafia which kills develops. It is this mentality that forms the *mafioso*'s way of thinking, that he must kill anybody who treads on his toes.'

I saw evidence of how the 'Ndrangheta works that afternoon when I walked to the city's new law courts, about a mile and a half up the road that runs beside the Torrente Calopinace, across the road from the Carabinieri headquarters and the prison. The jagged stars of two bullet holes in one of its large windows gave a sinister look to a fast-food outlet; a fading notice on its door said that the business was shut for holidays but it actually seemed closed for good. No day passes without cars or property being set alight or shots being fired at doors or windows, the 'Ndrangheta's unequivocal messages of intimidation.

'I thought that I could do something for this desolate place, this accursed region, for me the most beautiful in the world,' Nicola Gratteri replied when I asked him why he had become a magistrate. An experienced member of Reggio Calabria's anti-Mafia team, Gratteri had been in the magistracy for twenty years, a prosecutor for fifteen of them. He was born in Gerace and grew up in a part of the province around Locri called the Locride. Just say Locri, a town where the Mafia's word is law, and Italians think murder. 'I know the Locride's people and its criminals well. I went to middle school there and had classmates whom I later prosecuted and who were sent to prison.' German police would tap Gratteri's local knowledge after the murders in Duisburg of six Italians from the Locride in August 2007; I had heard that many *mafiosi* in the north of Calabria had migrated to Germany and intended to find out more when I reached that part of the region.

Sharp, fast talking and bouncing with energy, Gratteri was just the man to tell me how the 'Ndrangheta works, how hard it is for the authorities to tackle and how magistrates who are in the front line deal with violent death. Investigating magistrates, like policemen, get as close to violent death as anybody in Italy, except perhaps police doctors, pathologists and undertakers. 'In our world it is necessary to be clear-headed and detached, to avoid emotion. A kind of automatic process has to kick in when a magistrate arrives at the scene of a murder to take charge of investigations. It must be the same for a surgeon stitching up a patient; seeing a needle dig into flesh might make others squirm but it is just a part of the job for him. And it is like that for us when we deal with murders,' Gratteri explained. No, he replied, when I asked him if he remembered his first murder case. He had forgotten the first of the many killings he had investigated.

One of the aspects of crime, life and death in and around Reggio Calabria that struck me was the enormous quantity of arms that the 'Ndrangheta has to hand. But Calabria's *mafiosi* have always liked to be well armed, for defending, retaliating or attacking first. 'In the 1950s and 1960s, the armouries of the clans would usually contain a dozen shotguns, a dozen pistols and a couple of sticks of dynamite. Nowadays they hold much, much more.

'Arms and explosives have flooded into western Europe from the Balkans. The wars there and Yugoslavia's break-up have been a disaster for Europe and we are much less safe than before. Is it easy to buy arms? Well, four hundred euros will buy a Kalashnikov and nothing is easier than buying pistols.' That suits the 'Ndrangheta whose clans keep on good terms with the Albanian Mafia, their arms supplier.

'Like any small state, every *locale* needs an army,' Gratteri told me, explaining how the 'Ndrangheta is organised. The *cosca* or *'ndrina*, as a clan is called, is based to a large extent on blood families. Clans who are linked ally themselves into a *locale*, which is the basic geographical unit in which the 'Ndrangheta is organised, almost always coincident with a village or a district of a city or town. A minimum of forty-nine associates is needed to form a *locale*, which is commanded by a trio of bosses called the *copiata*, comprising the *capo bastone* (the boss), the *contabile* (who manages finances and sharing revenues) and the *capo crimine* (who runs the *locale*'s criminal activities). 'You could describe a *capo crimine* as a *locale*'s minister of war or minister of defence,' said Gratteri.

'Membership of the 'Ndrangheta is inherited, passed from father to son, so with a family of six or seven children, each of whom has another six or seven children, and taking account of all the cousins and in-laws, a clan can easily have three or four hundred members.' Staying in the family business may seem to make sense to young people in Calabria, as indeed in all the regions of the Mezzogiorno, where legal work is hard to find and unemployment about three times that in northern Italy and even higher among school leavers and university graduates. I remembered what Scicolone, the trade union leader in Gela, said about the street being life's only training ground for youngsters, the place where they bump up against criminal organisations, and their myth of easy, immediate success and gospel of violence.

'These blood relationships help explain the enormous strength of the 'Ndrangheta and our difficulty in penetrating it. Only rarely do members decide to cooperate with the authorities,' said Gratteri. Funerals, christenings and first communions provide occasions for family gatherings and kinship solidarity, in no part of Italy more than in the South. But weddings are probably even more important by sealing, as they do, unions between families. And as well as ending *faide*, feuds between different families, marriages extend the networks of the clans that form the Calabrian Mafia.

A wedding day should have been the last day for Giovanni Alampi, an ally of the Serrainos. Alampi's elimination had been decided some three months earlier, and one attempt had already failed before the hurried decision, taken on the day that Pasquale Libri was shot at long range while taking the air in Reggio Calabria's prison, that action should be immediate. The Libri family asked Giacomo Latella to move at once in exacting revenge and he did so, assembling a two-man hit team and organising logistic help from the clan that controlled the area where the action was planned.

Alampi arrived at a friend's wedding at around eleven o'clock on that morning in September 1988 and went to the wedding banquet in the afternoon in a restaurant on the single-carriageway road that, after the autostrada ends at the exit for Croce Valanidi and San Gregorio, hugs the Ionian Sea and sweeps around the instep of the Italian boot. He left the restaurant in the company of a friend at about half past six in the evening and was about to get into his car when two men on a powerful motorcycle came towards him and began shooting. Alampi threw himself to the ground and was unharmed, but his companion was injured when a bullet hit his arm.

The attempt failed because the hit team was unable to carry out its plan of stopping beside Alampi and shooting at close range. There were many people at the wedding banquet, police were patrolling the highway and heavy Sunday evening traffic was a problem. Moreover, the driver of the motorcycle was worried that he might be recognised; his mother and a sister were both there. Giovanni Alampi survived on this occasion but he had only weeks to live.

During the autumn that followed the attempt on his life Alampi had kept out of sight, but towards the end of November he began to lower his guard. Around four in the afternoon of 3 December he was with his brother Antonino negotiating the sale of a load of wood. Having watched him for about two weeks, this was the moment for which observers for the hit team had waited. They quickly tipped off the killers, who arrived in a large dark car from which one of them, wearing a hood, jumped out and opened fire with a 12-gauge shotgun, first hitting Antonino Alampi and then his brother Giovanni who was trying to escape. Antonino had light wounds to his head but Giovanni was already dead when he reached hospital.

Alampi's killers had been waiting in a stolen BMW in one of the many bergamot groves in the area, which was not only the centre of the Latella family's territory but also the centre of world production of natural bergamot. There were also plans to shoot Domenico Serraino, a cousin of Francesco Serraino, the boss of the clan, from a bergamot grove in front of his home. He was in fact killed when he made one of his rare excursions onto the balcony of his bedroom to smoke, but the killing was a drive-by shooting with a 12-gauge shotgun at about fifteen yards and the car used was abandoned by the Fiumara Valanidi in San Gregorio, where Italy's bergamot consortium has its offices.

The attackers of Giovanni Ficara, a brother-in-law of Giacomo Latella, dumped their car in the same place. Ficara was the target of a bazooka attack two days before Christmas 1990. Known as the *orefice* (goldsmith), he was about fifty yards from his jeweller's shop, when his armour-plated Nissan SUV was struck from behind by a bazooka round fired by attackers who were unaware that the vehicle had been fitted with an extra sheet of steel.

After Ficara tried to ram his attackers' car he found himself trapped and under fire from shotguns, pistols and a Kalashnikov sub-machine gun. Ficara's SUV was struck at the front by a second bazooka round, catching fire and, as the police later described it, 'visibly damaged both front and rear'. The bazooka rounds used against Ficara, and in a successful double murder, had come from a batch of thirty of Slav origin. Amazingly, Ficara escaped with light injuries despite his attackers' efforts.

I was due to visit the bergamot consortium, had done what I wanted in the city and, after two nights there, moved to a tourist village at Lazzaro, just off the coastal road and not far from the restaurant where the hit team had failed to kill Alampi. The best thing about the Magna Grecia was the water that came from its taps, drinkable and suitable for showering, unlike the brackish liquid in the centre of Reggio Calabria where underground water courses had been infiltrated by seawater. A narrow alley outside the tourist village gave a glimpse of the sea but not even the view across the water to Sicily made up for the rusting railings, crumbling plaster and wretched air of the houses suspended above the stony beach.

After settling the modest bill for modest lodgings and wondering about bergamot whose groves seemed to play a part in many local murder cases, I drove a few miles back to San Gregorio. More than ninety per cent of the world's natural bergamot essence is produced in the small strip of Calabria's coast that runs from near Palmi on the western side through Reggio Calabria and around the toe of the boot and north of Brancaleone on the Ionian Sea. When Henry Swinburne wrote about his travels in Calabria, he described the groves of oranges and other citrus fruits as marvellous and noted that traders in Reggio Calabria did a profitable business in exporting the essence of lemon, orange and bergamot to France and Genoa. Nowadays Reggio Calabria calls itself the Bergamot City.

Some people say that the bergamot tree had exotic origins in China, Greece, Turkey or Spain before finding its ideal habitat around Italy's toe. 'But the likeliest explanation is a spontaneous mutation of bitter orange or lime,' Francesco Crispo, head of the bergamot consortium, told me. Chance played a part in giving bergamot (*Citrus bergamia*) the role it has today. Essence from the fruit's peel was probably first used commercially in 1660, in a painkiller concocted by a Piedmontese alchemist. He moved to Cologne, which is why his chemical formulation using bergamot essence would later be called eau de Cologne. Taken up by Europe's lords and ladies, the perfume industry was born.

'The value of the essence of bergamot lies not just in its own fragrancy and freshness but also in its capacity to combine and fix the different elements that make a perfume. It reinforces lighter scents and brings out hidden ones,' explained Crispo. Fragrant on the nose, bergamot essence is clear, greenish-yellow and oily to the touch. About two hundred kilos of the lemon-like fruit are needed to extract one kilo of essence in a process that is as much cold cutting as cold pressing, the fruit turned against metal points that score the peel which, gently pressed, releases the essence in the same basic, once-manual process that has been used for the past hundred and fifty years.

All but one of the fragrances carrying the name of Gianfranco Ferré contain bergamot essence; its selling power is such that the firm decided to call one of its products Bergamotto Marino, for which the essence is provided by fruit from a special grove near Brancaleone where, according to the firm, 'the fruit's very thin peel absorbs marine aromas carried by the winds that waft along the coast'.

The global giant Procter and Gamble has a division called Prestige Products that owns the Jean Patou brand and has manufacturing agreements with fashion houses like Gucci, Dolce & Gabbana and Laura Biagiotti. Its products rely heavily on natural bergamot. 'It is a noble, elegant and sophisticated substance that gives diffusion – how a perfume displays itself on the skin over time – and power to perfumes' top notes,' Sumit Bhasin, Prestige Products' director, told me. Users of fine perfumes expect consistency and makers must avoid batch-to-batch variations. 'The quality of bergamot essence in Calabria is unbeatable and that is why Procter and Gamble buys there.'

That Calabria, which often presents an ugly face, should produce an essence without which the world's most wonderful fragrances cannot be made and that this essence should come from a small area of the region appallingly scarred by bloodshed was a surprise. It is yet another of the Mezzogiorno's contradictions, beauty and brutality going hand-in-hand around the Italian toe.

The murders of the Turoni brothers, Santo Nicolò, Pasquale Libri, Francesco Alati, Giovanni Alampi and Domenico Serraino were part of a much wider conflict between mafia families in southern Calabria. Indeed, while the Valanidi trial dealt with twenty-four murders and sixteen attempted murders, the killing was as great elsewhere and hostilities between Reggio Calabria's clans began well before January 1987, when the first murders with which the Valanidi trial was concerned were committed.

Reggio Calabria's mafia war began in October 1985 with the explosion of a car bomb in the town of Villa San Giovanni, about ten miles north of the city, the port from which ferries cross to Sicily. The perpetrators of the crime hoped to kill Antonino Imerti, known as the *nano feroce* (savage dwarf) and the leading figure in the local criminal community, but they failed and killed only the lesser *mafiosi* who were with him. Holding the De Stefano family responsible, members of the Imerti clan soon got revenge with the killing of Paolo De Stefano, near his home in his clan's stronghold in the desolate northern outskirts of Reggio Calabria.

The mafia war was a turf war, a question of territory. According to the court in the Valanidi trial, the bloody conflict had no ideological foundations. 'Much more prosaically, it was a conflict between the interests of opposing groups of organised criminal bands that aimed at winning territorial supremacy in order to gain monopoly or control over the revenues flowing from the activities from which organised crime makes its money: public works contracts, extortion, the monopoly of services to construction companies and exclusive rights in illicit trade.' Villa San Giovanni was ruled by the Imerti family and huge opportunities for enrich-ment looked likely there as the government of the time planned to build a bridge between mainland Italy and Sicily, and the Calabrian side would be on the Imertis' turf.

Following the outbreak of hostilities between the De Stefano and Imerti families, most of the 'Ndrangheta's clans in and around Reggio Calabria lined up on one side or the other. The conflict was transformed from a local affair between the forces of two families into a war between the forces of several; the Serraino were among those who backed the Imerti family while the Latella family and the Libri family supported the De Stefano. Moreover, the war involved more than just Reggio Calabria's leading mafia families; even minor clans openly backed the Imertiani or the Destefaniani. However, a few remained neutral, some feeling particularly vulnerable and others reckoning they could profit by sitting on the sidelines.

Clans had used arson to flush out their opponents, big-game rifles to shoot them, car bombs to blow them up and bazookas to show that their homicidal intentions were serious. With the kind of firepower on which the families could call, it is surprising that by the time the 'Ndrangheta's war in Reggio Calabria ended it had only claimed six hundred lives. The killing stopped suddenly early in the autumn of 1991, an armistice brokered by the boss of San Luca, a town about twenty-five miles east of Reggio Calabria, across the Aspromonte.

After talking to Francesco Crispo at the bergamot consortium, I took the autostrada to by-pass Reggio Calabria and travelled north to where the mafia war had begun. At Campo Calabro, about a mile inland from Villa San Giovanni where the first bomb exploded, I stopped to learn more about bergamot from Mimmo Capua, whose long-established firm is the market leader. From his elegant office Capua, the octogenarian grandson of the founder, could look across the Strait of Messina and see Mount Etna on clear days.

Capua remembered better times in the bergamot business. Reggio Calabria produced about three hundred tonnes of bergamot essence each year during the 1960s. This had now fallen to about a hundred tonnes, harvested from only three thousand acres of bergamot groves. Working with four extraction lines at Campo Calabro and buying product from others, Capua's firm was responsible for around half of all exports of bergamot essence. 'But we sell much more lemon and orange essence,' Capua told me. Diversification seems sensible; the market for bergamot essence, under attack since the arrival of synthetic bergamot in the 1970s, has suffered. Calabria is still the world's producer of natural bergamot essence, but it costs four times as much as the synthetic product.

A further call to make, I drove north after leaving Campo Calabro, away from Reggio Calabria. The autostrada climbs steeply soon after the exit for Villa San Giovanni, its carriageways soaring on hair-raising viaducts suspended over deep ravines above the small town of Scilla where, according to Homer's Odyssey, a six-headed monster called Scylla snatched oarsmen from Odysseus's boat. Close by, on the Sicilian side of the strait, a whirlpool called Charybdis threatened to suck Odysseus and his band to oblivion as they struggled north. But apart from the viaducts, there was nothing to fear on my short trip to Palmi, probably best known as the birthplace of Francesco Cilea, composer of the opera *Adriana Lecouvreur*, but also a place where the 'Ndrangheta calls the tune. There I was to meet Stefano Musolino, one of the investigating magistrates attached to Palmi's court.

'How did you react when you saw your first murder victim?' I asked, but Musolino had yet to face that part of his job. He became a judge when he entered the magistracy in 1997 and had only recently transferred to the prosecuting branch. There had been no murders while he had been on duty, but he did not expect to be unsettled when called as duty investigating magistrate to the scene of crime in his first murder case. Musolino, who comes from Reggio Calabria, was a seventeen-year-old student when the mafia war exploded. 'Murder seemed a daily event. Probably everybody in Reggio saw at least one dead body in the street in those years; I must have seen half a dozen. Two people were killed beneath my home in a quiet part of the city. Other places were far hotter,' he told me as we stood talking in the bar across the square, where he ordered a cocktail of almond milk and coffee, for me an agreeable new experience.

After we had returned to the court he introduced me to a young colleague for whom seeing a murder victim for the first time had come as a shock. 'I will never forget my first murder case,' grimaced Eliana Franco. She was the magistrate on duty in Palmi when, late one morning in November 2004, she took a call from the police in Taurianova, a large town about ten miles away. She was told there had been a shooting in an olive grove outside a town called Oppido Mamertina. Olive groves of low, bushy trees in Tuscany and Puglia help form landscapes of pastoral tranquillity, but the huge trees around Taurianova, Oppido Mamertina and nearby Cittanova, local species called *ottobratico* and *sinopolesi*, make a canopy that lets through little sunlight and creates a sense of foreboding and unease.

Walking in August 1847 under olive trees to Castelnuovo, as Cittanova was called until 1852 when a royal decree changed its name, Edward Lear noted the shade they gave. The following day, trudging from Oppido Mamertina to Palmi, he complained about the interminable groves of tall, grey olives. Olive oil is an important business now as it was then, and Eliana Franco's first murder case arose from a dispute over a purchase of land. Her case was one of double homicide, of a father and his son. When she reached the scene, the father had been taken to hospital, where he later died, and the son was lying on the ground. 'They had been ambushed by a pair of killers. The engine of their car was still running and they had been hit, several yards from the car, by bullets from a 7.65 pistol.'

Doing business with a gun is not unusual in Calabria. Franco's second murder case, three months later, was a straightforward settling of accounts in an ambush that left one man dead and another injured. 'Taurianova and Cittanova are hot places. They may seem calm on the surface but there is always violence bubbling beneath,' said Franco about this part of the patch where she works.

Much as Franco was shocked by those two murder cases, she was spared the horrific scene in Taurianova that greeted a colleague in May 1991. Two killers had shot a butcher, used a cleaver to sever his head, tossed it in the air and used it as a target. After bullets had blasted it higher, the bloody head fell and smashed on the ground. The murder of the butcher was one of four that day in Taurianova, a response to the killing on the day before of a local politician and man-of-respect, as powerful people close to the Mafia are sometimes called, who had been pinned by bullets to a barber's chair while being shaved. The *faida* took twelve lives in the town in just two weeks.

After leaving Palmi I drove inland past olive groves, through Oppido Mamertina and Taurianova, to Cittanova, a town of about ten thousand inhabitants, where I registered at the Casalnuovo hotel near the centre. I went there to learn about the *faida* between the Facchineri and Albanese families which began in March 1964, the result of a dispute about grazing rights, when a man close to the Facchineri family was murdered.

Blood is repaid by blood in this part of Italy, and Antonio Albanese, the suspected murderer, was killed in revenge. The feud exploded in full fury in 1970 and over the next decade thirty-two murders and nine attempted murders shattered the town, brought grief and bitterness to many families and led to a retreat by the Facchineri family. They returned with a vengeance on 7 July 1987, when five people belonging to the Albanese family and its allies were murdered in the space of a few minutes, three of them in the town's public gardens. Over the next four years there would be twenty-seven murders and nine attempted murders in the town. In the autumn of 2006 the mayor expressed concern about safety and public order and a growing feeling of alarm. The magistrate Eliana Franco was not alone in sensing that trouble might be brewing once again.

Two boys of seven and nine were among the victims of Cittanova's feud, gunned down while tending animals simply because they were from the Facchineri family. Another innocent victim was a town councillor belonging to the Communist Party who was standing outside the party's offices in Cittanova's main street, next to the intended target, when the killers drove by. 'Remember, there were also many people who opposed violence and wanted only that the town should break free of economic and social backwardness,' Girolamo Demaria, secretary of Cittanova's Democratici di Sinistra, the Italian Communist Party's successor, told me when we met in the party's offices.

Demaria was a close friend of Francesco (Ciccio) Vinci, an eighteen-year-old high-school student and another of the feud's innocent victims, shot in December 1976. Vinci was a political activist who belonged to the communist youth league but his politics were not the reason for his murder; that was a matter of mistaken identity. He had offered to take the place of a cousin related to the Facchineri family and drive into the countryside outside the town to pick up his uncle. Killers were waiting by the cemetery; their shooting severed Vinci's femoral artery and he died from loss of blood before help arrived. 'Ciccio's murder hurt me badly. He was my best friend, we lived close and saw each other every day. Such a blow alters one's life. For some of us it increased our commitment to fight for change.'

Massimo D'Alema, Italy's prime minister in 1998 and foreign minister in 2006, was national secretary of the communist youth league when Vinci was killed. 'I well remember the sense of dismay that hit us all, of a such a young life torn from his loved ones, his friends and comrades,' said D'Alema, thirty years after the murder.

The Vinci family has never got over the profound grief of Francesco's murder, as I learnt when Demaria took me to meet Caterina, one of the young victim's sisters, in her house near the centre of Cittanova where she had often cared for him when their mother was out. 'Our father could never come to terms with the fact that Francesco had been killed. He was the only boy and the youngest in the family. Three girls and then Francesco. We never had time to get to know him. Really, our lives ended then,' remembered Caterina, nine years older than Francesco, thirty years of sadness colouring her words.

'So young, so innocent about everything. How do I feel? Anger, anger, anger inside me every time I see family of those who killed him. And to think that one of the three murderers was at school with him.' Caterina had shown me into the first-floor living room, used for special occasions and when there are guests – the cabinets of chinaware and the family's best furniture reminders of Victorian sitting rooms – and her husband offered me a glass of limoncello, a warming lemon-based alcoholic drink that he had made. 'I would like to say a lot more about Francesco but my mind freezes when I think of him,' she said. While her father worked abroad, her mother brought up the family and tried to make ends meet by harvesting olives. 'It was the only work here, very hard work, and Francesco helped.' Like most families in Cittanova, the Vinci family was accustomed to hardship. And it also had to live with sudden, bloody death and the anger and emptiness this brings.

Few in Reggio Calabria were unaffected by the mafia war; the conflict that exploded in the city and surrounding districts was such that it is hard to imagine that it did not leave a mark on all who lived through it. However, the impact of violence, of a *faida*, is far deeper in a small town like Cittanova where everybody knows everybody and scenes of murders are passed each day. But reactions to killings are personal. 'Family relation-ships mean some people take one side or the other. Others turn inwards and suspect everyone else. A few give vent to their anger and anguish in a commitment to fight for change, for the better,' said Don Giuseppe (Pino) Demasi, the vicar-general of the Oppido-Palmi diocese who is also the parish priest in Polistena, about five miles from Cittanova.

Ordained in 1975, Don Pino was born in Cittanova, grew up there in the 1950s and 1960s and was nineteen when the *faida* exploded. '*Tanti morti*, so many dead.' His decision to enter the church arose partly from his horror at the bloodshed, although the appalling economic and social condi-tions that afflicted the town also counted; Don Pino's father, like Vinci's, had been one of millions of southern men who travelled north, to Italy's industrial cities or across the Alps to Switzerland or Germany in search of work. Poverty provides the soil in which the 'Ndrangheta thrives. Condi-tions have improved greatly since then, the 'Ndrangheta is more widely seen for the evil that it is, and Don Pino thinks that people are more aware of its strength. 'But the Mafia is everywhere around here, and in Cittanova the *faida* may erupt again and shatter the equilibrium.'

Hope for Calabria depends on the Calabresi, but the signs are not encouraging. Large numbers of young people demonstrated in Cittanova after Vinci's murder, some carrying banners proclaiming 'Ciccio, you will always be with us'. The town's mayor said that the Mafia would not win, that things would change, but the killings just continued. Among those who gave vent to their outrage in Cittanova in December 1976 was a group from Locri, a town of about thirteen thousand inhabitants on the other side of the Aspromonte mountains, on the Ionian coast. They would have been around forty-five years old when high-school and middle-school students took to the streets in Locri itself in October 2005 to protest against the murder there of the deputy chairman of Calabria's regional government. Locri was another place for me to visit.

Checking out of the Casalnuovo, where I would later return, I headed east from the town, past the public gardens where three people had been murdered about twenty years before, climbing the winding road that cuts through the Aspromonte. This is where the 'Ndrangheta grows marijuana. 'When you cross the Aspromonte from Cittanova to Gerace and Locri you can see how dense the vegetation is. The trees are enormous and it is dark a few steps from the road. Even from a helicopter you cannot see the large plantations of marijuana, with giant plants eight feet tall, that the 'Ndrangheta cultivates, but they are everywhere in the national park,' Nicola Gratteri had told me. 'However, this is business for low-level *mafiosi*. The top families deal in cocaine,' he added.

Then, dropping away from the summit about three thousand feet up, enjoying sweeping views of the Ionian Sea, I drove downhill into Gerace, the magistrate Gratteri's pretty home town. Edward Lear had stayed there with the Scaglione family in 1847 and thought it was by far the nicest place he visited in Calabria, sited high above the coastal plain, every rock, sanctuary and house in the town seemingly positioned and coloured specially for painters. Over a period of many years, an Italian-Scots painter called Clotilde Peploe stayed in the Scagliones' house and at a gallery in London I had seen works she painted while there. One was called *Heart of the Mafia*, which seemed appropriate; a note beside the painting described the area as wild and almost uninhabited, 'often used by the local Mafia ('Ndrangheta) to hide kidnap victims in the 1970s'.

Down to Locri on the coast, to the Palazzo Nieddu del Rio, where the region's deputy chairman, a doctor, had been shot five times in the chest at very close range late on a Sunday afternoon as he left the building, arriving dead at the hospital where he had worked. His death added another name to the list of more than twenty murder victims in and around Locri between January and October 2005.

Members of Magistratura Democratica, an association of progressive magistrates, were holding a conference in the Palazzo when I visited Locri. One of the speakers was Anna Maria Pancallo, a leader of the hundreds of students who took to the streets on the day after the murder, some with plain white sheets stretched between them, others with banners carrying words that said how deeply young people in the town and the surrounding area were affected by the shooting: 'The Mafia kills, silence does too'; 'United for a Locride without Mafia'; 'Free us from the 'Ndrangheta'; and 'Enough words ... now facts'.

'Nobody had spoken publicly in Locri about the Mafia before, nobody had ever shouted out against it,' remembered Pancallo, a slight, bright young woman, sitting in her father's small publishing house and printing works on the town's main street. Yet, the ranks of the youthful activists had soon thinned to about twenty and probably little would remain of their commitment when they left the town to study at university as she planned to do.

'What happens here is at the extreme edge of experience, definitely not like central Italy, for example. The local context is hard to understand for those who have grown up in normal middle-class Roman families like me,' observed Ilaria Auricchio, a young investigating magistrate, one of a team of eight in Locri, her first post. During her first three years as a magistrate she dealt with four murders and two attempted murders. 'These were not recorded as mafia murders, those are handled by the anti-Mafia people in Reggio, although the Mafia is often an element in ordinary crime.'

At the end of January 2007, about fifteen months after the murder of the Calabrian politician, Pasquale Adorno, president of Reggio Calabria's appeal court, recalled the events in Locri when part of the population, led by youngsters, had given a cry of rebellion against the Mafia. 'Thanks to them, for the first time, Locri could be spoken of as a place of hope, an example to be copied, a voice to be listened to.' However, Adorno noted that an explosive device had recently been set off in the hospital in Siderno, a town near Locri, and another had been defused in Locri's own hospital a few days later.

Wanting to see more of the Aspromonte and San Luca, about which Gratteri had told me, I drove south along the coast to spend the night in Brancaleone. The following day I continued around Capo Spartivento to Melito, not far short of Lazzaro where I had stayed earlier, turning inland to follow a road that flanks the Aspromonte for about thirty miles. I had decided to visit the Sanctuary of the Madonna of Polsi. My interest had been aroused partly by Lear's travels. On foot, he had pushed deep into the Aspromonte and thought that it was unlikely that any other foreigner had ever been to such remote corners of a region whose cities and towns were themselves infrequently visited. He engaged an extra local guide to reach Polsi. The few black-robed monks who lived there wondered why Lear and his English companion had travelled to such an out-of-the-way place; no outsiders had ever done so before.

But I was also interested in Polsi because GianCarlo Bregantini, the bishop of Locri, had told me that *mafiosi* no longer meet there. From a small mountain village called Denno, mid-way between Trent and Bolzano in northern Italy, Bishop Bregantini, a friendly, grey-bearded man always ready to support voluntary and charitable associations, had for many years spoken loudly against the evil of the 'Ndrangheta. On the day that I met him, he had been giving encouragement to a cooperative whose crops had been ruined by *mafiosi*. His transfer to another diocese after thirteen years in Locri, ordered by Pope Benedict XVI in November 2007, would raise a chorus of complaints from Calabria's churchgoers and threats of a boycott of the church. 'Out of obedience I came here, and out of obedience I leave,' Bishop Bregantini would tell his flock.

The Madonna of Polsi and the Mafia – the sacred and the profane, I thought as I left the prelate's office. Apparently the 'Ndrangheta's bosses used to gather in Polsi under the cover provided by the tens of thousands of faithful who make a pilgrimage to the sanctuary on the first Sunday of September. It is at the bottom of a high mountain valley, one road winding down to it and another leading up and away, on the far side of a cluster of buildings and the church. Tonino Perna, who had been chairman of the national park, had told me that the access road was clear but he was wrong. As the car slipped and slithered down a steep and twisting muddy track, I wondered if my decision to visit Polsi had been wise.

'How can I get out?' I asked Don Pino Strangio, the cheerful priest who looks after the sanctuary. Don Pino is also the parish priest at San Luca, the village through which Lear passed to reach Polsi and where I wanted to go. I was worried that this way out might be even worse than the way in, and from beside the church it seemed so. 'You shouldn't have problems,' said Don Pino, asking one of his helpers to lead the way on a motorcycle. I was soon out of the valley, going downhill, along a track that follows the course of a seasonal river and into San Luca. This is the village that Gratteri calls the 'Ndrangheta's heart, a village riven by a *faida* where the bosses' power is such that they could even stop a station for the Carabinieri from being built there.

At the beginning of 2007 Pasquale Adorno, the judge in Reggio Calabria, spoke about a recent murder in San Luca. 'A double attack by a killer squad bloodied Christmas Day in San Luca, with one woman murdered and three people injured, including a boy just five years old, events that could be a prelude to a reopening of the conflict between the clans.' Retaliation arrived quickly, a week later, when a shepherd with a long criminal record was murdered in San Luca. But even more blood would be shed in Germany, in Duisburg, where six men from the Locride were gunned down. The priest of San Luca for almost thirty years, and related to some of the *faida*'s victims, Don Pino would take the funeral service of the three of Duisburg's dead who came from the village. He appealed to the mourners to condemn the Mafia and to remember that justice means choosing the state. But how many times before have such words been spoken, and then forgotten?

Every now and again Calabria makes the news, usually news of crime or criminals, but interest quickly fades even in the bloodiest events and where the victims are public figures. Many killings make the local media but go no further. Describing Calabria as a *buco nero* (black hole), Ilaria Auricchio, the young magistrate in Locri, said, 'It is a forgotten region.'

6

———

GIOIA TAURO

Losing Business

THE WORLD HAS FAILED STATES and rogue nations – Zimbabwe, Somalia, North Korea and others where the usual rules of civil and democratic society are missing. Italy has Calabria, the long toe of the Italian boot where the law seems to be that which the 'Ndrangheta lays down rather than that set in Rome.

A black hole, as some people describe it, or a region without a future, as Italy's daily business newspaper called Calabria in June 2006 after the body of an elderly farmer was found near the beach at Briatico, a small town about sixty miles north of Reggio Calabria? The farmer had been lured into a trap late at night and shot; the murderers had loaded his body into the car that he had driven to the encounter and taken the car to where they set it on fire, leaving a smouldering wreck that the police would find, charred human remains inside. The victim had been active in an anti-racket association set up by local businessmen and his murder was one more example of the 'Ndrangheta's strength and the weakness of Italy's institutions in the region.

How can an economy thrive when organised crime is so strong, I wonder, and of course it does not thrive. Calabria's economy languishes, as it always has. In terms of gross domestic product per capita, a common measure of economic wellbeing, the region is poorer than any other in the country. People in Calabria produce less than two-thirds of the wealth produced by the average Italian and less than half of what comes from people in the country's most productive region. Calabria's five provinces sit geographically and economically at the bottom of the one hundred and three provinces into which Italy is divided.

Cittanova and the comfortable and reasonably priced Casalnuovo hotel was my base while I met businessmen in the south of the region and visited places where planners had tried, unsuccessfully, to create industries. The problem of southern economic backwardness is a long story, recognised but unsolved after Italian reunification in 1860 and during Mussolini's twenty-year fascist dictatorship. Following the second world war, the government thought that building infrastructure, like roads, railways, electricity grids and water systems, would be enough, but it was not and policy turned to industrial intervention in the 1960s.

Italy's large state holding corporations, their interests ranging from steel, shipbuilding, chemicals and oil to electronics, car making, food and textiles, were required to channel forty per cent of their investment towards the Mezzogiorno. Grants and low-interest loans were splurged on manufacturing companies to encourage them to go south but this policy also failed. Private firms built factories as far north in the South as was possible in order to benefit from incentives, partly to be closer to markets but mostly to avoid the inefficiency, corruption and organised crime with which the deep South is afflicted.

Even so, Sicily got oil refineries and chemical works, as I saw in Gela, and a small car-factory that I saw from the train as it left the station in Termini Imerese; Puglia got state-aided food, chemical and engineering plants; factories for many industries were built in Campania; and even tiny Basilicata benefited from new enterprises. As for Calabria, few were willing to step into a dark region that seemed even more alien and less hospitable after riots erupted in Reggio Calabria in July 1970 over the choice of Catanzaro as the region's capital. Deaths, dynamite attacks and barricades over the next ten months did not change the government's mind, although it did enact a measure called the Pacchetto Colombo (named after Emilio Colombo, prime minister at the time) to placate the Calabresi who felt excluded.

The 1960s and 1970s were decades of grand projects, so Colombo's package of three mammoth schemes to launch the economy in southern

Calabria fitted its time. Yet Liquichimica's petrochemical plant at Saline Ioniche, on the coast about fifteen miles south of Reggio Calabria, would soon be abandoned, to be one project on a long list of failed schemes for encouraging the Mezzogiorno's economic development. Southern Italy has some monstrous examples of industrial wreckage, cathedrals in the desert as they are often called, and the one erected at Saline Ioniche is among the more shocking.

Nowadays, it is one of only two large industrial complexes along the hundred and fifty miles of Ionian coast between Reggio Calabria and Crotone. The other is also in Saline Ioniche, a railway repair works where work ran dry. I had noticed Liquichimica's deserted plant as I drove along the coastal road, its large storage tanks, port facilities that should have taken ships of forty thousand tonnes, tall chimneys, and the pipes, tubes and ducts that go with petrochemical plants now rusting and crumbling by the sea.

Liquichimica planned to make bioprotein for animal feed as well as citric acid, of which it produced some experimental batches in 1973, but the plan was sunk by Italy's institute for public health which banned the bioprotein as cancerous. The company went bust and, although the state-owned group that acquired the assets kept some plants running elsewhere, the factory in Saline Ioniche was closed for good. The few people who had been hired stayed on the books and were paid for being idle until they retired.

'The Bible tells us that we are called by God to look after the Earth. He has entrusted this Earth to Man, not for Man to destroy but for Man to make it flourish,' Vittorio Mondello, the archbishop of Reggio Calabria, growled across his desk at me. The archbishop thinks that the abandoned plant at Saline Ioniche is one of the more disgraceful examples of the disregard of the Italian government and Calabresi for this part of the Bible's teaching. 'Billions and billions of lire were thrown away building a factory that would never produce anything. The Calabresi were hoodwinked by the promise of jobs,' he added, his expression becoming even more severe.

However, what seemed to anger the archbishop most is that bergamot trees were ripped out to provide the site for the factory. 'There used to be a wonderful bergamot grove but it was destroyed to create nothing. This is the awful truth.' Liquichimica created an eyesore not jobs, hurting the environment and the Italian taxpayer.

The 'Ndrangheta's clans were probably the only winners; they certainly profited from the building of the plant, a project that was worth about three hundred billion lire, a huge sum at the time, but that is long ago and long forgotten. And forgotten also are the lost geological report that advised against the site because the ground was unstable and the suspicious death in a road accident of the head of Reggio Calabria's civil engineering department who stubbornly insisted that the report's findings should be accepted and another site found for the plant.

Investment and the creation of jobs in the south of Calabria were the aims of the three-pronged Pacchetto Colombo. The project at Saline Ioniche, state aided but in the private sector, promised much but delivered nothing while hopes that the state's own big project, the construction of Italy's fifth major steelworks, would do better were quickly dashed. The state holding corporation already operated four large steelworks but the project for a fifth, near Gioia Tauro, about thirty-five miles north of Reggio Calabria, was badly timed as oil shocks hit the world economy in the 1970s and countries in the developing world began to produce cheap steel.

Nevertheless, work began on a site near Gioia Tauro. Building the petrochemical plant at Saline Ioniche brought destruction of a bergamot grove but development caused damage on a far greater scale north of Gioia Tauro. Though its name is still on the map, the village of Eranova was razed and its community of nine hundred people dispersed. 'I was its last priest,' Pino Demasi told me sadly. After being ordained in 1975 he had been sent to San Ferdinando, about five miles from Gioia Tauro, and Eranova was part of the parish. 'The decision to build a steelworks was terrible. Hundreds of acres of wonderful citrus groves were grubbed up.'

Yet to have continued with building the steelworks in the face of the adverse economic conditions would have been folly and common sense prevailed. The project was abandoned. Calabria's hopes of jobs and the expectations of the region's Mafia then shifted to the large power station that the state electricity corporation promised to build. Anti-Mafia investigators would discover that the Piromalli clan that controls Gioia Tauro had reached agreement in 1987 with the clan controlling Rosarno, a town about seven miles to the north, on how to split the enormous appetising opportunities that the power station's construction offered. That year was also when Gioia Tauro lost its mayor, killed because he had given offence to a member of the family of Giuseppe Piromalli, the clan's boss.

In 1989 the anti-Mafia high commissioner began investigating the contracts signed by the electricity corporation with construction firms. This was the beginning of the project's end. Magistrates acted early in 1990, laying charges against the corporation and contractors and seeking the preventive seizure of works; in July that year the site was sealed and work brought to a halt. Not long after, the corporation's chairman gave parliament's anti-Mafia commission details of contracts worth more than five and a half trillion lire (about two billion pounds) at Gioia Tauro. If the 'Ndrangheta had been disappointed by the steelworks' cancellation, they certainly compensated by making money from the project for a power station. Complying with a ruling by the government, the corporation had favoured local firms and reserved certain kinds of contracts for Calabrian firms, an invitation to the 'Ndrangheta that could not have been clearer.

The project was abandoned in May 1994 and the state electricity corporation's tortuous involvement with Gioia Tauro ended like that of the state steel corporation. 'The decision was necessary,' it said, 'because the conditions of certainty and consensus for undertaking a project involving such high investment do not exist.'

No permanent jobs were created at Gioia Tauro in almost a quarter of a century following the Pacchetto Colombo's announcement, and while construction work on preparing the site and building the port had created temporary employment, it also provided rich pickings for the 'Ndrangheta. By 1993 it was clear that the project for a power station would run aground but, after this second aborted scheme by a state-owned company, the private sector stepped in and the saga of Gioia Tauro ended better than the failed attempt to create jobs at Saline Ioniche. That Gioia Tauro would eventually have a major project was due to a far-sighted shipowner who saw that the huge, unfinished port could be transformed into a transhipment terminal for container ships.

Container transhipment ports act as distribution centres where large ships arrive and discharge containers for onward transport by smaller feeder vessels, and the large ships are loaded with those brought in by the smaller ships. 'The idea was absolutely new to Europe in the early 1990s, and in this part of Calabria we are strategically placed, right in the middle of the Mediterranean, close to the routes that ships follow from Suez to Gibraltar,' Tim Halhead, the port's operations director explained to me. With the boom in world trade, particularly that involving Asia, transhipment became big business in the late 1990s. Having begun operations in 1995, only two years after the shipowner had conceived the idea, within ten years Gioia Tauro's port was handling the equivalent of around three million twenty-foot containers annually and competing for leadership of container transhipment in the Mediterranean.

A success story, but not free of the 'Ndrangheta. Nothing in Calabria escapes its involvement and a business such as Gioia Tauro's port is a powerful attraction. Wherever there is a mafia family, it aims to control its turf and this means taking a cut on whatever economic activity is undertaken there. In Gioia Tauro's case, the transhipment terminal operates on the turf of formidable mafia families and these tried, unsuccessfully, to extort one dollar and fifty cents for every container handled when the port began operations.

Yet territorial control extends beyond simply squeezing local businesses. According to Nicola Gratteri, the anti-Mafia magistrate whom I met in Reggio Calabria, the families in and around Gioia Tauro reached agreement on how to divide management of the port's structures, control of the port being important for developing other businesses, like arms trafficking with Bosnia and Croatia, drugs trafficking and cigarette contraband. 'We seize quintals of cocaine every year but probably only discover five per cent of the total that arrives in Italy, mainly in containers by ship.'

Senior managers in the port play down the 'Ndrangheta's presence and point to the importance of security and what they do to keep it tight. 'Gioia Tauro is no different from Rotterdam, Southampton or other ports where I have worked,' said Halhead. He believes that the finding of drugs or arms should be a cause for celebration as this shows that security measures are working.

However, strikes around the beginning of 2007, called by a local independent trade union unconnected with Italy's large national labour organisations, posed worrying questions. Large container ships follow strict schedules set many months ahead and shipping lines need total reliability in the ports that they use. There is increasing competition between the Mediterranean's main container ports like Algeciras and Valencia in Spain and a terminal near the Suez Canal. Ships go elsewhere if Gioia Tauro has trouble, so the strikes caused huge concern to the port's parent company in Germany.

Certainly Cecilia Eckelmann Battistello, the company's managing director in Hamburg, was surprised that people in Calabria, a region with such a sickly economy, should put the business and jobs at risk. Seen from northern Europe, the disruption was incomprehensible. What was behind it? 'The Mafia,' Eckelmann Battistello told me bluntly. And Pasquale Larosa, local secretary of the CGIL national trade union, called on the authorities to investigate the possibility that the Mafia was connected to the disruption at the port. Some of his members had been subjected to intimidation, and intimidation in Calabria is not a matter to be treated lightly. 'Calabria is not like Lombardy or Piedmont. Intimidation must be taken very seriously here.'

During my visit to Corleone I had met Giacomo Zappia, the chairman of a cooperative of young people who work land confiscated from Gioia Tauro's *mafiosi*, and promised to call on him when I arrived in Calabria. We met in his offices in a run-down building on the town's outskirts, near the CGIL's, before going for a snack lunch. 'Let's go here, this bar is fine,' he said. Other cafes nearby carry an *odore di mafia* and are best avoided. He then took me along the main road out of town, the Via Locri that leads to the autostrada for Reggio Calabria and across the Aspromonte to the Locride and the Ionian Sea, the road down which I had driven earlier from Cittanova.

Zappia wanted to show me what determined anti-Mafia magistrates and the courts can do in a Mafia-dominated town that the local clan considers its own. Properties on both sides of the road have been confiscated from the Piromalli family and people acting as fronts for it. 'Look over there, on the right where the Italian Red Cross and the anti-racket association have their offices,' Zappia's finger pointed to a nondescript building with signs outside, 'and on the left, at that piece of land where there's a church.' Non-profit bodies and government organisations are often allocated confiscated property that once belonged to the Mafia.

Rusting shutters, lowered many years before, are also a sign that a building was at one time among the 'Ndrangheta's assets. Zappia stopped in front of a four-storey apartment block, paintwork fading, plaster crumbling, where unpruned bougainvillea hid the ground floor. 'Mafia before, now confiscated,' he said. And what is true in the town is true also in the countryside where abandoned citrus groves, ivy weaving upwards to strangle branches and bamboo plants growing higher than the trees themselves, are often evidence that the land had been owned by *mafiosi*.

A few miles outside Gioia Tauro, the Cooperativa Valle del Marro, of which Zappia is the chairman, took over about thirty-five acres of over-grown land at the beginning of 2005, the first such cooperative of young people in Calabria to be assigned land that had belonged to the Mafia, the Piromalli family in this case. They began grubbing up orange trees in the spring and were able to clear five acres by the end of the year and make their first small harvest in the summer of 2006.

Confiscated in 1986, the orange groves had been untended for twenty years and bringing the land back under cultivation again – with chilli peppers, a Calabrian speciality, and aubergines – was a huge job for the small cooperative. An ancient tractor, donated by the cooperative move-ment in Tuscany, threw up clouds of fine sandy dust as it worked land from which old tree trunks had been pushed aside to be sawn up. The tractor helped but, under the burning sun of the Calabrian summer, most of the job was exhausting manual work. When they began, the coopera-tive's members believed that, being too small and too much in the public eye, they would be immune to the 'Ndrangheta's attacks. But no business is too small or too much in the public eye, and all are expected to pay their tribute or suffer the consequences.

Five days before Christmas in 2006, *mafiosi* broke into the cooperative's store, stole equipment and damaged machinery. And that same night they sabotaged machinery for harvesting olives that the cooperative kept in Oppido Mamertina, where it worked olive groves that had been confis-cated from another of the 'Ndrangheta's clans. Zappia knew that the risk of further attacks would increase after planting in April. 'Poisoning and uprooting are easy.' Right on cue, *mafiosi* returned, started the tractor and used it to plough up the orderly rows of vegetables that the cooperative's members had planted and carefully tended. The newborn business was vulnerable and would be even more so after completing the clearance of the land and doubling the area under cultivation.

Zappia has a maxim, shared by some other young people in Calabria and elsewhere in the South: *lottare per rimanere, rimanere per lottare* – fight to stay, stay to fight. Business in Calabria is involved in a unending battle and Zappia's cooperative is as close as any to the front line.

Unlike the cooperative in Gioia Tauro, Pippo Callipo's firm is large and well established, but it faces the difficulties that all firms face in Calabria. With its offices and factory near Pizzo, about thirty-five miles up the coast, it is a thriving, private-sector business in a part of southern Italy where thriving, private-sector businesses are rare. Callipo runs the high-quality tunny-canning firm that his great-grandfather established in 1913. His sparkling modern factory on a winding country road a few miles outside the town processes around thirty tonnes of tunny every day, employs over two hundred workers and is a big cog in the local economy whose loss would be an enormous blow for the area around Pizzo itself and way beyond, in the region as a whole.

However, such things do not matter to mafia bosses. Like most businessmen in Calabria, Callipo has been a target for the 'Ndrangheta, his factory hit in drive-by shootings. Armed guards on contract from a private security agency approved by the police go on duty when the factory's working day ends and the canning lines stop. That gives some protection to the factory but Callipo's own safety is another matter. 'When I leave my office late in the evening I am always worried about some kind of attack until I reach the main road. The police are never around,' he told me as we sat eating a tunny salad in a small dining room near the factory's entrance.

After he was elected chairman of Calabria's businessmen's association in 2001 he learnt even more about how business in the region is under siege. Four words sum up Calabria's businessmen: isolated, ignored, powerless and scared. The situation was so bad that in June 2005 Callipo wrote an open letter to Italy's president, then Carlo Azeglio Ciampi. He wanted action in Calabria and hoped that his letter would get it. The Mafia, he said, held the region hostage and deprived people there of important constitutional rights like those of running a business and living in a normal society.

'Every morning it is the Mafia that provides the sad, desolate wake-up call, by means of its emissaries who go unpunished when they threaten and attack.' There is no lack of words from the state but solid commitment and action are missing. 'If necessary, the army should be sent in, because the state needs to reconquer this region. As matters stand, its sovereignty over Calabria is in crisis,' Callipo told Ciampi. Calabria remains backward because the state is unable to guarantee the physical safety of people living and working there, and without safety there can be no development.

Callipo thought that all that was missing was for a bureaucrat to place a sign at Calabria's boundaries to say that the region has been closed by the Mafia.

Seven months before writing to Ciampi he had written to the minister of home affairs, but got no reply. He met two senior officials from the ministry who thought that a questionnaire in which local businessmen were asked to explain the Mafia's existence might help. After workers employed by the firm belonging to the chairman of the provincial association of businessmen in Vibo Valentia had been shot at he wrote to the chairman of the regional government, but that produced nothing other than a proposal to establish a talking shop on the question of organised crime.

Following almost five and a half years as its chairman – well over the usual maximum of four years – he stood down from the leadership of the businessmen's association in July 2006. 'Security has not improved. Crime, or the threat of it, is the same as it was before,' he told me. The army had not been drafted to Calabria and the 'Ndrangheta continued its hold over the region.

Callipo's firm has also continued, despite the difficulties. Perhaps having been in business for four generations helps, or maybe operating in a business with distant historic roots is a factor. Tunny has been fished off Calabria's west coast for centuries, the Gulf of Sant'Eufemia Lamezia providing ideal breeding conditions for the Mediterranean tunny, Pizzo at its southern end being the oldest and most important of the region's tunny fisheries. Migrating in spring and early summer southeast across the Tyrrhenian Sea, great shoals of the large fish would turn down the Calabrian coast and would find their path barred at Pizzo by a large net barrier, one end anchored to a rock onshore, the other attached to a rectangular system of nets forming a set of five interconnecting underwater chambers. This way of catching tunny arrived in Calabria and Sicily with the Arabs about a thousand years ago.

Forced to swim away from the shore, the tunny would be trapped and their migration would end in a bloody climax in the final chamber, the *camera della morte* (death chamber). Callipo's great-grandfather set up his canning business in response to a need to preserve the surplus catch that was not consumed in and around Pizzo. The *tonnare* (the tunny fisheries, some of whose ruins can still be seen) disappeared many years ago, along with the brutal ritual of the *mattanza* (slaughter or massacre) once the fish were trapped in the final chamber. Nowadays, the eight hundred tunny that are canned every day in Callipo's factory arrive by lorry, the yellowfin frozen far across the world in factory ships in the Indian Ocean, but the highly prized Mediterranean bluefin arrives fresh.

Pizzo's *tonnara* caught the fish on their migration around the Tyrrhenian Sea, following the route that they had taken for centuries and arriving in the Gulf of Sant'Eufemia about a day after leaving Carloforte in Sardinia. Then the currents changed and it became an obsolete relic of a bygone age. 'Pizzo's economy was completely dependent on the *tonnara* for which a marquess had a licence from the King of Naples. Outside the fishing season people here were kept busy repairing the enormous nets that were needed and maintaining their boats,' said Callipo.

There is not much to Pizzo, a town of less than ten thousand inhabitants with a large church, a castle built by Ferdinand of Aragon towards the end of the fifteenth century and a footnote in history. Joachim Murat, marshal of France, Napoleon's brother-in-law and King of Naples from 1808 until 1815, died in the castle at Pizzo under a volley of musket fire. After Napoleon's defeat in 1815 Murat had tried to return to Naples from Corsica with a small band of loyal followers to lead a popular uprising against the returning Bourbons but was forced off course by a storm and driven ashore in Calabria. Having fled to Sicily at the end of 1798, the Bourbons were disinclined to mercy when they reclaimed their throne on Italy's mainland, and Murat was executed by a firing squad. Legend says that he told his executioners: 'Save my face, aim for the heart.'

Recklessness was part of Murat's character, as his brother-in-law readily recognised. According to Napoleon, Murat had tried with just two hundred and fifty men to reconquer a kingdom he had been unable to hold with eighty thousand. Almost two hundred years later the situation would be similar. 'The police forces have not been enough for the past ten to twenty years, so the Mafia has become even harder to beat,' Callipo complained to me.

Even so, he remains committed to his region and diversified in 2007 by opening a small factory in Pizzo to make *tartufi* (truffles) hazel-nut ice cream, a speciality of the town. Every initiative helps, but Calabria badly needs many more such new businesses to reduce the huge gap that separates its economy from that of the rest of Italy.

Without doubt the 'Ndrangheta is an important reason why Calabria lags behind, perhaps the main reason. A clothing factory near Callipo's tunny-canning plant was torched and an empty petrol can left nearby as a message to say that the *mafiosi* make the rules and that those rules must be obeyed. 'It is the same all over Calabria, nowhere is safe. Business gets no protection from the Mafia.' But there is another, darker aspect. Some politicians, *mafiosi* and businessmen are happy to work together. 'Calabria's murky waters suit many people, allowing them to hide their dirty business,' Callipo remarked, as we sat finishing our lunch.

'Businessmen talk among themselves but do not speak publicly because they are afraid. About three weeks before the deputy chairman of the regional government was murdered in Locri, I was warned by businessmen there that something bad was in the air.' Because he was an insider, not just one of them but the leader of Calabria's business community, the businessmen spoke to Callipo, but they are usually reluctant to speak out or talk to strangers.

Asking businessmen about how they cope with the Mafia makes me uneasy; it is trickier than asking about turnover and profits. I had spoken to Pina Grassi in Palermo, the widow of Libero Grassi, a businessman who was murdered by Cosa Nostra in August 1991 because he refused to pay the *pizzo* (protection money) and campaigned against his extortioners in newspapers and on television. 'We sent out about two thousand invitations to a public debate in May 1991 and only twenty people turned up. The Mafia had to kill Libero to set an example, to stop others from refusing to pay.'

'The situation has improved,' she said. But it is thought that around three-quarters of Palermo's businesses still pay the *pizzo* and so do people in the professions there. Extortion is low-level crime, but is nevertheless important for the Mafia, providing money to support the families of *mafiosi* who are in prison and a means for maintaining territorial control. Pina Grassi continues her husband's campaign but it is a lonely struggle 'with no help or encouragement from Palermo's city authorities or from Sicily's regional government'.

Girolamo Demaria in Cittanova introduced me to two men in the town who had also stood up to mafia extortioners; Rocco Raso, who runs a building materials business, and Luigi Molina, who has a gift shop in the main street. 'There was a climate of terror here. *Mafiosi* thought they ran the town and they asked me for an impossibly large amount of money,' Raso told me as we sat chatting in the Casalnuovo hotel. The 'Ndrangheta had not tried to squeeze him before and he spoke to other businessmen and learnt that they too were being targeted by one of the local clans.

Summoning up courage, a small group of extortion victims reported the matter to the authorities, who brought charges against four people, the first time that victims had reacted in this way. 'We were worried because the trial of the extortioners was underway in Palmi when Libero Grassi was murdered in Palermo,' Raso told me. He said that businessmen in Cittanova have not been troubled since they decided in 1990 that they could say no to the Mafia. 'Everyone had just kept quiet and kept themselves to themselves before. It was a turning point for Cittanova. We think there is little extortion here now but the situation is terrible elsewhere and extortion is rife in a neighbouring town.'

I had asked the owner of a bergamot grove in Valanidi, near Reggio Calabria, about the 'Ndrangheta and he told me that the good times had ended many years ago and that growing bergamot fruit to make bergamot essence is such a poor business that the 'Ndrangheta does not bother the firms involved. I did not press the question further, although anti-Mafia magistrates had told me that even the poorest businesses are affected and that, in any case, the Mafia also works indirectly, telling businessmen which transport firms they should use, where they should buy supplies and which people they should hire, for example.

And I had asked a businessman in Reggio Calabria how he deals with the 'Ndrangheta. From cordial, he turned glacial. 'That is a question I cannot answer. I have sued journalists before,' he said threateningly. As for the call that Pippo Callipo had made for greater effort in fighting the Mafia, the businessman thought that the owner of the tunny-canning business in Pizzo had been 'very imprudent'.

Fear is what keeps people silent, said magistrates in Reggio Calabria. And if local businessmen are scared, why should outsiders risk venturing into mainland Italy's furthest corner? Northern Italian companies avoid involvement in the South and foreign investors, if they consider Italy at all, usually stay as far to the north as they can. Economic development and jobs arrive only with investment, investment arrives only in conditions of security, and security is lacking. Such is the seemingly intractable problem that afflicts Calabria and much of the Mezzogiorno.

I heard more about extortion at Lamezia Terme, about fifteen miles north of Pizzo, at the northern end of the Gulf of Sant'Eufemia, where a firm on the main road to the town from the airport provides evidence that even having the police as neighbours in Calabria is no protection against the clans. The town's new police station is an imposing high-security building surrounded by high concrete walls, topped by tall steel palings on which notices say that it is patrolled by armed guards. This seems like a war zone, with bullet-proof vests as part of normal uniform and patrol cars that carry armouries to match the weaponry that *mafiosi* might have to hand. Next door, on the other side of the concrete wall, stood the blackened skeleton of a large three-storey building, stark proof of the impotence of Italy's institutions in the face of the Mafia.

Reinforced concrete pillars protruding from the rubble of cement, plaster and broken glass were what remained of the Godino family's wholesale tyre distribution business after an arson attack in October 2006. 'I was at home that evening, smelt burning rubber and thought little about it because there was a gypsy encampment nearby where they often burnt old tyres. Then I saw the flames and realised that the smell came from tyres we had stacked outside, not from the gypsy encampment. A window broke and suddenly the whole warehouse burst into flame,' Daniele Godino, a bright man in his late twenties, told me.

His father is typical of many Calabresi, emigrating to Canada when he was a teenager, accumulating savings there and returning to Lamezia Terme to set up his tyre business in 1981, after almost twenty years abroad. He had built the warehouse with the family home above it in 1996 and would start again on the same site. The Godino family knew that it was a mafia target; on four occasions the building had been shot at and bottles of petrol had been left outside not long before the arson attack. 'Lamezia is a difficult town that offers little,' said Godino. More than difficult; like many Calabrian towns, Lamezia Terme is also a mafia town where those who are against the Mafia face threats as well as difficulties.

Gianni Speranza, a bouncy secondary-school teacher who stood for mayor in April 2005 and won, was another of those who decided that the 'Ndrangheta should not be accommodated. 'The 'Ndrangheta has a long history in Lamezia. It has always been here and this was one of the first places, even before the Aspromonte, where the Mafia made kidnapping one of its main businesses. That was at the beginning of the 1970s. And the first magistrate to be murdered by the Mafia was killed here in Lamezia. An important change occurred in the 1980s when business, politics and the Mafia got together,' explained Speranza. Mafia infiltration of local politics was such that Italy's head of state dissolved the town's council in 1991.

The Mafia wasted no time in showing its disapproval of Speranza's election. 'I was elected on a Monday and two days later the door to the town council was torched and I received bullets in the post. The message was clear. Although I got the votes, they are still the power that counts.' He became mayor following a period of two and a half years during which Lamezia Terme was governed by a special commissioner. A decree signed by the Italian president in October 2002, dissolving the town's council for a second time, noted that some members of the town council that had been elected in May of the previous year had been in contact either directly or indirectly with the Mafia. 'These links with organised crime put heavy pressure on the councillors and compromised the council's freedom in how it takes decisions,' the decree said. (Thirty-two town councils in Calabria were dissolved between 1995 and 2006 because of mafia infiltration.)

Writing to the president, the home affairs minister drew attention to the gravity of the situation in Lamezia, where three warring clans were clashing over extortion, drugs and arms trafficking, and how to profit from private-sector business and public-sector work. In less than two years Lamezia had been bloodied by fifteen mafia killings and seven cases of serious injuries in which *mafiosi* were involved.

There were close family relationships between two members of the council in 2002 and two councillors in the council that had been disbanded in 1991, who had later been put on trial for mafia-related offences. Another four councillors, in a council dominated by rightwing parties in 2002, also had morally dubious connections. Companies in which Lamezia's council owned stakes had hired people with criminal records. Grants had been made to firms that had links with the criminal world. A consortium in which the public sector had a controlling interest was headed by a person whose commercial relations included close ties with businessmen who were under criminal investigation.

'It is worrying to think what might have happened if that council had continued to run the town,' Speranza said to me. Yet while the people of Lamezia elected a progressive mayor, they also gave their votes to the parties on the right that had provided the council that had been dissolved and would again form the governing majority. The town's first citizen would have to work with a council of a different political colour. And like Rosario Crocetta, the leftwing mayor of Gela in southern Sicily, Speranza had also attacked the Mafia when he campaigned for office and, as in Crocetta's case, the threats would mean that he could not move safely around the town and would need an armoured car and armed bodyguards.

'The fact that the Mafia is here does not mean that there are a lot of *mafiosi*, but it does mean they control the economy,' observed Speranza. Looking back at the history of an industrial area on the coast near the airport, he reflected on how his town, created in 1970 from the merger of three neighbouring towns, might have developed. 'This is a young town but, in almost forty years since it was founded, it has grown up with disappointment. After 1970's riots in Reggio Calabria, the Pacchetto Colombo promised Lamezia a large petrochemical plant that would employ two and a half thousand workers. The Società Italiana Resine hired two hundred people but construction barely started and the plant never entered production.'

Lamezia's hopes died in the decade that followed its birth. What should have been a huge industrial complex was abandoned, like the petrochemical plant at Saline Ioniche and the steelworks at Gioia Tauro, the other two large projects in the Pacchetto Colombo. The Società Italiana Resine (known as SIR) went bust and would be the centre of a major case of judicial corruption in Rome. And it would leave a large empty area by the coast, with a handful of completed buildings, where thirty years later Calabrian politicians and businessmen would place their modest expectations for the area's economic development.

The two and a half thousand acres of flat land that belonged to SIR lie between the north–south highway and the coast, their northern boundary neighbouring the airport. In March 1997 a consortium called Lamezia Europa was set up with the aim of developing part of the land and a protocol, drawn up two years later, tries to ensure that firms there are on the right side of the law. Physical security is a priority and the consortium, which began building access roads in 2001, has fenced the entire area and set up a surveillance centre.

Development of the area is seen as a way to ease the problem of unemployment in and around the town but it is a daunting task. Six years after building work began, less than half of the fifty-five firms that had agreed to set up had done so, there were a little more than four hundred jobs, and about one fifth of those were in a call centre. However, Tullio Rispoli, the manager of the consortium, was confident that the firms would together hit the target of one thousand jobs and hopeful that the number would reach fifteen hundred. Rispoli drove me around the site, mostly empty land running down to the sea. 'We have one of the last stretches of unspoilt beach along this coast.' 'Managing its development will be a challenge,' I said, thinking of all the developers, with or without mafia connections, who will try to get their hands on it.

Every yard of economic progress in Lamezia Terme, as everywhere in the region, is gained after an exhausting struggle that saps the energy of all but the most enthusiastic, committed and honest businessman, politician or local administrator. Every step must be won against the handicap of Calabria's distance and poor infrastructure, the deadweight of the region's black reputation, the entanglements of red tape and worse. As often as not, the town and its region seem to be slipping back, not edging forward.

7

SIBARI

Migrants

GIANNI SPERANZA, Lamezia Terme's mayor, wanted me to appear with him in a talk show on a local television channel. I was not keen but it was a way to learn more about the town and earned me a trip to the studio in the armour-plated car in which Speranza travels, an armed policeman driving, a second riding shotgun at his side.

'What are your impressions?' asked Nadia Donato, our host at City One. 'Three well-stocked bookshops in the main street is a good sign,' I told her, 'and there is fine scenery behind the town and a marvellous stretch of beach.' After a light lunch with Speranza and his bodyguards I had done some legwork, to the sea again, to the long-abandoned site that once belonged to the Società Italiana Resine (SIR), where the shore is still unspoilt, then back to the centre and a scruffy street beside the railway line. While sitting in their SUV outside a car dealer's, two young men had been shot dead there a few months before I nosed around. And along the street, outside Tonino's barber's shop, near the depot where Lamezia parks its refuse trucks, a twenty-six-year-old man had been gunned down in August 2004; less than six months later his brother would also die.

'You seem to have a crime problem,' I added. Yet it was easier to dodge the question than tell the truth when Donato asked me what hope, what future, Lamezia has. Its citizens had elected a mayor with the right name, Gianni Speranza, Johnny Hope. But what do you say about a town whose own mayor cannot move freely, whose election was greeted with an arson attack on the town hall and an envelope of bullets, a town whose council was dissolved twice in ten years because of mafia infiltration, where arson had been committed next door to a large police station, and where a feud between local mafia families leaves dozens dead? Indeed, as I write, Italy's business newspaper reports that Lamezia had another murder yesterday, of a businessman whom magistrates thought was connected to one of the town's clans, who had been a town councillor and was one of the causes of the council's dissolution in 1991.

I had recently put the same question about hope for the future to a professor in Palermo as my talk-show host in Lamezia asked me. 'A one-way ticket, low-cost,' he replied. But I was told that although the daily Ryanair service from Lamezia to Stansted is always full, it returns to Lamezia with as many passengers as on the outward flight.

The mayor's office had booked a room at the Grand Hotel Lamezia in the middle of the lower part of town. It faced a large railway station across the square, was near the autostrada's exit, close to the airport, and its less than grand appearance matched the far from smart location. While it was no hidden beauty, offered no luxury behind the faded facade, this hotel was really rather good. I got a decent dinner at half past ten, the large, quiet and comfortable room cost only fifty euros, and being near the station meant few steps for the papers in the morning.

Even better, my car remained where and how I had left it, not a burnt-out shell, no damage to the paintwork, its tyres still inflated. After what I have read about cars, with or without their drivers, being targeted by the 'Ndrangheta, it was hard not to worry about leaving the new Fiat unattended too long. It had sat in a walled car park at the back of the hotel overnight but even that seemed risky in Calabria, Italy's black hole.

After Lamezia I headed back to the Ionian coast again, although further north than before, to Catanzaro, Calabria's regional capital, where I had an appointment that afternoon with Luigi de Magistris, a controversial prosecutor. I had time to spare and turned off the highway that joins the two coasts, about five miles inland from the junction with the autostrada at Lamezia where I had joined it. Pushing along a country road into the hills I soon reached a village called Maida.

America celebrates the Fourth of July, but so does Britain, modestly and unknowingly for most Britons. I had crossed a valley that was a battle-field on 4 July 1806, the site of a British victory when forces led by Sir John Stuart defeated a French army commanded by Jean-Louis Eben-ezer Reynier. The British troops had landed at Sant'Eufemia, the part of Lamezia near where SIR had begun its factory, pressed inland, clashed with the French and forced them to flee towards Catanzaro. Reynier was unlucky or incompetent, perhaps both as five years earlier he had been blamed for the French defeat at Alexandria in Egypt, arrested and sent back to France.

The French celebrated the battle of Maida by setting up military tribu-nals in a vain attempt to stamp out brigandage, which was encouraged by the British and supported by most Calabresi, and by trying to stop locals from going around armed. The British celebrated their victory on the Edgware Road in London, where a patriotic publican called his newly opened inn the *Hero of Maida*. The stretch of road running north from the Regent's Canal to the beginning of Kilburn High Road would be called Maida Vale.

'Avoid the rush hour or spend ages reaching the centre,' the hotel's manager in Lamezia had advised me. But traffic was not a problem as I made my way uphill towards Catanzaro in mid-afternoon; neither was finding the centre and a place to park near the Palazzo di Giustizia, where bright yellow notices warned against standing outside. The building's cornices are dangerous, falling masonry a threat, Catanzaro's crumbling court building another symptom of the condition of Italy's justice system. In August 2006 the justice minister had replied to a parliamentary question about the crisis afflicting justice in the Calabrian capital and undermining the work of those fighting crime. Funds for running and maintaining cars used by Catanzaro's anti-Mafia forces had been halved during the preceding six years, nine of their fifteen armour-plated cars were more than ten years old and the authorities had difficulty in paying the petrol bill.

Before arriving there I had read a report by Pietro Antonio Sirena, the president of Catanzaro's appeal court. He did not say that bits were drop-ping off the building but mentioned structural problems, how some parts were unsuitable, and how corridors were the only space available to store court files. However, that was a minor concern, far overshadowed by the 'Ndrangheta. Sirena was worried about the Calabrian Mafia's close ties to business, to politics and to 'powers in the region that live on secret relationships which corrode parts of the state that were once immune to mafia influence'.

The 'Ndrangheta was attacking the region's political and institutional fabric. 'This assault creates a real risk of a crisis for democracy and of people's trust in institutions and democracy itself.' Infiltrating the parts of the public sector that handle large amounts of money is a mafia priority and it is there that *mafiosi* have created ties with government employees. 'This makes me think that recruiting staff in those areas needs to be reviewed.'

As I was led through a maze of corridors to Luigi de Magistris's room, I thought that Sirena's words were unlikely to have much impact in the corridors of power in Calabria and Rome, where politicians and bag-carriers owe their positions to keeping quiet and doing as little as possible to disturb the status quo. Even so, de Magistris was trying to shake things up, his investigations had upset people in the weeks before I met him, and one of his friends in Rome had asked me to avoid controversial topics, to stop de Magistris from making more difficulties for himself. Magistrates who are willing to investigate the doings of rich and powerful people come under pressure, as de Magistris told me. 'I receive fifteen to twenty critical letters every week. The intimidation is constant but I don't lose sleep.'

When de Magistris entered the magistracy in 1994 he became the fourth generation of his family to put on magistrates' robes, and he chose to do so as a prosecutor. His father, a judge in Naples, had upset the political establishment by sentencing a former health minister to nine years in jail for corruption when the *tangentopoli* (bribesville) scandal was still claiming high-level scalps.

De Magistris explained that what is new in Calabria is the Mafia's involvement in white-collar crime. '*Tangentopoli* was straightforward, just businessmen, bribes, politicians and public servants. Here we have a new dimension.' In Calabria, he said, powerful people are getting more powerful and richer through an all-embracing system involving huge flows of public funds from Rome and Brussels, the Mafia, politicians from left, right and centre, businessmen and banks, and jobs. Unemployment in Calabria is among the highest in Italy, so jobs are prized pickings in the undergrowth of political patronage and power. De Magistris set out a neat equation: 'Control of finance equals control of jobs equals votes.' As the regional capital, Catanzaro counts because it is where the money flows.

The young prosecutor was worried by the convergence of the interests of Calabria's professional classes with those of its criminal classes and by their infiltration into the forces of law and justice. 'Within the state there are those who are anti-state. Who are they? The virus has taken hold, but where is the anti-virus?'

After saying goodbye I hoped to find a hotel in Catanzaro Lido, but the city's seaside resort is a chaos of cars and concrete, so I headed north along the Ionian coastal road towards Sibari. The light was going and I had other disappointments, vainly chasing promising signs to places like Nirvana Village and Serene in the hope of finding a hotel with a beach. I pulled in when I reached Cropani Marina, drawn by garish red and yellow neon lights advertising the F40 hotel, restaurant and pizzeria, a hotel set back from the road.

I left Cropani in the morning, aiming to reach Sibari in the afternoon, about a hundred miles up the coast, and so had time to visit Crotone, an important colony in Magna Græcia where Pythagoras, a Greek mathematician and philosopher, lived. In Italy the names of local heroes are often given to airports so Crotone's airport is named after him, just as Venice's is called 'Marco Polo' and Palermo's is 'Giovanni Falcone and Paolo Borsellino'.

Anybody who has studied geometry at secondary school has probably not forgotten his theorem, but my interest in Crotone was in more than Pythagoras and the town's ancient Greek history. Part of the report by the president of Catanzaro's appeal court dealt with the town. In the autumn of 2006 he had been told by Crotone's prosecutor of daytime shootings in its centre and of innocent bystanders being injured as rival gangs settled scores. 'The clans are organised like armies with battlefield armaments that they even deploy on public roads.'

This slant on Pythagoras's town was very different from what I had read in a colourful and alluring brochure that a property developer had recently given me. This described Calabria as the southern Italian riviera, one of Italy's best-kept secrets, a place where dreams begin, and was selling Crotone for the quality of its bars and nightlife and all the amenities of a modern European city. Targeting Britons and other northern Europeans, the brochure said, 'There is always something going on here.' That is just what the prosecutor said too, although what he had in mind were not the exhibitions, opera and festivals that the property developer promised.

Wanting to reconcile these two views of Crotone, I called the salesman who had given me the brochure and asked about Calabria's mafia risks. Safer than Spain and France, he confidently assured me.

Four years before Crotone's prosecutor pointed out his local difficulties, the national anti-Mafia agency in Rome had noted that the 'Ndrangheta was present in force in Crotone province and particularly in Isola Capo Rizzuto, Cutro and Cirò Marina. The clans' enforcers had been busy threatening the owners and managers of clubs, restaurants and tourist complexes around Isola Capo Rizzuto, a popular holiday resort not far south of Crotone. Killers had used a Kalashnikov and pump-action shotgun in a murder only twenty yards from the Carabinieri station in Isola Capo Rizzuto. Yet with plans to build a holiday village at Cirò Marina about twenty miles up the coast, the developer was plugging the area as idyllic, warm and welcoming.

About a month after I drove through Cirò Marina, the calm of a Sunday evening in Piazza Diaz was shattered by gunshots. Locals and tourists eating dinner on the veranda of a restaurant overlooking the square were shocked and scared by the arrival of two men gripping pistols, their faces hidden by the visors of motorcycle helmets, who headed for a party of diners. Tables and chairs went flying as people dived for cover when the killers opened fire. Taken by surprise, the target, an associate of the bosses of the local 'Ndrangheta family, had no time to move, was struck in the head by two large-calibre bullets and died soon after. The murdered man's wife was hit in the belly and a bullet entered the arm of an eleven-year-old girl who was with the party. The two killers did their job, walked calmly from the restaurant and disappeared in a warren of side streets.

I had seen news of the shooting when I called Vincenzo Luberto, a magistrate with Catanzaro's anti-Mafia team whose patch runs up the coast to Sibari. I thought he was on holiday that week but guessed that the murder might have affected his plans. 'Holidays?' said Luberto with a hollow laugh, 'As long as they keep killing each other there is no such thing as holidays.'

For three young Neapolitans who were on holiday and were treated for minor injuries, being in Cirò Marina may have seemed little different from home where the settling of criminal accounts has left many districts in and around Naples with dead and wounded. 'If we cannot guarantee visitors and our local folk the possibility to eat dinner in peace or stroll in a public square, it's hard to see what credibility our efforts at promoting the town can have,' said Cirò Marina's mayor. Once seen, never forgotten is how the property developer described Cirò Marina. For those Neapolitans enjoying a pizza on a quiet Sunday evening, seeing the neighbouring table shot up, being hit by ricocheting bullets, sprayed and splintered by flying tableware and hospitalised would certainly have been unforgettable.

As for the developer's oasis of beauty, the words of Pietro Antonio Sirena in Catanzaro come to mind: 'I am also thinking about the interests of criminal groups in various businesses of the tourism sector, about the indiscriminate construction along the coasts of this splendid region, which are among the most beautiful in Italy and risk massive degradation.' In fact, some important stretches of Calabria's coast have long been ruined by development and Crotone itself, like Saline Ioniche, Gioia Tauro and Lamezia Terme, has suffered. Crotone's development as a centre for chemicals, minerals and metals began early, during the mid-1920s. Eventually the state oil, gas and chemicals group was involved but the businesses it took over ran into difficulties, lost heavily and were closed in 1994 when the government was preparing the group's privatisation.

Jobs have gone, leaving abandoned factories and more long-term damage than at first appears. One estimate puts the waste produced by Crotone's factories during the seventy years they were open at ninety thousand tonnes. Where the toxic waste disappeared is a mystery, however, like many things in the Mezzogiorno. Enormous quantities of zinc waste simply vanished. Investigations led by de Magistris in the second half of the 1990s revealed that around fifteen thousand tonnes of toxic waste were taken from Crotone to other parts of Calabria, and that the northern part of the Sibari plain got much of it. He told a parliamentary commission that his investigations revealed evidence of ties between the Mafia and politicians in the region.

The people of Crotone seem to hold a grudge against Sibari. In the twentieth century they sent it their toxic waste, including hazardous heavy metals like cadmium, mercury and lead, doing who knows what harm to the recipients' health. And about two and a half thousand years before they dumped dangerous metal compounds there, they razed Sybaris in one of the Greek-against-Greek struggles that marked the Greek colonisation of southern Italy.

Sybaris and Croton both came into existence towards the end of the eighth century BC, when Greeks from the same northwest part of the Peloponnese, overlooking the Gulf of Corinth, arrived in Calabria. They would have kept to the route that Greeks probably followed when they left for new lives in Magna Græcia; up the Adriatic to what is now Albania and then, helped by the wind, southwards to make landfall at Italy's most eastern point, near Otranto. From there they would have hugged the Apulian coast, rounding the tip of the heel, and continued their passage up and along the instep of the Italian boot. The migrants from Greece founded their colony of Sybaris in about 720BC.

All around the instep, the Greeks discovered land that is flat, fertile and well fed with water from the rivers that flow from the Apennine mountains, and Sibari with its broad, deep plain is particularly favoured. The colony became wealthy and powerful, and the city itself controlled much of the hinterland. Large harvests of grain, olives, grapes and other fruit gave the people of Sybaris a base for trade and the city became an important centre where textiles, ivory, ceramics, perfumes and silver objects arrived from Asia Minor. It must have seemed like some kind of paradise on earth at the time, or so the tales of the Sybarites' luxurious lifestyle would have us believe.

Croton was much poorer. The two cities had been founded about the same time and by people from the same part of Greece, so it is easy to imagine how those in Croton looked enviously at their northern neighbours. When political problems in Sybaris gave them cause for a war in 510BC, they won, putting the Sybarites' army to flight and holding the city under siege for more than two months until it fell. It was rebuilt but would never be the same again.

As I found when I drove into Sibari, there are no signs now of the luxury, opulence and soft living that the word Sybarite conjures up, just a small cluster of ordinary houses and shops, and little else. There is Il Sibarita, a gift shop selling perfumes and leather goods, a bar called La Caffetteria del Nonno (grandad's cafe) where a silent old woman served me a drink, and a railway station, a junction on the line that follows the coast around the Italian instep. Two or three trains pass hourly in each direction, mainly local trains, two-carriage diesels that rumble and grumble slowly to places such as Metaponto, Catanzaro Lido and Crotone.

And little exists of the ancient Greek city. The main excavations are disappointing, with none of the splendour that seizes the imagination at

Selinunte, Segesta and Syracuse in Sicily. Legend says that after the people of Croton sacked the captured city, they diverted the River Crati that flows through the plain, flooding the ruins and wiping out their rival for ever. Certainly, the archaeologists who have searched since the end of the nineteenth century for the site of Sybaris have had meagre satisfaction for their efforts.

The earliest dig, in 1879 at an inland site about two miles from the River Crati's right bank, uncovered a tomb from the fifth century BC but excavations in 1887 and 1888 yielded nothing. The breakthrough in the search for the ancient city came in 1932 when a doctor, an amateur archaeologist, was allowed to make a dig. Unlike earlier searchers who had looked in hills around the plain, he thought that the Sybarites would have built their city near the coast and that the stretch between the mouths of the Crati and the Coscile (also called the Sibari), to the north, was the most promising place. And so it was. Excavations there during the 1960s revealed three layers of the ancient city: the Roman colony of Copia from 194BC on top; the Greek city of Thurii that rose on the ruins of Sybaris in 444BC sandwiched in the middle; and the original Greek colony of Sybaris at the bottom.

Yet the site is disappointingly unmoving. Nothing dramatic. No columns, no temples, no amphitheatres, just a few walls and a long stretch of slabs that form a road. Thanks to money from Brussels there is a museum a few miles from the site, but this lacks exhibits that take the breath away. Nothing extraordinary. Nothing to make the average visitor pause, nothing like the Riace warrior bronzes in Reggio Calabria, no hoards of treasure like the silver coins in the small museum in Gela.

It was rather a let-down, I thought as I drove up the coast to Trebisacce, to a hotel opposite the beach, for a room with a view, a stroll after dinner along the front, the Ionian Sea shimmering in the moonlight, and onto a pier where people sat fishing, legs dangling over the edge. But the pier looked dangerous, no railings or lights, a strip of concrete and a drop for those who watch the moon, not where they put their feet.

One reason that brought me to Sibari was a story I had heard in Rome, from a yachtsman who used the marina in Sibari for a while, a story that made me wonder whether the Mafia might have been involved. Ernesto had sailed south to Calabria in 2002, renting a mooring in the Laghi di Sibari, a man-made lake separated from the sea by a broad beach but with access through a narrow channel about five hundred yards long. The winter of 2002/3 passed smoothly, and so did the summer of 2003. The problem arose the following year for hundreds of people, many of them foreign, who kept craft in Sibari. A young magistrate ordered the closure of the channel to the sea at the end of May 2004, infuriating boat owners who were confined to port as the season began. Taking away his yacht on a transporter, one angry German tore the page for Sibari from his mariners' handbook and vowed he would never return.

'All hell broke loose when I signed the order,' Baldo Pisani, the magistrate, told me. He had arrived in Calabria freshly qualified in October 2003 and should not have been surprised at the disturbance he caused. 'Everyone was against it, even the bishop.'

Not quite everybody, as I discovered when I called on the port authorities at Corigliano Calabro on the southern edge of the Sibari plain to ask Vincenzo Figoli, the harbour-master, about the marina. The Sibari plain was drained in the 1950s and the channel serves to keep it so by carrying rainwater, and water pumped from below its surface, out to sea. The channel is not meant for navigation but for water management; it acts to prevent the plain from flooding, and since this had occurred the magistrate's order referred to a risk to life and property. 'The River Crati carries a huge amount of sand, building up a beach to the north of the mouth, towards the channel's outlet, and this gets blocked by sandbanks,' Figoli explained.

Checks carried out in April and May of 2004 found a lack of buoys and leading marks made navigation dangerous in the channel, and Corigliano Calabro's port authorities had issued three orders forbidding passage through it in 2003. In any case, in the spring of 2004 the channel was completely blocked by sand, making navigation impossible for the marina's users. One of the disputed issues concerned the funds for dredging, and of course nobody wanted to pay. Eventually the channel was dredged and Pisani issued an order in mid-August that reopened it.

'I cast off, made my way cautiously out of the lake, down the channel to sea and I've never gone back,' said Ernesto. He had rented a mooring and was able to say goodbye for good. Stuck with properties whose value had collapsed, the two thousand home owners who had bought lakeside houses and apartments at the marina were less fortunate, I thought as I walked along a sad parade of shuttered shops and shut-down restaurants.

Figoli, the harbourmaster at Corigliano Calabro, had explained the complexity of the situation at the Laghi di Sibari, the legal ins and outs and the question of responsibility for keeping the channel clear. Yet a crucial question still awaited an answer. Who actually owns the man-made lake? If seawater, flowing up through the channel when no water runs down from the plain, is in the lake then the lake is owned by the state. But so much is done in the South sailing close to or over the legal line, sometimes unknowingly, sometimes from necessity. Treating rules as flexible is a way to cut red tape, to short-cut bureaucracy. I asked Figoli about Trebisacce's pier. 'Oh, that's not a pier,' he laughed, 'that's a jetty for fishing boats to tie up to, but the town's authorities want to use it as a pier.' He had overseen its construction a few years back, when the wooden piles of an old jetty had rotted and put it out of use.

Avoiding Marina di Sibari's large hotel, I drove inland along the plain's northern edge, passing through Francavilla Marittima where part of Crotone's toxic waste had been sent. From there the road winds upwards into the hills, towards the Pollino National Park and about eight miles from Francavilla Marittima I took a turning to the right where a sign points to Civita-Çifti. A small village, not much more than a thousand people, it perches stage-like on a hilltop with the Pollino mountains as its backdrop, the Sibari plain below. Like Vena di Maida near Lamezia Terme and thirty other villages in Calabria, Civita (Çifti is the Albanian name) is a community of Albanian-speaking Italians whose ancestors, refugees from the Ottoman Empire, arrived soon after their leader Skanderberg died in 1468.

Civita's Arbëreshë, as Albanian speakers are called, are proud of their spotlessly clean village, its ethnic museum, traditions and church with its icons, mosaics and Greek-Byzantine rites. The young curator showed me round and I stayed that night in her family's guest-house, the Nido d'Aquila, where a Swedish couple also had a room. 'This is our secret, a holiday place that nobody else knows,' confided Magnus Bard, a cartoonist with a Stockholm newspaper, as he worked in water colours on the terrace. I wondered as we chatted over dinner if the 'Ndrangheta had found their way to Civita or whether Civita was a secret from them too. 'Let me know,' said Bard. And I did.

The following morning brought a five-mile drive down winding roads to Cassano allo Ionio, Sibari's capital of crime, where I had an appointment with the lieutenant who commands the Carabinieri in the town and a small outlying station at Sibari. Born in the Veneto in northeast Italy, far from Calabria and all its problems, Giorgio Feola had arrived two and a half years before in what he described as an epicentre of crime. And that small Albanian-speaking village too? 'Well, no. Civita is a crime-free island in a sea of crime.'

As for Cassano, before calling at the Carabinieri's new station on the edge of town, I walked around, even took some photos, and nobody appeared to mind. It all seemed calm, no sign of crime, but appearances deceive. 'There is evil hidden everywhere beneath. All businesses pay the *pizzo* and politicians have mafia ties. *Omertà* is the undisputed rule. Normal legality just doesn't exist. That's the way things are,' explained Feola. 'After a murder the victim's family do all they can to obstruct the police, taking the corpse home from the scene of the crime. Every time there is a murder the women, dressed in black, go into the street and wail and scream while the men, impassive, think only of vendetta.'

Feola has been threatened but that does not deter him from going out, although he never moves without a gun. 'I live armed, night and day,' he said. His twenty years as a carabiniere included postings to Sicily and Kosovo but Feola thinks none of the places he has served is as bad as Cassano.

He worries about what is bubbling below the surface. A fragile equilibrium had recently been broken when the boss of one of Cassano's three mafia families returned after four years in jail on a murder charge. Italy's snail's pace justice had yet to bring his case to court and the maximum period in custody had run out. 'He is scared of being killed himself.' And Cassano's fragile peace faced another threat, from the disclosures of a rare *pentito* who was helping the authorities. In Calabria, where nobody talks, he was unusual. The threat of death had set a twenty-five-year-old talking, Cassano's first *pentito* ever. 'He couriered dirty money and had been stopped by chance in the north of Italy, where he was taking half a million euros to be laundered. His *capo* said that if the money wasn't repaid then he would die,' Feola explained.

'Look out of the window and you can see the group of buildings where the Abbruzzese family lives,' he continued, pointing to anonymous apartment blocks. A large family of gypsies, the Abbruzzesi, had arrived from further south in Calabria in the 1980s and had taken over a part of the town. Their arrival signalled the start of a bloody war as Cassano's two incumbent mafia families did not take well to having trespassers on their turf.

The lives of Calabria's migrant *mafiosi* become easier when they move to where their faces are unknown, their ways of working poorly understood and there are opportunities for crime. Germany was such a place in 1995 after Operation Galassia swept up hundreds of *capi* and *gregari* belonging to clans in and around the Sibari plain. Moving to Germany made sense for those who dodged arrest; hundreds of thousands of southern Italians had emigrated there in the decades after the second world war, taking jobs in Germany's booming economy, and it was an obvious refuge for survivors of the police and prosecutors' blitz. Moreover, the 'Ndrangheta already had German business interests such as the drugs trade, defrauding Germany's social security organisations, robberies and dealing in stolen cars. And the 'Ndrangheta's German clans were busy in extortion too, squeezing fellow Italians but avoiding locals who might have complained.

Connections with Calabria are strong, as the German police discovered when they investigated a gang trafficking arms and cocaine. It had been working on orders from Calabria and most of the arms that were smuggled and part of the illicit revenues had been sent south to 'Ndrangheta associates in Crotone and Cirò. It is no surprise that the gang met in bars, pizzerias and clubs owned or managed by Calabresi from those two towns.

Yet Germany has become important for Calabria's clans not simply as territory for its traditional crimes and rackets, and as a hideout for *mafiosi* on the run. It is also a place where huge sums of dirty money are sent: revenues from extortion and trafficking in drugs and arms turned into investments in shares on Frankfurt's stock market, holiday homes on the Baltic, and commercial ventures like hotels, restaurants, pizzerias, bars and ice-cream parlours, registered in the names of family members who act as fronts. These investments explain the low profile in Germany of the 'Ndrangheta's clans. Avoiding the attention of the authorities meant that there should be no killing, no mafia wars like those that bloody Calabria. However, in the early hours of 15 August 2007 a hit squad from the Locride gunned down six Calabresi outside Da Bruno's restaurant near the railway station in the centre of Duisburg, a stronghold of the Nirta family from San Luca.

The massacre in Duisburg made San Luca's feud an international affair. Probably nothing has so shattered the Rhineland city's calm since 1944, when more than two thousand British aircraft added to the devastation that had already come from bombing. About four thousand Italians live in Duisburg, a city of half a million, the steel capital that makes a third of German steel, and Italy's soccer team had stayed there when it won the World Cup in 2006.

It is easy to imagine what Duisburg's respectable burghers thought about the slaying. How would the half million citizens of Sheffield, once Britain's steel capital, feel if six Italian men were shot as they left Dino's, La Bella Roma or Pavarotti's on the city's London Road? Six dead – the killers also murdered the target's five companions – is an enormously serious crime, a multiple homicide that showed the 'Ndrangheta's ferocity and the value it places on human life.

According to Italy's anti-Mafia authorities, the 'Ndrangheta's clans found it easy to work in Germany, stamp their mark and win respect from the German underworld. One reason for their trouble-free infiltration was the relaxed way that the German police first treated the threat, probably because they saw the Mafia as an Italian problem and thought that it was nothing to do with them. But other factors helped the 'Ndrangheta to penetrate widely and deeply into Germany, of which one was the lack of a German law similar to Italy's on mafia association. And there are a large number of families who have never been in trouble, have clean records with Germany's police, yet are parts of Calabrian kinship networks and willing to help the clans.

Maps which plot where clans are found show the 'Ndrangheta's frightening strength, particularly in the south and west, in the *Länder* of Bavaria, Baden-Württemberg, Hesse and North Rhine-Westphalia. In each of these regions around ten different clans have found a new home, some present in more than one town, usually only one clan per town, though Munich has more. It is said that a picture is worth a thousand words, and the five pages of maps in the annual report prepared by the Direzione Nazionale Antimafia for the judicial year 2002, certainly give readers graphic evidence of the 'Ndrangheta's migration to Germany. Among the coloured dots on three of them are those representing the Nirta family, involved in San Luca's *faida*, and present not only in Duisburg but in other towns in North

Rhine-Westphalia as well as in Munich and other parts of Germany. The maps in the report reveal the wide spread of the Farao clan from Cirò: into Arnsberg in North Rhine-Westphalia; into Waiblingen and Bruchsal in Baden-Württemberg; and into places like Kassel, Homberg, Hanau and Darmstadt in the Hesse *Länd*. According to the report, the Carelli clan from Corigliano, on the southern edge of the Sibari plain, where I met Vincenzo Figoli the harbourmaster, is also present in Germany, having migrated to Regensburg and other places in Bavaria, to Frankfurt and to towns in North Rhine-Westphalia.

People in Duisburg were not alone in being shocked by how a Calabrian feud had travelled to their city. Elsewhere in Germany people probably began wondering about their Italian neighbours, and not only those from Calabria, and some might have started looking with suspicion at cafes, restaurants and pizzerias with Italian names. If being Italian became harder in cities and large towns like Hagen, a steel town of two hundred thousand people about fifty miles east of Duisburg, where the Nirta clan also has a hold, it became even more so in small towns. What did people in Warstein, a town with a population of about twenty-five thousand on the River Möhne in the east of North Rhine-Westphalia think when they heard about the massacre in Duisburg? Famous for its brewery, twinned with the village of Pietrapaola, about twenty-five miles from Cirò, Warstein is another place that the Direzione Nazionale Antimafia says that the Nirta clan has reached.

However, Germans should not be surprised to find the 'Ndrangheta doing business among them. Investigations revealed that *mafiosi* from Calabria were active in Germany as long ago as the mid-1980s. In 1989 a group of Calabresi was arrested for counterfeiting banknotes and towards the end of 1992 a senior German police officer drew attention to the Mafia's increasing activity. In the early 1990s a front for Cirò's Farao clan in Stuttgart, who ran a chain of restaurants, was found to have given substantial financial support to a high-ranking politician of Germany's Christian Democrat Party. And as the Warsaw Pact disbanded, the Soviet Union fragmented and the Balkans fell apart, so arms trafficking grew and the German police discovered that Germany was where clans from Cirò and Corigliano were in this business, working with Albanians.

While knowledge of the 'Ndrangheta's presence in Germany goes back to well before the Duisburg murders, only since then has the average German begun to be concerned. Many Germans probably thought of Rudesheim as just a pretty village on the Rhine, famous for its wines, and did not connect it to the Farao clan. Southeast from Rudesheim, in the foothills of the Bavarian Alps, in the corner of Germany that juts towards Austria and Switzerland, Kempten is a town of about sixty-five thousand and a centre for dairy farming. It describes itself as having two thousand years of history and Italian flair and likens its town hall square to an Italian piazza. No mention, obviously, of the 'Ndrangheta, but after the shootings in Duisburg many locals probably know that Corigliano's clan has migrated there.

Easy communications by road, rail and air, the disappearance of checks at national borders in continental Europe and the arrival of a new genera-tion, comfortable with foreign travel, other cultures and different languages, have certainly helped the Mafia. Large numbers of children born to parents from southern Italy grew up in Germany in the 1970s and 1980s, speaking Italian, probably the dialect of their parents' towns and villages, and the language of their host country. 'The young Calabresi, very sharp twenty-five to forty-year-olds who work for the bosses, move as easily between Germany and neighbouring countries as we move around Reggio Calabria,' Nicola Gratteri, the anti-Mafia magistrate from the Locride who helped the Germans on the Duisburg murders, told me.

Migration is at the heart of the Mezzogiorno's story. Poverty forced one and a half million penniless rural labourers abroad between 1881 and 1900, mostly to the Americas. A further four million followed in the next fifteen years and Naples became Europe's busiest passenger port, its quaysides the scene of countless tearful farewells as grandparents, parents, brothers, sisters, wives and children said goodbye to kin who might never return or whom they might never see again. In 1910, New York City alone had an Italian population of about six hundred thousand, and it was in that flood of migration around the beginning of the twentieth century that the Sicilian Mafia crossed the Atlantic and sank its roots in America.

No jobs and poor prospects continued to drive southerners from home when the second world war ended. Many Calabresi migrated north to Italy's industrial triangle, Piedmont, Lombardy and Liguria, where the post-war economic miracle brought back life to old and war-damaged factories and opened new ones too. And travelling with the honest workers were

Calabresi with ties to the clans who helped the 'Ndrangheta to estab-lish itself across much of the north, from the Veneto in the east through Lombardy to Piedmont in the west. In doing so it was even able to influence politics in some places, as locals discovered in Bardonecchia, a ski resort west of Turin, for example, where infiltration by Calabrian *mafiosi* brought the dissolution of the town council in 1995. The authorities believed that some Calabresi working there in the construction industry were linked to the 'Ndrangheta, had suspicions that a residential complex had benefited from planning irregularities and thought that the town council was suscep-tible to criminal influence.

Migrating north, on night trains, in shabby clothes, their few belongings packed in cardboard boxes tied with string, southerners crossed the Alps to France and Switzerland as well as Germany in the post-war decades. Others travelled further, to countries such as Canada where, in the 1950s, a prosecutor gave the name Siderno Group of Organised Crime to Calab-rian criminals. Some sources say that two heavyweight Calabrian mobsters in New York were behind this gang, named after a town about three miles north of Locri. One was Frank Costello, born Francesco Castiglia in 1891 in Cassano allo Ionio, the town on the Sibari plain that Giorgio Feola, the Carabinieri lieutenant, told me was thoroughly bad. The other was Albert Anastasia, born in 1902 in Tropea, a town on the coast between Gioia Tauro and Pizzo. Anastasia's thirst for blood was notorious among America's mobsters and earned him the title of Lord High Executioner. During the 1930s and 1940s he headed Murder Inc., the Mob's military arm, responsible for hundreds of killings, and he himself would be murdered in 1957 as he sat in a barber's chair in midtown Manhattan.

The presence of these two Calabresi, bosses who had carved their careers in crime during the 1920s and 1930s, at the top of the American Mob in the years after the second world war shows that the Italian contribution to America's organised crime was far from just Sicilian. Mass migration around 1900 took Italians to America from Sicily, Campania and Calabria. Like Costello, who was four when he arrived in New York in 1895, some were still too young for crime, but others were already active.

More than a century later, the problems remain. In 2004 a senior anti-Mafia magistrate wrote that, thanks to mass migration, no continent can consider itself immune to the 'Ndrangheta. Calabria's *mafiosi* can draw on their capacity to adapt to any environment, he said, even those that are hostile and far away.

Indeed, by the 1970s the 'Ndrangheta was in Australia, dealing in drugs and with enemies in its traditional way, although Calabrian gangsters had been held responsible for murders and other mob crimes even in the years before the second world war. Much closer to Calabria than Canada or Australia, no more distant than northern Germany and spared the waves of Italian emigration on which the 'Ndrangheta was carried, Britain has been at the edge of its interest, and perhaps this will continue. But Britain has probably not been left untouched. According to Gratteri, the Ursino and Macri clans from Gioiosa Ionica, about three miles north of Siderno, have been involved in trafficking drugs from Turkey and Pakistan to Britain.

Australia, America, Canada and even Britain seemed far away as I travelled north from Reggio Calabria to Sibari, but so did Rome. Calabria still has a distant feel and Edward Lear's description of it as a region to which few foreigners travel still holds true. Less than four per cent of those who visit the Mezzogiorno stop in Calabria, despite its relics of Magna Græcia, dense forests, mountains and long stretches of coast. Two hundred and twenty miles separate Capo Spartivento, the region's southern point, from Calabria's boundary with Basilicata, near the mouth of the River Sinni on the Ionian Sea, to where I travelled, and the distance up the west coast to Praia a Mare is about the same. Yet the distance that separates Calabria from the rest of Italy, Europe and the world is more than miles and more than simply an economic gap. There is a cultural separation too.

Nicola Gratteri's words about Calabria come back: 'desolate ... accursed ... beautiful'. During my journey there I saw the contrasts and the colour and discovered something of the best that the region offers: its scenery, its food, its cautious hospitality and Calabria's people, the priests and magistrates, businessmen and ordinary workers with whom I spoke. But from them I heard of the region's worst and this, alas, is what outsiders also hear. Hundreds of thousands of Calabresi have left their land, countless law-abiding people who contribute to the societies of which they are now part, many bearing the burden of surnames of criminals who have disgraced the region from which they come. They do not make the headlines, but the 'Ndrangheta, Italy's bloodiest and most impenetrable Mafia, inevitably makes news that is never good.

8

SCANZANO JONICO

Contagion

WHEN HENRY SWINBURNE journeyed through southern Italy on horseback towards the end of the eighteenth century he entered Calabria on the Ionian coast, travelling south from Basilicata, the small region that lies in the instep of the Italian boot. I was heading north along the Ionica SS106 state highway, a notoriously dangerous road that I had come to know since arriving in Calabria.

Soon after crossing the boundary between the two regions I reached the River Sinni. Locri Epizefiri, Riace, Crotone, Sibari and now Heraclea, between the Sinni and the River Agri about four miles to the east, the relics of long-dead colonies established by people from ancient Greece dot this coast. A battle took place on the Sinni in 282BC between an alliance of Greeks led by King Pyrrhus of Epirus and the rising forces of Rome that had already seized Crotone, Locri and Reggio Calabria. Although defeated here by superior numbers whose forces included war elephants, and at Asculum in Puglia the following year, Rome would conquer the South and put an end to Magna Græcia. From Pyrrhus's victory in Puglia would come the pyrrhic victory where the winner's gains fail to make up for losses, a victory not worth winning.

I had passed another large yacht marina called Marinagri that was nearing completion near the mouth of the Sinni. It had run into legal problems, though of a kind different from those at the marina in Sibari, and was under investigation by the magistrate whom I had met in Catanzaro. Despite the harm that such construction causes, jobs are the main reason southern Italians accept it, legal or illegal.

Having earned a name as somebody willing to speak on touchy issues, I was in Policoro to take part in a debate on legality in Basilicata. The year before I had been asked by the mayor of Tramutola, a village in the upper Agri valley, to name a subject on which I would be willing to speak during its summer festival and I had suggested politics, ethics and legality; hardly something to attract holiday crowds, but the square was full. The speakers in Policoro were the same as those with whom I had shared the platform then, a lawyer and an activist priest.

'Let's be honest and admit that there's a moral question concerning crime and justice in Basilicata and this involves politicians,' said Vincenzo Montagna, a criminal lawyer with a practice in Policoro. He thinks that there has been a sharp decline in the moral climate since the 1990s when large sums of money arrived, first to compensate the victims of 1980's earthquake and help reconstruction and then with the discovery of Europe's largest onshore oilfield near Tramutola. 'The notion bandied around that Basilicata is a crime-free island in a sea of crime is just a myth,' Montagna told the people who had gathered in the grounds of Policoro's thirteenth-century castle to follow the debate.

'I'm tired of the complacent claims that Basilicata is a happy region, untouched by problems that neighbouring regions face. That's hypocrisy. Whatever is bad gets hidden and whoever exposes the truth gets criticised,' complained Marcello Cozzi, an outspoken priest more comfortable in an open-necked shirt than dog collar. As in Sicily and Calabria, the people of Basilicata are generally silent where crime is concerned, sticking to the rule of *omertà* that stops people talking. According to Don Marcello, Calabria's 'Ndrangheta treats Basilicata as home turf.

Indeed, in January 2007 the president of the appeal court in Potenza, the region's capital, spoke about proof of the 'Ndrangheta's presence in Basilicata. Massive efforts by the police and the trials that followed round-ups during the preceding decade had broken up the region's clans, and although the criminals who had replaced them were not as dangerous, constant attention was needed to stop organised crime from taking hold again. Basilicata's aspiring *mafiosi* were in contact with the Mafia in Calabria and in the cities of Bari and Taranto in Puglia, said the judge, and like most of the criminal fraternity in the South they were interested in trafficking drugs and arms, and in extortion.

'The situation is clearly not comparable with that in the three neighbouring regions,' said the appeal court's president, 'and this in itself is definitely positive.' In fact, only the regions of Molise in central Italy and the Valle d'Aosta in the northwest bettered Basilicata in terms of the number of reported crimes per inhabitant. Even so, the team of anti-Mafia magistrates in Potenza worried about links between politics, crooked business and organised crime and believed that infiltration of the public tendering process and public services by criminals was a serious threat.

After leaving Policoro I turned inland along the Agri valley, the Pollino National Park that Basilicata shares with Calabria away to my left, its highest peaks rising to more than seven thousand feet. This expanse of almost half a million acres of barren mountain on the Calabrian side and forest on the northern slopes is home to roe deer, golden eagles, wolves and many other species of wildlife. I had only had a brief glimpse of the southern part when I stayed in Civita but had travelled deep into the Pollino on the Basilicata side in the summer of 1984, almost a decade before the park was established. I had gone to a small village called San Severino Lucano, almost three thousand feet above sea level and one of the villages nearest to Monte Pollino, to meet Emilio Colombo.

The man responsible for the Pacchetto Colombo that was meant to take industry to Calabria is, in fact, from Basilicata. Born in 1920 in Potenza, Colombo was for decades one of Italy's most powerful politicians. Elected to Italy's post-war constituent assembly in 1946 and a member of its first republican parliament two years later, Colombo was an important force behind agrarian reform, became a powerful figure at the top of the Christian Democrat Party and went on to hold many ministerial posts, including agriculture, foreign affairs, industry and finance, during Italy's economic miracle. He was prime minister from 1970 to 1972 and was appointed senator for life in 2003.

Back in 1984 it was a long trek along winding roads to San Severino Lucano, but the bespectacled Colombo, elegantly dressed as always in a dark double-breasted suit, a little white of shirt-cuff flashing at the wrist, had arrived by helicopter to make a short speech, walk around the village, shake hands, smile and joke, and lunch in the mayor's home. He had insisted that I should sit next to him. Colombo's liking for chilli pepper was well known in his constituency and he had dosed his pasta generously with the intense red pods brought specially for him.

'When Alcide De Gasperi made his first visit to Basilicata in 1950, it took three and a half hours to reach Potenza from Matera. None of the roads was surfaced and we arrived covered with white dust thrown up by the wheels,' Colombo remembered. Leader of the Christian Democrat Party and Italy's prime minister from the birth of the republic until 1953, De Gasperi saw a far different Italy in Basilicata on that exhausting journey than he had known in his home region. He was born in Trento province when it was part of the Austrian Empire and had been a member of the parliament in Vienna between 1911 and 1918. De Gasperi died in 1954. He would have had to live many more years to travel the sixty miles from Matera to Potenza in just an hour as people do today.

Twenty-nine years after that journey from Matera to Potenza, Colombo had followed De Gasperi by being awarded the Charlemagne Prize for his contribution to European unity. For Colombo, the most significant aspect of progress between showing De Gasperi Basilicata and talking to me had been the huge improvement in communications. 'Isolation belongs to the past. Today's road network allows Basilicata access to the rest of Italy and indeed contact with itself, without having to cling to mountainsides or scale their peaks,' he had told me as we sat together in San Severino Lucano on that sunny day in 1984.

The Basilicata that De Gasperi saw in 1950 had changed little from the region about which Carlo Levi wrote in his book *Christ Stopped at Eboli*, describing the people and poverty he found when the fascist regime banished him in 1935 to Aliano, the village where I was now headed as I turned inland from the coast. A deep sense of exclusion, of existence at the very edge of the Italian state pervades Levi's book, a work on the South that remains a classic more than sixty years after its publication. He chose the title because a villager had told him that the people there were not Christians but simply beasts, or even less than beasts. Christ had stopped short of Aliano, at Eboli, in fact, south of Salerno near where the northwest border of Basilicata and Campania touch.

Aliano, which Levi called Gagliano in his book, was a village of miserably poor people, slaves to superstition, prisoners of poor land from which they scraped subsistence. Malaria was endemic in the lower part of the valley, serious medical conditions went untreated, infant mortality was high, malnutrition constant, and meningitis and typhoid were illnesses of poverty and poor hygiene that often struck. A doctor from Turin, Levi was forbidden to practise by the regime, but he did so all the same. To the right as I drove up the Agri valley the arid grey clay, emerging steeply from the plain in stark, rounded hills, gouged with deep ravines, seemed lunar in its desolation. And it was towards those hills that I turned.

Wearing handcuffs and escorted by two carabinieri, Levi arrived in Aliano from Grassano, where banishment had initially taken him. A few unmetalled roads wound across the bare countryside, descending into valleys carved out by small rivers and then climbing from them. A few villages stood alone on the hilltops. Some of that feeling of emptiness remains today. At Aliano, Levi reached a dead-end; the road finished there, at the bottom of the main street of the village, a cluster of houses perched on a ridge with ravines dropping sharply on both sides. There were, Levi wrote, no real shops in Gagliano, a community of about twelve hundred people.

I had visited Aliano in the late 1970s, approaching from the north like Levi did. By the standards of Milan or Rome it was still extremely poor. Agricultural labourers continued to go to and from the patches of land they farmed riding on the backs of mules, and they continued to stable these mules beneath their houses in the village. Levi wrote of how he had been awakened by the sound of mules' hooves on the paving stones as peasants began their daily journeys of three or four hours to the fields.

Now those mules have gone and probably their owners too. What I remembered as a stable is now a restaurant, and looks an elegant one. The streets are neat and clean, the houses well kept or being restored. I walked along the main street to where Levi's escort had left him and got talking with an elderly man near the church of San Luigi Gonzaga, Aliano's patron saint. 'I was eight years old when Levi arrived and he lived nearby,' he told me. Aliano had changed, and not all the changes were for the better. 'Young people don't want to work any more. Years ago, some children in a family tended the flocks, others worked the land. No longer. And house-wives nowadays don't even want to do the washing.'

Seeking another view on Aliano, I stopped at a cafe near the post office in the village centre. It is called the Carlo Levi and there were several tables outside at which groups of mainly middle-aged and elderly men sat playing cards, a scene repeated in countless other villages in the Mezzogiorno. 'Oh, the old guys,' said the young woman behind the counter, 'they play from mid-afternoon until well into the evening.' When I asked what the village offers its young people, she said that there is nothing, although some young-sters get drunk. That is a new problem. The old problem of a lack of work has never gone away.

Levi wrote that there were two thousand men from Gagliano in America. Those who returned would often waste their savings buying patches of land from which it was impossible to grub a living, would quickly sink back into poverty and, from time to time, regret their decision to return. As Colombo had told me in 1984, large-scale migration had finished by then, partly because the demand for unskilled labour elsewhere had dried up. But the problems about which Basilicata's best-known politician had spoken to me almost a quarter of a century ago have not been solved. Young people continue to leave the village, as many of their predecessors did.

I walked back along Aliano's main street, past a bust of Levi with its inscription 'From Turin, his love for the people of the South' that had been placed near a children's playground, and past the house where Levi lived. Below a high forehead and receding hairline, the eyes seem lost in the past, the mouth set without expression, and the greeny-grey metal bust offers few clues to the man who died in 1975. He is buried in the cemetery of the village to which he had taken an alien northern culture and whose own ways and stories he would record for posterity.

Leaving Aliano, I drove back to the river and continued north for about forty miles, past the Pertusillo dam and its reservoir that helps give Puglia its water and Grumentum where Roman forces beat those of Carthage twice in a decade; in 207BC the Carthaginians lost eight thousand men. Grumentum would be set alight by Saracens in AD872 and razed by them about a hundred years later.

I would stay for several days in Tramutola, the village where my wife was born and spent her childhood and which I have known since 1972. Like Aliano, it too has changed greatly. Flies are no longer a nuisance in the summer. Chickens used to roam the streets, many houses had stables then and pigs were kept in cellars and fed on kitchen scraps. Slaughtered in the weeks after Christmas, the poor beasts were dragged squealing into the streets, turned on their backs and killed by a knife plunged into an artery in the neck, the blood caught and mixed with cocoa and sugar as filling for a sweet pie called *sanguinaccio*.

But Tramutola's streets served as more than open-air slaughterhouses. I remember my surprise when, talking in 1973 to my wife's nonagenarian grandfather, a gnarled, moustached figure dressed in a black jacket who would sit leaning on his stick outside his house near the church watching the people pass, I noticed behind him a young girl squatting in the gutter of a road leading to the hills behind the village. This was one of two accepted places for villagers to relieve themselves.

Vito Sacco spoke nostalgically to me about his journeys to America, to Boston, Massachusetts, before the first world war. He had also worked in Argentina, to where most of his many children emigrated before or after the second world war when legislation had closed the doors to the United States. Migration would later take people to places closer to home. During the 1970s and 1980s the village's streets would be crowded in August and around the end of the year with cars bearing number plates from Switzerland, Germany and the north of Italy. No more. The children of those migrants have settled where their parents went, their ties with the village now tenuous. Once very poor, the village is no longer so; the oil that brings money to the valley was first found in the 1930s beneath the woods nearby.

While I was there I wrote an article for *The Economist*, looking at the issues that the lawyer Vincenzo Montagna and Don Marcello had raised in Policoro. It caused a minor local controversy. A day or two later, when I was about to leave, I found that somebody, probably wanting to let me know that the article was unwelcome, had slashed one of my car's tyres. How much this would have displeased my father-in-law, always a most tolerant and generous man. For the first time I felt uneasy in Tramutola, knowing and understanding the small village less well than I thought.

I left Tramutola and headed down the valley, past Villa d'Agri and the wellheads and oil centre near Viggiano, a town whose black Madonna draws pilgrims from afar, and back again to the coast. Until the agricultural reforms after the second world war, the Ionian coastal plain for mile after mile on both sides of the boundary between Calabria and Basilicata was woodland with ash, oak, poplar, tamarisk and willow, and Mediterranean scrub close to the sandy seashore. Thousands of acres, many of them left uncultivated, belonged to an aristocrat called Luigi Berlingeri. 'My father told me how Berlingeri had over twelve hundred acres of woods just for a hunting reserve,' said Filippo Mele as we sat drinking coffee outside a cafe in Scanzano Jonico, a small town near the mouth of the River Agri. Mele, whose father had been an agricultural labourer, moved up the social ladder, attending university, graduating in medicine, becoming a family doctor in the town and serving as its mayor between 1988 and 1991.

Mele lives in what used to be a smallholder's single-storey house, built in the 1950s when agricultural reforms led to the sale of plots of land of about twelve acres at affordable prices, attracting people from mountain areas behind the coast. Its first owners could not have imagined how Mele has transformed the house, turning what had been a stable into a dining room, extending the building, laying a terrace and installing remote-controlled gates in walls that enclose carefully tended lawns.

'Tourism arrived here around the beginning of the 1970s. There was a boom during the 1990s and there are now about twenty thousand hotel beds along this stretch of coast,' said Mele, a talkative man who moonlights for a regional newspaper. It is easy to imagine how tourists might have reacted had a plan gone ahead for a national storage for nuclear waste on the plain between the coastal highway and the sea. Certainly the locals were angry, anxious and active in opposing the plan supported by the mayor – not Mele but a rightwing successor. They occupied the site and blocked the coastal highway and railway line for fifteen days in November 2003, forcing the authorities to backtrack and giving a good story to Mele and the foreign press.

Mele took me along narrow country roads criss-crossing the plain, a patchwork of fields, orchards and vineyards, dotted with farm buildings and small houses, usually identical boxes like his home used to be. As we drove towards the sea, the land, impoverished by salt, became noticeably less fertile. He turned left and stopped at the corner so I could look at a grey stone tower, like a pyramid with its pointed top cut off, built when Spain ruled these parts as a lookout post to warn of invading Saracens. A white road sign had slipped down its steel support and was lying slanted across some red plastic tape. We had turned into Viale Carlo Enrico Bernasconi, the C of Carlo missing, the sign bent and defaced. Bernasconi was a close colleague of Silvio Berlusconi and the man responsible for the film library of the media tycoon's empire and for its film production and distribution business. He had been found guilty of false accounting in a case involving Berlusconi and given a prison sentence that he did not serve.

However, Bernasconi continued to be in the news long after his death in 2001. Prosecutors in Milan would allege in a trial that began in March 2007 that he gave six hundred thousand dollars to David Mills, an English lawyer, after Mills had given helpful testimony in two cases involving Berlusconi, whom he had assisted in creating a complex network of offshore companies. Initially Mills wrote to his accountants to say that the payment had been made because he helped Berlusconi negotiate some 'very tricky corners, to put it mildly'. Subsequently Mills, who has always denied any wrongdoing and has stated that he has 'never been bribed by Mr Berlusconi or by anyone on his behalf', said that this letter outlined a scenario in order to obtain tax advice and that the money had been given to him by another client.

'A road named after Bernasconi? Why?' I asked Mele. The reason lies a few miles from the crossroads near the Saracen tower, a tourist village that stands between the road and the sea. At the entrance a sign says that this is the Polo Turistico Integrato di Scanzano Jonico, that it benefits from state aid and that this aid was approved by Berlusconi's government in 2001 and 2002. This is a venture of the Compagnia Italiana Turismo (CIT, a large tourism group that was once state owned), which was declared insolvent by the court in Milan in March 2006. Bernasconi was one of CIT's directors and Scanzano Jonico's town council thought he deserved a road named after him.

Mele wanted me to see another white elephant, on the main road just outside Scanzano Jonico. 'There it is, the Centrale del Latte di Scanzano,' he said, pulling his car to the side of the road. A quasi-public-sector dairy set up in the 1950s to collect milk from farms in the area, it had closed more than ten years before. Grass and weeds the size of bushes were growing where the large asphalted parking area had broken up, fittings had rusted and weather had worn away large patches of the white paint on the hangar-like building.

The dairy is tied to an unsolved mystery and a poster on a hoarding near it recalled the murder in July 1993 of Vincenzo De Mare, whose black and white photograph showed a balding middle-aged man, a smile playing at the corners of his mouth. Placed there by followers of Libera, the anti-Mafia association that I had encountered in Sicily, the poster had a message. It read, 'So that no murderous hand should go unpunished and so that remembering him should be a commitment to seek the truth.' De Mare drove a lorry for the dairy and there are suspicions that he had refused to transport toxic waste illegally and that white-collar criminals behind the trafficking had engaged killers to murder him. Mele saw barrels that he believes contained chemicals stored in the long-closed dairy on an occasion when he got through the fence and looked inside the building.

Trafficking in toxic waste is not the only trafficking around the Metaponto that worries locals and the authorities. Trafficking in nuclear waste is another concern, and magistrates have investigated various rumours. Certainly trafficking in waste is a business in which the Mafia has a long record.

'Let's eat at the Tavernetta del Barone,' said Filippo Mele, as he drove into Scanzano Jonico's main square where I had left my car. Over an excellent seafood lunch Mele told me about the crime wave that hit the coast in the second half of the 1980s and ran into the 1990s. 'The clans seized control because the police forces were asleep. Politicians and carabinieri even went fishing with the local boss, who had a pact with the clans in Calabria and Puglia. The authorities only woke up when bombs began exploding and guns started shooting.' Money that arrived with the growth of tourism and an expanding fruit-farming sector was behind the violence that in one town alone left seven murder victims in one year.

The time had come to leave Basilicata and move east to Puglia. I had learnt of a region different from the one I thought I had known for many years. My father-in-law had told me that Basilicata was too small and poor to interest the Mafia. I had asked Emilio Colombo about organised crime when I met him in 1984 and he had described the region as having progressed without attracting Campania's Camorra or the 'Ndrangheta from Calabria. 'The region has remained immune to the sickness of organised crime and we are fighting to ensure that this continues to be so,' Colombo had said. But that fight was lost. Touched at its borders by regions where organised crime is virulent, a constant menace, Colombo was wrong to think that his could avoid infection.

9

OTRANTO

Trafficking

METAPONTO, about ten miles east of Scanzano Jonico, is at the end of Basilicata's Ionian coastal strip, a few miles from the region's boundary with Puglia. Pythagoras lived there after he left Crotone in 510BC, and founded a school of thinkers that is believed to have worked out that the world is round and goes around. But like other cities established by the ancient Greeks, Metaponto suffered from the swings of power and flows of war – Spartacus passed through and left a massacre in his wake – and little now remains.

Signs point inland to Matera, the second of Basilicata's two provincial capitals and famous for its Sassi, the rock dwellings in ravines that carve into the city's centre where almost fifteen thousand people lived until the authorities rehoused them. Carlo Levi recorded his sister's description of the Sassi in *Christ Stopped at Eboli*. She may have looked into one of the ravines from near the same point that I would many years later, the Sasso Caveoso with its caves that served as homes, stacked one upon another, the road outside one serving as a roof for that below. Luisa Levi said that they were like a schoolboy's idea of Dante's Inferno, openings in the cliffs where animals and people lived side-by-side. The government in Rome passed laws in the 1950s to clear the Sassi of those who lived there, later enacting legislation to protect them, and Unesco listed them as a World Heritage site in 1993.

I was heading for Taranto, however, and continued along the coastal highway. Passing the tall stacks of an oil refinery and steelworks belching smoke, I reached the old city and the swing bridge over the narrow channel that joins the Gulf of Taranto to a large expanse of water called the Mare Piccolo, the little sea. A flagpole in the fifteenth-century Aragonese castle guarding the channel was flying the flag of a three-star admiral, the Italian navy's commander-in-chief.

Early in January of 1963 I had been in a British destroyer entering and leaving the Mare Piccolo and still remember the bitter cold when we got underway, the flurries of snow cutting through the air as we left harbour, the walls of the channel so close that we could almost touch them.

Taranto bears the weight of history for the navies of both nations. One night in November 1940 Swordfish aircraft of the British Fleet Air Arm, flimsy biplanes like relics from the first world war, had taken off from the aircraft carrier *Illustrious* and delivered a heavy blow to the Italian navy whose main units were moored there. Three of Italy's six battleships were hit by torpedoes that the aircraft launched, one of them damaged beyond repair, and the Italian fleet withdrew to Naples, away from the action. Even today, almost seventy years on, the Fleet Air Arm celebrates a victory that would be the model for the Japanese attack on Pearl Harbor one year later.

One of the battleships that the aircraft attacked was called the *Vittorio Veneto*, a brand-new giant of almost forty-seven thousand tonnes that had entered service earlier in the year. It was broken up in the 1960s, though a successor, a cruiser with the same name, joined the Italian fleet soon after, and this was berthed in Taranto when I passed through, and walked by the fascist-era officers' club and along the terrace of the gardens above the dockyard. Forlorn and empty after being placed in reserve, its grey paint flaking and rusting, its red pennant number 550 still visible on the hull, bows flaring steeply to a point, the cruiser was moored with its stern to the jetty in the way typical of Mediterranean ports. Apart from a frigate lying alongside the cruiser, the dockyard was deserted, a graveyard of naval memories.

I pressed on out of the city, driving south along the coastal road beside the Ionian Sea through small resorts where hotels have names like Eden, Paradise, Silver Beach and Golden Bay, and past ribbon-development of villas and apartment blocks, many built without planning permits. My destination was Otranto, a town near Italy's most easterly point where the southern part of Puglia's Adriatic coast bulges towards the Balkans. The hotel where I would stay would be the Albania, which seemed fitting as Albania, its mountains visible on clear days, lies across the Otranto Channel, the Adriatic's narrowest part.

'Ships of the Italian navy with sophisticated electronic equipment were in continuous touch, telling us what they were seeing on their radar plots. On one occasion they had thirty-five contacts, each blip on the screen a small boat loaded with people from Albania and headed at high speed across the Adriatic towards our coast. Two of our lads were cross-eyed trying to keep track and decide which contacts offered the best chances of interception,' Amedeo Antonucci, a lieutenant colonel in the Guardia di Finanza, a financial police service responsible for customs and border controls known as the GdF, told me, describing operations on one dark night towards the end of the 1990s. Antonucci is head of the GdF's unit responsible for air and sea patrols in Puglia, a frontier region where every kind of trafficking makes money for criminal organisations.

As I learnt in Calabria, there had been a flow of migrants from Albania to Italy many centuries ago. The modern migration began in July 1990 with the arrival in Otranto of a raft carrying six men. A massive and dramatic exodus occurred the following year, a first wave in March when about eleven thousand Albanians arrived in Brindisi, some fifty miles north of Otranto. A second wave took place in August when a ship called the *Vlora* berthed in Bari, the regional capital, crowded with what some estimates put at fifteen thousand people. Photographs of the ship and its huge human cargo, packed on deck and clinging to the superstructure, made news throughout the world, and shocked and scared many Italians, helping to create the stereotype of the lawless, aggressive Albanian in the country's collective imagination.

The flow of people across the Adriatic resumed after disorders followed the collapse of Albania's financial system in 1997, caused by Ponzi-style frauds, and the downfall of the country's government. In April 1997 the European parliament passed a resolution that condemned the continued violence of armed groups. 'Unscrupulous criminal bands are exploiting this situation,' it said. However, while matters improved in Albania, conditions in neighbouring Kosovo deteriorated sharply and Italy, just over forty miles away across the Otranto Channel and the Balkans' closest El Dorado, became a magnet once again. A report prepared by the European Commission, the World Bank and the IMF noted how the explosion of conflict in Kosovo at the end of March 1999 quickly brought an exodus of hundreds of thousands of Kosovar Albanian refugees. 'That was when the Albanian Mafia began smuggling migrants and trafficking in people,' said Antonucci 'and our work got tougher.'

We met on the quayside of the harbour in Otranto and drove down the coast to Castro, where Antonucci wanted to show me a memorial to two colleagues killed by Albanian criminals. The GdF was out in force on the night of 23/24 July 2000 and at around four o'clock in the morning, not long before dawn, one of the patrolling vessels saw an inflatable boat, a craft that Italians call a *gommone*, speeding towards the coast, and alerted other units. After picking up the message, one of the GdF's inflatable boats turned towards the contact and hove to at a distance, keeping the suspect vessel under observation.

The *scafisti*, as the drivers of fast boats engaged in illicit traffic are known, noticed that they were being watched and tried to get away, heading south at high speed, taking evasive action, turning often and sharply and reversing course. Cornered eventually near Castro, they set their inflatable boat running towards their pursuers in a final bid to escape, shoved the throttles open and dived into the sea. Antonucci had pointed to a *gommone* belonging to the GdF when we were in Otranto and to the crumpled hull of a fast motor boat moored alongside. 'A *gommone* is like a torpedo and that's the kind of damage it does.'

The four men of the crew were tossed overboard when their boat was struck and despite quick reaction by colleagues in other boats only two were picked up alive. The body of one was found around midday in the sea off the Zinzulusa grotto. The search for the body of the second continued for the rest of July and throughout August but was fruitless. 'The currents are strong and variable along this coast. Who knows where his body may have finished, or how many bodies of people desperate to get to Italy have been swept away and never found?'

Steps at the end of a car park lead down to the grotto, along a steep path carved in the rock on the high northern cliff of an inlet. 'To those who fell while doing their duty', begins the inscription on a plaque remembering the two men who were killed, a sculpture in white stone above it showing people being helped from the water.

The GdF crew could easily have closed on the Albanians when they were putting their passengers ashore but had preferred to wait in order to avoid putting lives at risk. 'Our first rule is to consider the wellbeing of the people being carried,' Antonucci told me. In March 1997 an Italian navy warship had collided with a vessel carrying about a hundred and fifty people and more than a hundred had died, a black event that probably focused minds on how the problem of human trafficking and migrant smuggling at sea should and should not be tackled.

Puglia's Adriatic coast from Capo Santa Maria di Leuca, where a tall white octagonal lighthouse marks the tip of the Italian heel, to Otranto is a coast of wonderful scenery. Often the road between Santa Maria di Leuca and Castro runs through tidy olive groves, terraced upwards inland and down towards the sea. From Castro to Otranto, the land is open and the road that follows the wild, rocky coast dips occasionally to small inlets with sandy beaches.

'Scafisti know every inch of this coast, every bay, every tiny landing place where they can leave their passengers. They drop them on beaches, on rocks that jut into the sea, on the steps of seaside restaurants, on the private landing stages of villas, at the bottom of cliffs,' said Antonucci as we drove north from Castro back to Otranto. The problem of migrant smuggling and human trafficking from Albania has, however, eased significantly since Italy placed a mission of its own forces on the other side of the Adriatic in 2000 to train the local police and prevent the departure of boats from there. But it does continue, as interceptions regularly show, and it is a business that the Albanians manage on their own, avoiding contacts with Puglia's own criminal organisations. The scafisti can cover the cost of a boat in two trips by charging between three thousand and four thousand euros per passenger for the one-way journey.

Albania's migrant smugglers and human traffickers are indifferent to the fate of their human cargoes, ready to dump non-swimmers overboard or place child hostages near their boats' motors to deter the GdF from blocking their escape. 'Albanian mafiosi have nothing to learn from their Italian cousins where brutality is concerned. But our men never shoot at sea. Life is sacred. With the way that boats roll and pitch who knows where shots might go?'

Back in Otranto, he took me aboard the *Fusco*, a large fast patrol boat carrying a 30mm gun, its two powerful diesel engines giving it a speed of around forty knots. Everything was neat and shipshape on deck and on the bridge and below, and the engines and equipment in the machinery spaces sparkled. One hundred and fifteen feet long and displacing thirty-five tons, the *Fusco* carries a crew of thirteen and is good in rough seas. The vessel joined the GdF's fleet in 2006 equipped with powerful communications, command and control systems to meet the challenges that the *scafisti* pose.

Forty knots is fast, but not fast enough to catch the criminals who operate in the narrow channel of the southern Adriatic. The GdF's high-speed patrol boats, forty-two feet long and carrying four-man crews, can plane at seventy knots in calm seas. Crewing these patrol boats, the same breed as offshore racers, calls for strong stomachs, good muscle tone and a sense of adventure. 'Giving chase at speeds over fifty knots in complete darkness – *scafisti* choose moonless nights for their business – requires nerves of steel. They do all they can to escape and certainly don't heave to when we try to board them.'

A high stone wall built to protect the old town of Otranto against invaders rises steeply from the water across the harbour from the quay where I stood talking with Antonucci. A massive castle, whose construction began in 1485, finishes one end of the wall while a tower built in 1481 stands at the other. But perhaps not even these would have been enough to deter the Turkish invaders who besieged the town in August 1480, or save its people who capitulated after fifteen days and were massacred in the cathedral where they had sought refuge. A large twelfth-century mosaic pavement would have been where many of the victims waited, desperately hoping that the siege would be lifted, knowing that their deaths would be bloody should the Turks seize the town. Probably some sat, stood or prayed in the dimly lit crypt, a silent, uneasy forest of pillars of different marbles and various styles. They were soon called martyrs and the bones of more than five hundred of those fifteenth-century victims are preserved in a chapel, the stone used for their beheading beneath its altar.

Part of the cathedral's northern wall, its plain grey stone blocks and a side door to the crypt, was framed by the window behind the desk of the mayor. 'Remember that Otranto was Byzantium's last foothold in the West and became an eastern outpost of the West with the arrival of the Normans,' said Luciano Cariddi, a thirty-nine-year-old accountant who was elected mayor in 2007. Being Italy's easternmost town, where the sun rises on the Bel Paese, is a cause for celebration. 'On the last night of the year we hold a concert in the square, after which many of us go to Capo d'Otranto, Italy's most easterly point about five miles to the south. There we have a symbolic lighting of the old lighthouse and wait for dawn, a chilly wait if a tramontana wind is blowing from the north.'

Otranto's main problem is coping with the huge influx of summer holidaymakers who visit the town, a picturesque place, boosting its population from the usual five thousand to more than sixty thousand. That is the kind of problem that the mayors of many southern Italian towns would be glad to exchange for theirs. The Mafia has apparently left Otranto alone. 'It is untouched by crime. I've often wondered why this is. Perhaps it suits our local Mafia to keep things quiet here. Many towns in the Salento are badly troubled by the Sacra Corona Unita,' Cariddi told me.

Organised crime is recent in Puglia, beginning in the 1970s, and has roots outside the region, in neighbouring Campania. Official reports tell how Raffaele Cutolo, a Neapolitan *capo*, initiated a large number of Apulian criminals into the Mafia in 1979, and how towards the end of the year a group of bosses, including Cutolo and *mafiosi* from Sicily and Calabria, met in Galatina, a town about twenty miles west of Otranto, roughly in the middle of the Salento, as the part of the region that forms the Italian heel is called.

According to some accounts, the Sacra Corona Unita, inspired by Calabria's 'Ndrangheta, was born two years after Cutolo's meeting with the other *mafiosi*. And its birthplace was a cell in the jail in Trani, on the coast north of Bari, Puglia's capital, where the founder, Giuseppe Rogoli, was imprisoned. Many say that the year was 1983, that the founding was on 1 May and that the prison was in Bari but, whichever the account, Rogoli, from Mesagne, about six miles from Brindisi in the north of the Salento, is held responsible for the Sacra Corona Unita and bringing Mafia-style organised crime to Puglia. 'I swear on the tip of this dagger bathed in blood, to be always faithful to this body of free men, active and declared members of the Sacra Corona Unita, and to represent its founder Giuseppe Rogoli everywhere.' Such is the oath of initiation.

Fortunately, thanks to numerous arrests and a lack of coordination between bands, organised crime is less virulent in Puglia than in the three other large regions of the Mezzogiorno. Yet locking up Apulian *mafiosi* or remanding suspected *mafiosi* in custody may help to strengthen the Mafia in the region. Reporting early in 2008, the Italian government's executive committee for intelligence and security, known as Cesis, noted the role of Italy's prison system in sustaining Puglia's mafia organisations, 'both because initiations into the Sacra Corona Unita traditionally take place during imprisonment and because bosses who are serving prison sentences are able, even from inside jail, to direct the operations of their clans'.

While a relaxing of rivalry between clans means less blood on the streets, the mafia truces in the provinces of Lecce and Brindisi that Cesis noted simply mean that *mafiosi* are putting their energy and resources into building their businesses rather than killing each other. One month before Cesis published its report, the president of Lecce's appeal court pointed out that local mafia organisations were strengthening their international connections in the drug trade, confirming the kind of internationalisation of the Sacra Corona Unita that investigations had uncovered over recent years. The consolidated relations between Salento's Sacra Corona Unita and Albanian criminal gangs have allowed it to become a go-between and to act as a guarantor for them in their dealings with other Italian mafia organisations. The authorities had, said the president of Lecce's appeal court, made numerous and significant discoveries of shipments of cocaine, marijuana and heroin, a large part coming from Albania for delivery to clans in the Apulian heel.

After leaving Otranto I drove up the coast before turning inland to take the state highway to Lecce. The mayor had told me that tourism and agriculture are the town's main activities, and that the cultivation of rootstock for vines is an important niche occupying about a hundred and thirty nurseries. Eurovitis is one of many that lie on the coastal road a few miles outside town. 'We have been doing the grafting of cultivated vines since the late 1980s,' said Antonio De Matteis, a member of the family that owns the business, 'and growing the American species of rootstock for far longer.'

A group of six women were sitting in a large basement when I called, some snipping long streamers of American vine to cuttings of just over one foot long, others clipping off buds to leave the cuttings clean. After treatment and storage, De Matteis's staff would graft small sections of the vines that produce the varieties of grape that make up the wines we enjoy onto the American cuttings, a phylloxera-resistant rootstock. 'We work with a firm in northeast Italy that exports to many of the world's wine-growing countries,' explained De Matteis as we walked around one of his fields, streamers of the American vine up to fifty feet long sprouting from large knobbly roots and trailing across the ground.

However, this part of Puglia is best known for its olives and olive oil, and olive groves cover large areas of the Salento and further north. Their importance in the landscape is such that the regional authorities have decided that those ancient, stubby, gnarled trees whose trunks and branches compose the strangest arboreal sculptures should be preserved for the future. They planned to make a survey to identify the centuries-old trees on which preservation orders should be placed, and I saw many that looked suitable as I drove north.

Brindisi was a scruffy city when I passed through many years ago. It has not improved, although the harbour is more impressive than I remembered it. The large, well-protected eastern and western arms form the only safe natural harbour on Italy's Adriatic coast, important for the ancient Greeks in colonising southern Italy, and for the Romans, who occupied Brindisi in 266BC, in expanding their empire to the east. The Appian Way joined Brindisi to the capital from the second century BC and one column and the remains of another stand where the great road ended at the harbour's edge. Virgil died there in 19BC after returning from a journey to Greece.

But I was interested in recent events and I found a memorial to one a few miles north of the city, set at the edge of a road that runs parallel with the busy dual carriageway carrying traffic between Brindisi and Bari. I had turned off state highway 379 where a sign points to Iaddico, an area of countryside as road maps show nothing with that name. On a narrow country road two members of the Guardia di Finanza had been murdered by cigarette smugglers in February 2000.

A small ornate monument, supported by a white marble triangle, stands on a base of the same stone, and a vineyard behind it gives way to fields. A bunch of faded blue and white flowers made of plastic sits in a cup beneath the words: 'Man is never so serene as when he has done his duty properly.

You will always be in our hearts.' And above the inscription, separated by a cross, are the names of the two young members of the GdF who were mortally injured near that spot.

On a night in late February, the two were members of a four-man team in one of six patrol cars of the GdF's Brindisi flying squad, engaged in one of its many operations to combat criminals smuggling cigarettes into Italy. The team had chanced on a convoy of vehicles carrying cases of cigarettes that had just been brought ashore. But it was an uneven encounter and, when the law officers tried to stop them, one of the convoy rammed their patrol car, a standard Fiat Punto offering no more protection than any other small saloon. Several of the GdF's vehicles moved quickly when radio contact was lost and could not be re-established, and what they found was an awful, blood-chilling sight.

All four men in the GdF's patrol car were seriously injured; one was found to be dead when he reached hospital, and a second died soon after. Their car had been struck by a Range Rover whose front had been fitted with a massive steel ram, and the criminals had fled leaving behind thirty-five cases of cigarettes. 'One human life is worth more than all the cigarettes in the whole world,' Antonio Tummillo, a colonel of the GdF, told me sadly when I met him in the force's regional headquarters in Bari.

Cigarette contraband began in Puglia in the mid 1970s when the Neapolitan Camorra, under the pressure of a clampdown on the west coast, started to transfer its traffic to the Adriatic, giving birth to the Apulian Mafia at the same time. Smuggling cigarettes may seem unimportant but it involved hundreds, perhaps thousands, of people in Puglia, bringing them the easy money that goes with crime and into contact with hardened criminals. It would become a big business, particularly around Brindisi, yielding the Camorra massive revenues and giving its finances a huge boost.

'The gangs were so well organised that they were even able to offload cargoes in the port of Brindisi itself,' said Tummillo, showing me photographs that an observation helicopter had taken of one such arrival. Mostly, however, the cases of cigarettes were brought ashore along the sandy coast that stretches north from Brindisi towards Bari and south into the Salento.

After leaving Iaddico I had pulled off the main highway and driven about a mile to the Costa Merlata, the crenellated coast, and stood on the sandy beach of a cove. Behind me was a small hotel that claims to be 'the hotel of your dreams', a white single-storey building with palms on its terraces called La Darsena, the dock. The hotel's name prodded my imagination and I wondered as I looked out to sea if this place had been used for landing contraband. Boats could have made their way in without difficulty, avoiding the rocks in the centre of the cove over which waves were breaking by keeping close to the rough arms of low, rocky outcrops topped with ground-hugging vegetation that curve away from the beach.

At least fifty people were involved in every shipment, organised into human chains to unload the cases of cigarettes from the boats into waiting lorries, jeeps and cars, bands in contact with control centres that would warn of the threat of police raids. Offloading was completed in less than two minutes.

'We never found smugglers who were armed,' Tummillo told me, 'but tackling them was extremely dangerous all the same.' As well as rams in front and fearsome steel buffers behind, the vehicles that the criminals used often carried cans of oil and bags of nails that were sprayed and sprinkled behind if they thought they were being followed. Some vehicles were fitted with powerful rear spotlights to blind followers. 'Our main worry was that our *finanzieri* would be injured or killed in the frequent chases that took place on main roads and country lanes across the region. At times speeds reached well over one hundred miles an hour and we had chases that took our cars from Brindisi to Bari, seventy-five miles of nail-biting, gut-tightening, high-speed tension.' The smugglers may not have been armed but they murdered and threatened nevertheless, killing bystanders, forcing vehicles off the road and caring only about their contraband.

Although some carried more, most boats carried around a hundred and twenty cases of cigarettes, every case containing five hundred packets of twenty cigarettes. Nowadays a packet of Marlboro costs four euros twenty cents from law-abiding tobacconists, and three-quarters of that goes to the government in excise duties and value added tax. So the corrupt officials in countries where cigarettes transited, the criminal organisations abroad and in Italy and the distribution chains involved in contraband, including the smoker, would split around three euros on every packet brought illegally into Italy; every cargo carried by a high-speed boat would have been worth around two hundred thousand euros at today's prices.

Much of the contraband came across the Adriatic from Montenegro, where numerous Italian *mafiosi* had made their base, a five-hour return journey with the throttles full open, jerrycans of petrol stowed among the cases of cigarettes for refuelling the thirsty engines while at sea. 'These were men of respect for people in Montenegro,' said Tummillo.

However, the criminals did not rely on only one country of supply for their business. Some criminal groups used ships cruising off the Greek islands of Corfu and Kefallonia as floating warehouses. Loaded with cigarettes in Greek ports like Patras and Igoumenitsa, the ships' cargo manifests showed destinations such as Bar and Kotor, ports in Montenegro, and transferring the contraband in international waters allowed the smugglers to avoid the increasing difficulties of operating directly from there.

The flag of Belize hangs in the office of Amedeo Antonucci, the lieutenant colonel whom I had met in Otranto, a reminder of the *Janet V* operation he led that ended the activities of one such smugglers' ship. Early in December 1999 a patrolling aircraft of the GdF sighted the *Janet V*, a small cargo vessel carrying the Belize flag and known to have been involved in smuggling cigarettes, heading southwest in international waters off the coast of Corfu. When a high-speed boat came alongside, was loaded with cases of cigarettes and set off into Italian territorial waters, Antonucci and his team moved into action. The Montego Bay convention on the law of the sea in their hands, they boarded the *Janet V*, its hold still stacked with cases of cigarettes, just before it could slip back into the safety of Greek territorial waters. Two of the four Greeks in the crew had criminal records for smuggling, while the fifth member, an Albanian, held two passports, one of which was false.

Although the smugglers succeeded for many years in carrying on their illicit trade in cigarettes across the Adriatic, Italy's police forces were able to thwart them once the authorities in Rome finally decided that the crime should be tackled. In fact, a massive drive against the criminals began immediately after the murder of the two members of the GdF in February 2000; it was called Operazione Primavera, operation springtime, and involved the despatch of almost two thousand special forces to Puglia, including some from the Carabinieri's parachute battalion.

The emergency operation continued until the middle of June 2000 and led to the confiscation of several thousand tonnes of tobacco and, as a bonus, nearly forty-six kilos of heroin, almost fourteen kilos of cocaine and large quantities of arms and explosives. The police made over five hundred arrests and seized more than two hundred cars and almost fifty armoured off-road vehicles. They discovered twenty-four warehouses where cigarettes were hidden on their way from the illicit stocks abroad to smokers in Italian towns and cities.

Over a long period the GdF seized hundreds of tonnes of cigarettes each year in Puglia – in 1998 alone they took almost six hundred tonnes from the gangs that ran the racket – but the amount that slipped through the GdF's net was huge. Even so, a clear measure of the success of Operazione Primavera is that seizures in the following seven years slumped to an annual average of less than thirty tonnes and the number of boats caught also fell heavily. By early 2008 three years had passed since the GdF's most recent seizure, a single boat in 2005 and itself the first since 2002.

After Operazione Primavera the smugglers thought about moving their operations further north, to the neighbouring region of Molise or to the Abruzzo, even higher up the Italian coast, but dropped the idea because they lacked the local knowledge and contacts essential for carrying on their business. Yet, as I would see when I reached Naples, the city where the contraband cigarette trade began, the problem has not disappeared. Near the railway station and in the narrow side streets of the centre, many small stalls offer smokers a wide range of contraband brands.

The smugglers have found means of bringing in their cigarettes other than stacked in high-speed boats that on calm dark nights race across the narrow stretch of sea between Puglia and the Balkans. They now arrive hidden in lorries or containers along regular transport routes, perhaps entering the country through road borders in the north or, continuing the Balkan connection, reaching Puglia on the many trans-Adriatic ferry services into Brindisi and Bari. Numerous shipping lines, with their large ferries and frequent services, carry hundreds of lorries every day from ports on the eastern side of the Adriatic like Igoumenitsa, Patras and Bar.

Lieutenant Colonel Antonucci's fleet of patrol boats and *gommoni* had a quieter time after Operazione Primavera hit the cigarette smugglers, and an increase in political stability in Albania and the arrival of the Italian mission brought a sharp fall in the number of people that the *scafisti* carried across the Adriatic. Indeed, some of the GdF's units were transferred to

Sicily to help tackle the large flow of illegal immigrants who begin their journeys in North Africa. But the Italian authorities have not dropped their guard. Drugs traffickers still use fast boats for transporting illegal substances into Puglia, particularly marijuana, grown widely in Albania, of which the authorities in Puglia generally seize several tonnes each year.

But criminals rely more on other methods for trafficking in drugs and arms. 'Heroin arrives in small loads, is carried in cars and lorries or in the many fishing boats that fish in the Adriatic,' Tummillo told me, 'and arms are usually transported in lorries or containers.' Early in 2008 his men in Bari discovered two missiles hidden beneath a cargo of fruit and vegetables in a German lorry that had just arrived from Greece.

Colonel Tummillo's office in the GdF's headquarters, a well-kept block built during the fascist period, overlooks the port. From the large windows he can see the lorries and trailers manoeuvring along the quayside and watch the busy movement of ships and ferries in the harbour. Looking out, it was hard to imagine the port as the scene of a terrible disaster in which mustard gas killed and injured hundreds of servicemen and civilians.

The second world war brought death, destruction and suffering to many places in the Mezzogiorno: heavy fighting damaged Gela when American soldiers landed in July 1943; even now the centre of Palermo bears the scars of bombardment; both Messina and Reggio Calabria were bombed; Allied landings near Salerno, vigorously opposed by German defenders, brought great damage in the area; and the abbey of Monte Cassino between Naples and Rome was razed. The list of southern villages, towns and cities over which war was fought is long, but while Bari was still almost untouched in late November 1943, it would soon earn an unenviable distinction. According to some historians, the worst disaster caused by chemical weapons in the second world war happened in the city.

As autumn turned to winter in 1943, Allied forces had taken Sicily and advanced through Calabria. They were beyond Naples on Italy's western coast and the British Eighth Army had taken Puglia and the neighbouring region of Molise and crossed into the Abruzzo, where its progress was halted on the River Sangro. With its large port, Bari was important for the advance up the Adriatic coast and its docks were crowded on 2 December with ships offloading or waiting to offload their cargoes. But the port had attracted the attention of the German high command, which had a large fleet of bombers standing by when the pilot of a reconnaissance aircraft reported activity there that day.

The Allies had underestimated German strength and Bari was poorly defended. No fighters were based there, those at other airfields in Puglia were not allocated to defence, the radar system was unserviceable and the port well lit. Flying in low as night arrived, the German aircraft were unopposed and dropped bombs that would sink seventeen ships and badly damage six. One that went down, after blowing up, was the *John Harvey*, an American Liberty ship, and among its cargo of munitions were bombs filled with mustard gas.

Italians call mustard gas *iprite*, named after Ypres, the battleground in Flanders where it was first used in July 1917, as much to disable the British troops as kill them, though kill them it did as well. The gas blisters the skin, damages the eyes and bronchial tubes and causes bleeding. The writer Vera Brittain, a nurse during the first world war, described the gas as an invention of the Devil. Its effects on soldiers were horrifying, as she wrote in *Testament of Youth* about those she treated, 'burnt and blistered all over with great mustard-coloured suppurating blisters, with blind eyes all sticky and stuck together, and always fighting for breath, with voices a mere whisper, saying that their throats are closing and they know they will choke'.

At least the doctors and nurses of the first world war who treated soldiers affected by mustard gas knew what they were dealing with. In Bari, on the night of the bombing and during the following days, the staff of hospitals found themselves faced with a worryingly unknown and puzzling condition. The *John Harvey*'s cargo of mustard-gas bombs was secret and the ship's crew and specialised army personnel onboard who knew of the existence of the bombs all died. While doctors soon suspected that they were faced with the effects of a toxic gas, only at the end of December did a report establish that mustard gas was the cause. About one in seven of the soldiers and sailors who were treated eventually died, a mortality rate more than six times that of those similarly affected during the first world war.

When the *John Harvey* exploded, mustard gas was part of the highly toxic mixture of smoke, vapour and particles of fuel and solids that burst into the sky and fell into the water and onto the city. Nobody knows how many civilians died from its effects in December 1943 and at the beginning of 1944, but the list of victims did not finish with the war. Five members of the crew of a fishing boat died in July 1946 after their nets brought up one of the American bombs. Other episodes have occurred over the intervening decades and cases of contamination along the coast still cause concern.

The bodies of the British servicemen who died as a result of the bombing lie in a war cemetery southwest of Bari, not far from the road to Taranto. I was interested in a district called Japigia on that side of the city, and the criminal clan whose turf it is, and arranged to meet Giuseppe Scelsi, a magistrate in Bari's anti-Mafia group whose office is in a newish building away from the city centre, opposite the vast Cimitero Monumentale where many of the civilian victims of the German raid are buried.

Even now some people express doubts about whether the Mafia, or a Mafia, operates in Puglia. Quick to recognise that Sicily has Cosa Nostra, Calabria the 'Ndrangheta and Campania the Camorra, they are sceptical about the presence of mafia-style organised crime in the Italian heel. Talking to Scelsi would give me insights into this particular southern criminal reality.

I had read a document written several years before by Michele Emiliano, an investigating magistrate in Bari, that examined judgements of various trials in the region. Apulian courts had, he said, tended to underestimate the significance of the local Mafia by simply using the expression organised crime instead of Apulian Mafia. There is an important difference between organised crime and mafia crime, however, and Italy's penal code makes a clear distinction. Article 416 concerning criminal association, for which the penalty for membership runs from one to five years in prison, is followed by Article 416b which deals with mafia-type association, where prison sentences for membership range from three to six years, and criminals convicted of organising or leading mafia associations draw heavier sentences than those given to the organisers or bosses of ordinary criminal associations. Article 416b applies to 'the Camorra and other associations, however they are called locally, that use the intimidatory strength of membership to pursue aims like those of mafia-type associations'.

Many people in Puglia, including some magistrates, were reluctant to admit that their region was infected by the Mafia. Documentary evidence of criminal oaths, the statutes of clans and the names of their members produced by prosecutors were not enough in 1986 to convince a court in Bari to rule that the people on trial were *mafiosi*. And nine years later, Bari's assize court of appeal avoided labelling the Società Foggiana, described by Emiliano as one of the oldest, best organised and most dangerous criminal organisations in Puglia, as a mafia association. The appeal court in Lecce had, however, by then branded the Sacra Corona Unita as *mafiosa*. Yet despite this judgement in Lecce early in 1990 and the overwhelming evidence that the Mafia was active in Puglia, the government later in the year excluded it from a list of regions where organised crime was a serious problem.

Having parked my car near Bari's cemetery, I crossed the road and went into the building where the prosecution service has its offices, offered my small backpack to a courteous carabiniere for checking, made my way to the third floor and found Scelsi's office. A man in his fifties with shaggy long hair, yet smartly dressed in an elegant brown jacket over a blue shirt with a striped tie, offered me his hand and waved me to a chair. Scelsi had joined the magistracy in 1981, attracted partly by the idea that as a magistrate he would be able to help further the cause of social justice. His first post was as a judge in Tirano, a small town in the Valtellina valley overlooked by the Alps northeast of Milan, an experience that lasted five years and often involved cases concerning the environment.

An enormous distance, both geographical and cultural, separates Tirano, a few miles from the Swiss border and the Engadine with Saint Moritz at its centre, from Puglia, its sunshine, its closeness to nations like Albania, Montenegro and Greece, its southern way of life and the struggle against the Mafia. 'Don't forget that the Valtellina was once part of the Austrian Empire,' said the magistrate. And the Mafia was not one of the problems that the Habsburgs faced. 'Life was very different there,' said Scelsi about his period in Tirano. He returned to Puglia and was a member of the anti-Mafia team in Bari between 1994 and 2002, rejoining it a few years later following an obligatory break when he was assigned to other work.

'Puglia occupies a very particular geopolitical position. It's a platform for east–west traffic.' Not long after he spoke with me, he and a colleague spent six hours questioning the prime minister of Montenegro, Milo Djukanovic, whom they were investigating for collusion in the smuggling of cigarettes. Elected for the first time in 1991, Djukanovic served three consecutive terms until 1998, when he was elected president, a position he held until 2003 when he became prime minister once more. After spending seventeen months away from office, Djukanovic became Montenegro's prime minister again in February 2008, and as such enjoyed immunity when he travelled, at his own request and with no risk of arrest, to Bari to answer the magistrates' questions a few weeks later. Recognising Djukanovic's immunity, the investigating magistrates would subsequently ask that their investigations be formally closed.

Scelsi's investigations covered the years between 1994 and 2002, when Djukanovic either headed Montenegro's government or was the country's head of state. Thousands of tonnes of cigarettes were imported every year into Montenegro during that period, and a good part of those huge quantities were then exported illicitly, by high-speed boats based in ports like Bar, across the Adriatic to Italy. Moreover, Italian criminals found official complicity and a safe place to hide in Montenegro.

For a long time the smuggling of cigarettes enjoyed wide local support from ordinary people in Puglia. 'Earning money by helping the smugglers was rather like having an invalidity pension, a form of social shock absorber in a region where unemployment is high. Efforts at suppressing contraband were not particularly vigorous and the smugglers were tolerated,' explained Scelsi. And while drugs are now a major problem facing anti-Mafia officials, public tolerance of narcotics seems to have grown. 'They've become acceptable, probably thanks to the increasing use of cocaine. The heroin pusher is seen as dealing in death, but the cocaine pusher is seen as selling fun.'

Cigarette contraband on a vast scale like the authorities faced in the Italian heel and drugs trafficking are very much the Mafia's business and were at the heart of a major trial that Scelsi conducted against Savino Parisi, the boss of the Japigia district of Bari, and dozens of other Baresi. It ended in December 2004. There had been an Italian criminal cartel operating in Montenegro, with mafia practices of affiliation, division of areas of interest and the use of violence to settle disputes. In a submission to the court, Scelsi said that *mafiosi* on the run from the Italian authorities were protected by paying off people who counted in Montenegro and that Italian criminals bought, maintained and fuelled their boats in Montenegrin ports, controlling those ports with armed guards.

Obtaining guilty verdicts against people accused of being *mafiosi* requires showing that the criminal groups to which they belong are mafia organisations. 'That needs proof that the organisations are structured in certain ways and that they work in certain ways,' Scelsi told me. When he was investigating Parisi and the clan that dominates Japigia, he and his team looked for evidence to support their assertion that the outfit headed by Parisi was a mafia organisation. He had no doubts that Parisi, who had spent much of the 1990s in prison and was eventually freed in 2005, was its boss.

A clear hierarchy is a feature of a mafia clan. As Scelsi noted, numerous witnesses identified Savino Parisi as the undisputed head of the organisation that controls Japigia, below him a small group of *uomini di fiducia* (trusted men) and *gregari* (foot soldiers) underneath who push drugs, rob, guard arms caches and keep an eye on what is happening in their part of the city. 'There are actually five grades of affiliates, with four grades below the *uomini di fiducia* at the top.' People who are not part of the organisation but can be called on when needed form the base of the pyramid. There are rituals and procedures to be followed, rules that must be obeyed, channels and methods of communication that have to be used, punishments that are meted out, and duties and obligations that must be respected.

'Nobody in the Parisi clan ever complained when they were in jail,' one man told the authorities, pointing out that prisoners' families were provided for and lawyers paid from the clan's funds. However, there is a dark side to the paternalism that bestows largesse and large sums of money for baptisms or weddings on the families of criminals in jail. 'Mafia power', Scelsi reminded me, 'is exercised by intimidation, subjugation and *omertà*, the rule of silence.' Although Parisi was described as 'a man of peace', he led a well-armed clan that could count on a large number of affiliates not only in the Japigia district of Bari but also in nearby towns, such as Bitonto, which was considered a protectorate of the clan.

But whatever its influence outside Japigia, it is over its own stronghold that the clan has an unrelenting grip, and as I learnt in Sicily and Calabria maintaining control over their territory is a feature of Cosa Nostra and the 'Ndrangheta. The Parisi clan's guards and patrols watch street corners in their district. How public contracts should be awarded, to whom social housing should be allocated and who should get jobs are all part of mafia business, in Puglia as much as anywhere in the South. Moreover, Puglia's *mafiosi* look on prison as their territory. 'Bari prison was managed by Bari's criminal organisations,' said Scelsi. And while one section of the prison was recognised as being the turf of the Parisi clan, Parisi himself was the boss in every part of it.

Human trafficking and prostitution are out of bounds for members of the clan, but with drugs and arms trafficking, cigarette contraband and money laundering it is already well diversified. 'These illicit activities are helped by Puglia's strategic position at the European Union's political and geographical edge, by weak social structures on the other side and the powerful force that mafia crime exerts.' And, of course, violence, the threat or the reality of it, is always present. 'There are many thirty-year-olds with bloodied hands in Bari,' Scelsi told me just before we said goodbye.

The nearest that Scelsi and his magistrate colleagues in Bari are likely to get to Puglia's *mafiosi* is in the usually secure surroundings of courts and prisons, but Luigi Liguori often finds himself closer in conditions that are much less safe. Chief of Bari's flying squad, Liguori has been an officer in Italy's state police since 1985. I went to meet him, taking the lift to the fifth floor of the police headquarters, walking past the door of the fifteen-strong homicide unit to the corner where Liguori has his office.

Nattily dressed in a dark blue-grey suit with a thin brown stripe, and a shirt to match the stripe, Liguori welcomed me with a genial smile on his round, open face. He seemed cheerful for somebody who deals all the time with serious crime. 'I've been fortunate, I've always been in the flying squad,' he said, no trace of irony in his voice. His first post when he entered the police after finishing a degree in law was with the flying squad in Genoa, where he was caught up in investigations into drugs trafficking and Gela's Stidda which was operating in the city. And after spending five years in the Ligurian capital he moved south to Puglia, to a town where nobody else wanted to go.

There may be no shortage of bloody-handed thirty-year-olds among Puglia's *mafiosi*, as Scelsi says, but when Liguori arrived they were up against a thirty-year-old who was willing to match violence with steel. He took up his post in Bitonto, the town about ten miles inland from Bari that is one of the protectorates of the Parisi clan, in October 1991 and immediately upset the local mafia fraternity. 'They didn't like policemen who took photos, watched and followed them around,' he remembered about his first two months there, 'and five days before Christmas they set off explosives outside the police station.' Liguori had an armed bodyguard for the rest of the year that he spent in Bitonto. 'But I never move without my pistol,' he told me, mentioning that fear goes with the job of policing in mafia regions, and opening the drawer of his desk to point to the gun he keeps inside.

After Bitonto, Liguori spent ten years with Puglia's anti-Mafia service and had headed Bari's flying squad and its hundred and fifty officers for five years when I met him. 'Tell me about yourself and how you see the region's Mafia,' I asked Liguori, over a long-armed cantilevered lamp decorated with yellow Post-it notes that stretched across the desk between us.

He told me that he is a Calabrese, born and brought up in Corigliano, a town in the Sibari plain that I had visited on my way north. 'Puglia's Mafia is an imported Mafia, but that doesn't mean that organised crime here is softer, easier than in the more notorious places. In fact, *mafiosi* here try to show that they are more *mafiosi* than those in Sicily and Calabria, murdering just to show that they can kill as ruthlessly as Cosa Nostra and the 'Ndrangheta.' Before I met Scelsi, a senior magistrate had told me about the authorities' concern over the widespread availability of firearms around Bari, particularly heavy weapons. 'The local criminal community possesses worrying quantities of arms but often we also come across arms that are held by people above suspicion.'

That is an issue that troubles anybody who looks at the Mezzogiorno: the uncertainty about where legal lines are drawn and who stands on which side in the battle against the Mafia. As Liguori explained to me, the Mafia in Puglia is Levantine, concerned principally about trade and the business that it can do, but it does not shrink from violence and even indulges in violence for violence's sake.

Across the road from the windows of Liguori's corner office I could see the massive Castello Svevo, a castle built for Frederick II in the thirteenth century. Behind it lies the *città vecchia*, the old city of Bari, a warren of narrow streets and passages where a visitor loses his way more easily than he finds it. The old city was peaceful when I visited but it had been a dangerous place not many years before, when mafia wars had brought shoot-outs and innocent bystanders died. In the crypt of the Basilica of San Nicola where the Orthodox liturgy is celebrated every week, I watched as an elderly lady bent to kiss an icon and leave a yellow rose, candles flickering weakly and dim lamps overhead.

The picture is dark. 'The sickness lies in civil society. The whole of the South is infected. The Mafia is like grass. You keep cutting but it always grows back,' the chief of Bari's flying squad told me bleakly.

10

EBOLI

Roadworks

SOME ITALIANS SAY the South begins in Florence. But for the politicians who set southern policy after the second world war and for the civil servants who managed it, the Mezzogiorno began not far south of Rome, in Pomezia on the edge of the Pontine marshes. I had not counted the miles before reaching Bari but the map in the guidebook of the Touring Club Italiano shows that the distance along the most direct route from Gela, where I began the journey on Sicily's southern coast, is over four hundred miles, and that the Apulian capital is almost three hundred miles from Rome. I was still in the deep south.

One thousand miles separate Monte Bianco, on the Alpine border with France, from Reggio Calabria; more than from Bayonne in southwest France at its frontier with Spain to Strasbourg in the northeast where France and Germany touch, and more than from Land's End to John O'Groats, Britain's toe and top. And when the ferry from the mainland lowers its ramp in Messina, a journey to Mazara del Vallo in Sicily's southwest corner, almost as close to Africa as to Palermo, adds another two hundred and fifty miles.

Carving around or boring through mountains and soaring over valleys, autostrade built in the 1960 and 1970s cut the times of journeys sharply, but even today few Italians in the north or centre lightly undertake travelling by road to the furthest parts of Calabria or to Sicily. Neither does rail offer much of an alternative for those heading south; the fastest express from Rome to Reggio Calabria takes almost six and a half hours and other trains two or three hours longer.

If Italy's extreme south seems distant early in the twenty-first century, how far it must have seemed to travellers in the 1870s and 1880s, the early years of reunified Italy, or in the closing decades of the eighteenth century when the South was ruled by the Bourbons. The historian Fernand Braudel described the challenges of communication and trade that faced France in the eighteenth century as the 'tyranny of distance'; the journey from Paris to Marseille took eight days in 1785, even after road improvements allowed fast stagecoaches to go full gallop. Yet the tyranny of distance was harsher and continued far longer in southern Italy than in France.

Even so, foreign travellers seeking ancient history, culture and the exotic were undeterred. Felix Mendelssohn went as far as Paestum, on the coast south of Salerno, before turning back to Naples. The German composer was one of a number of travellers from northern Europe who, from around the end of the eighteenth century, visited the South, mainly Naples and Sicily. Travels in Sicily even took Jean Houel, a French painter, to Corleone in 1770. Goethe expected Sicily to be the high point of his journey to Italy and spent six weeks there in the spring of 1787. As I had learnt, the British aristocrat Henry Swinburne travelled all around Calabria in 1777, keeping mainly to the coast. William Hamilton, Britain's envoy to the Kingdom of Naples, visited Calabria in 1783, soon after the region was devastated by an earthquake, landing at Pizzo and travelling to Reggio Calabria on horseback.

Another adventurous British traveller was Edward Lear, the writer and painter whose story I had encountered in southern Calabria, who spent nearly two months there in the summer of 1847, unworried about attacks by brigands. Yet seventy years before Lear's journey, warned of Calabria's wildness, Swinburne had expected to encounter them. One year after Swinburne completed his journey, Hamilton reported that troops had been sent against bandits in the region. That was just one of many sweeps. In fact, lawlessness was widespread around the beginning of the nineteenth century. The road from Naples eastwards across the Apennines to Puglia was very dangerous but bands operated from Molise in the northeast of the kingdom all the way down through Calabria.

Hampered by the lack of roads, the troops who tackled the brigands were further handicapped by the tortuous topography in much of the Mezzogiorno, and the position of Naples in the most northern part of the Kingdom of the Two Sicilies, formed when the Kingdoms of Naples and Sicily were brought together in 1816, would have stretched the most efficient government. Although the Bourbons would build more and better roads, at the beginning of the nineteenth century the kingdom's network centred on the city's needs. Four main roads, the royal highways, radiated from Naples: one to the border with the Papal States, and the others to the Abruzzo, Puglia and Calabria.

Before leaving Bari I tried to discover where the royal highway to Naples had passed but found no trace on the modern maps I opened. Perhaps it went through Bitonto before rising into the open, windswept Murge uplands and the mountains further on. In any case, I was heading for Eboli, about twenty miles south of Salerno, a route that crosses Trajan's Via Appia, whose end is marked by the columns above the harbour in Brindisi, and goes through Altamura where the Appia Antica passes on its way to Taranto.

I had travelled often along the autostrada south of Salerno but had never once turned off to Eboli, although the connection with Carlo Levi's book had intrigued me. Now I had another reason to be interested in the town. After years of construction and disruption to traffic, the autostrada from Salerno had been upgraded this far and I wondered how the Mafia had infiltrated the work and was infiltrating work further south, in Calabria.

I thought that I had first written about the Mafia at the end of 1998, but looking through my files I found an article on the Italian construction industry written eight years earlier for the *Financial Times*. 'Breaking the Grip of the Mafia', says the title. 'The battle against organised crime is delicately balanced,' explains the subtitle, using the words of Antonio Bargone, the deputy chairman of parliament's anti-Mafia commission with whom I had spoken.

About twenty years have passed since Bargone, a lawyer from Brindisi, told me that the Mafia's widespread involvement in the construction industry is inevitable. 'It is part of their strategy to obtain political dominion. Organised crime can weave itself into the entire social fabric through public works contracts that boost its presence and widen its sphere of influence,' he said then, adding that one reason the Mafia owned construction companies was to launder money obtained from crime. Its hold on the extractive industries and earthmoving was tight, and through this it was able to coerce legitimate firms. 'These activities give employment to thousands of people, thereby extending the Mafia's influence,' Bargone told me. Although no longer a member of parliament, he served as a junior minister in the ministry of public works in the centre-left administrations that governed Italy between 1996 and 2001 and had special responsibility for autostrade.

Not much had changed since he spoke to me in 1990. In November 2002, acting on instructions from anti-Mafia magistrates, police in Catanzaro arrested various managers and members of the technical staff of Anas, the state highways agency responsible for the autostrada from Salerno to Reggio Calabria. Four days after those arrests the managing director of Anas met the prefect of Salerno and other authorities to discuss progress in upgrading the road and the mafia risk. 'Anas is in the front line in the battle against mafia infiltration of public works and for a long time has been working actively with the forces engaged in the struggle against organised crime,' he said after the meeting.

Before travelling south I had called at the head offices of Anas in Rome to talk to senior engineers responsible for the autostrada's upgrading. One was Gavino Coratza, the general manager, who had worked for Anas for thirty years, mainly in Sardinia, and had moved to Rome in 2005 to head the agency's new-construction division. 'You know, work on the Salerno to Reggio Calabria autostrada is much more than modernisation. Effectively, we are building a completely new road.' Conceived in the 1960s, the two hundred and seventy-five miles of autostrada had been built quickly, to old standards, and began carrying traffic in the early 1970s.

'It goes through the toughest terrain in Italy. It's a mountain motorway where stretches are often under snow in winter. There's not only sun in the South, there's also snow,' said Vincenzo Marzi, the civil engineer who heads the project. When the politicians and planners decided that the autostrada should be built, the choice of where it should pass was strongly influenced by politics. 'It would have been far easier to have built it near the railway and the main road that follow the coast.' Instead, the autostrada went inland through mountains, across the empty spaces of northern Calabria to pass close to Cosenza, the political fief of a powerful minister.

In part, however, the new road was also seen as a way to open up and carry economic progress to one of Italy's most backward areas.

'In the 1990s we realised that the autostrada urgently needed improvements and that this would be a huge commitment in terms of both engineering and money. Although we didn't have a detailed picture of how it would be financed, we estimated that it would cost in the region of nine billion euros,' Coratza explained. And, of course, such a massive financial commitment drew the mafia clans through whose territories the autostrada runs, from Salerno in the north to Reggio Calabria at its southern end.

'We are not discovering the wheel. We know about the places where we are working and the special environmental factors that are found there,' said Coratza, environmental factors being code for Mafia. 'The fact is, we're not policemen. The Mafia is a matter for the state.' Apparently, some staff at Anas were reluctant to work on the project and Coratza understood their uneasiness. 'Contractors can buy new diggers and earthmovers but human lives are not something you can buy.'

Marzi had been working on the project since 2003 and had travelled many times up and down the autostrada, checking on progress and talking to the site managers, engineers, surveyors and workers who were making the road far safer for the tens of thousands of drivers who find themselves on various stretches every day. 'It's an extraordinary project. We have a dedicated team of people who are not just time-card punchers.'

I slowed to a new speed limit, left the highway that carries traffic from Potenza, weaved through the works at the Sicignano junction and followed the signs for Salerno about thirty miles away. Work was well advanced on a complicated twenty-mile section to the south and had begun to the north, in the direction of Eboli, where the autostrada passes through wooded countryside, mountains all around. A single-track railway winds its way through a valley below the road, which suddenly opens out into a broad three-lane affair that passes through well-lit tunnels.

Soon I reached Eboli, where the autostrada narrows once again and where, as Marzi had warned me, the exit was still being planned. The town offers nothing in particular, a main street with a few cafes and diffident staff. 'So, so. Like any other town in the world,' was a non-committal reply to my question about Eboli. Nothing I found records the man who made Eboli famous, no statue or plaque in the town's large square. Yet, speaking with the young secretary of the Democratic Party, I discovered that Carlo Levi is not forgotten. 'Levi and mozzarella made from buffalo milk are the two reasons why the town is known,' he told me.

There is a much better reason to leave the autostrada at Eboli, however, than the town that nestles beneath the Picentini mountains; Paestum lies on the coast, towards the south of the Sele plain, and here I again encountered relics of ancient Greece. Neptune's city Poseidonia, or Paestum for the Romans who arrived later, was founded towards the end seventh century BC by Greeks from Sybaris and the temple of Apollo (or the temple of Neptune, as it is often called) is among the finest and best-preserved examples of Doric style anywhere. Arriving at Paestum late in the afternoon, I saw it and the temple of Hera close by and the more distant temple of Athena as the sun was slipping through the horizon behind them. Visitors had left, a few pines and cypress trees rose dark green from among the orderly grey stone blocks lining the ground, and the setting sun cast a warm glow on the pale columns of the temples which seemed they would stand forever untouched by time.

The Greek temples had stood at Paestum for about five centuries before Christ, who stopped at Eboli, as Levi wrote. Eboli represented the place where civilisation ended, halted in front of the mountains that close the southern end of the Sele plain, the Picentini mountains inland and the Cilento extending to the sea. Certainly the mountains to the south contrast sharply with the fertile plain.

After staying overnight not far from Paestum I rejoined the autostrada at Eboli and headed towards Salerno, the autostrada's northern end. Large construction sites were busy as I drove down the steep hill to where the autostrada finishes, the road for Rome swinging off to the right, the autostrada that runs from Salerno to Naples continuing straight ahead, the direction that I took. Many years had passed since I last went this way, along the twenty-mile section from Salerno to Pompeii, completed almost fifty years before, and showing its age, with blackening concrete, unlit tunnels, tight bends and speed limits as low as thirty miles per hour.

Along an even older stretch of autostrada, though it was being modernised, the traffic increased significantly after Pompeii. Telling of far better times, dilapidated villas once elegant with their gardens of pines and palms and views across the Gulf of Naples stand close to the road after Torre del Greco, a town where years ago many jewellers thrived making cameos and working coral. Soon after Ercolano I could see Naples, its port and a decommissioned oil refinery off to the left, and then on past Portici, where Italy's first railway train wheezed in 1839 along tracks that ran about four miles to the centre. The Bourbon Kingdom of the Two Sicilies was backward in almost every respect but it could boast of Italy's first railway and its first steamship, launched in 1818.

Arriving in Naples by train or plane arouses a sense of trepidation. What will the city bring? Arriving by car sharpens the edge of adventure. I registered at the Clarean, a small, comfortable and modern hotel in the large square in front of the main station, the square a place with a bad reputation and not without risk, or so I was told, though the city has worse. The Clarean is convenient, near the underground railway beneath the station, and a tram line passes close by. A narrow street called Spaccanapoli that divides the old centre of Naples is not far and the court is just fifteen minutes' walk past the station, in a modern district of tall office blocks. I would go there several times during the days I spent in the city.

My first call was on Franco Roberti, deputy chief prosecutor and an experienced anti-Mafia magistrate whose name and telephone number had been given to me by Armando Spataro, a friend in Milan. The two had joined the magistracy at the same time, in 1975, and both had been friends of Giovanni Falcone and had helped him form Movimento per la Giustizia, an association of magistrates with a platform for efficiency and an emphasis on ethics. A photograph on the wall beside Roberti's desk on the twelfth floor of a building occupied by the magistrates who investigate crimes and prosecute criminal cases shows Falcone, hands clasped, a smile on his face.

In 1991 Roberti had applied to be transferred to the national anti-Mafia directorate because he expected that Falcone would be its head, although political manoeuvring and infighting in the magistracy's governing body obstructed Falcone's appointment in the early months of 1992. 'I told him at Easter that if he didn't go then I wouldn't either. A month later he was murdered. I've never got over Giovanni's death. It was an awful loss for me personally and a huge setback in the fight against the Mafia. He had something extra and this was why the Mafia killed him. Had he lived the Mafia would have been badly damaged.' Roberti spent eight years with the Direzione Nazionale Antimafia, three of them in Palermo. And after a four-year break between 2001 and 2005 when he worked again in Naples, on cases involving terrorism, Roberti went back to anti-Mafia work and to tackling the Camorra.

Mafia infiltration of the construction industry and public works is matter on which the Neapolitan magistrate is an expert. As he told me, the involvement of the Camorra and Calabria's 'Ndrangheta in the modernisation of the autostrada from Salerno to Reggio Calabria is just one of the projects from which the clans have made money. 'Reconstruction after the earthquake that killed thousands in 1980 and devastated towns and villages south and east of Naples was a great opportunity for the Camorra. About one half of what reconstruction cost the public purse went to them.' It is estimated that the cost was around sixty trillion lire, equivalent to about thirty billion euros or twenty-four billion pounds, so perhaps as much as twelve billion pounds was transferred from the Italian taxpayer, and possibly from taxpayers elsewhere in Europe, to the Mafia in and around Naples.

Sharing the money that arrived from Rome and elsewhere kept everybody happy. 'Politicians took bribes from firms and won the electoral support of the Camorra. Main contractors got money for putting their names on projects for which they signed contracts, doing no work but simply sub-contracting to local firms that belonged or were linked to the clans,' Roberti explained, telling the rotten story of how politicians, business and the Mafia worked hand-in-hand. Black books and false invoices were the norm, generating huge sums of money for paying bribes and other illicit ends.

Yet what polluted construction in Campania in the 1980s and 1990s had not been cleaned up when I spoke with Roberti. 'You should know that the Camorra's clans offer services, in finance, in security and in anything to do with construction. There used to be the figure of *camorrista-imprenditore*, the *mafioso* who also ran a business. Now he has been replaced by the *imprenditore-camorrista*, the businessman who is involved in the economic activities of criminal groups, either because he is threatened or because he decides freely to be so.'

As well as submitting false invoices for work not done, and for which they are paid, the Camorra's clans have been adept at infiltrating roadworks in other ways. 'The state's response to the ability of criminal businesses to find ways around laws and to avoid the efforts of the police and the judiciary has been neither quick nor effective.' Big business for the clans, earthmoving provides an example of where they dodge laws that cover public works. By giving sub-contracts to lease plant without the labour to drive it, main contractors can legally, at least on the surface, pass work to firms under the Camorra's control. 'Production of concrete is another example. Many producers are tied to the Camorra.' Often these firms simply pour concrete while charging three times the rate for this way of supplying it by claiming that they have provided the concrete under pressure, a method that makes concrete stronger when it sets. I had heard in Sicily of other mafia frauds involving concrete. 'How safe are many structures?' asked Roberti.

He had undertaken an important investigation into the Salerno to Reggio Calabria autostrada a few years before I met him that had revealed evidence of infiltration by the Camorra. 'Further confirmation of this disquieting scenario has recently come from the statements of a leading figure in the world of organised crime that is active in the Sele plain, in particular in the area between Eboli and Campagna, who referred explicitly to the work involved in the construction of the third lane and bridges in that stretch of the autostrada,' he wrote then.

'Public works are very important for the Mafia,' Roberti told me just before I shut my notebook. And keeping out the Mafia ought to be important to the state, but keeping public works free of the Mafia has never seemed a priority for Italy's politicians. 'The Mafia and the Camorra have always been around; alas, they are there and we must live with this reality,' remarked the minister of public works in Silvio Berlusconi's government in August 2001. More than a decade earlier, when I was writing on the construction industry, Antonio Bargone had told me, 'People are becoming accustomed to live with the Mafia rather than trying to combat it.' Schools, hospitals, railways, ports, roads, bridges: the more money the state spends on construction in the South, the more the Mafia pockets.

11

———

NAPLES

Turf Wars

WALKING FROM THE HOTEL to the court to meet Franco Roberti had taken me through bustling backstreets bearing the names of Italian provinces that form a grid near the station. Market stalls take over from traffic in the morning, and inexpensive clothes and shoes were heaped on some of them, kaleidoscopic displays of fish, fruit and vegetables on others, and jostling shoppers slowed the passage of people with places to go.

Mountains of rubbish five or six feet high rose from pavements and gutters, making a carnival mix of coloured carriers holding household waste, large black rubbish bags and empty cardboard boxes of different sizes. But there had been no party. This was Naples during its mammoth garbage crisis of 2007 and 2008. And these were some of the street corners of the city that made news around the world and, I would discover, were not as bad as others.

There were similar scenes in the Centro Direzionale, the city's equivalent of London's Docklands, built in the 1980s and 1990s to a plan drawn up by Kenzo Tange, a well-known Japanese architect. Some places had obviously become accepted as points where rubbish could be dumped. But this new district had already started to slide into urban blight. Efforts to keep the escalators moving to the decks below the large piazza, above which tall office buildings tower, appear to have been abandoned years ago, their side panels ripped away to expose the motors and belts, graffiti spoiling the walls beside them.

The court stands in the far corner of the Centro Direzionale, beyond the church, across the piazza where the engines' roar from aircraft climbing steeply after take-off bounces noisily between the blocks. Poggioreale, the old prison of Naples built at the beginning of the twentieth century and connected to the new court by an underground passage, is also beyond the church. Justice is a major business in and around the city. The court fills three huge, ominous dark grey blocks and a low, long pale-coloured building above which they loom. 'Yes, that's the court,' nodded an elderly lawyer who was passing, 'but justice should be a matter of quality not quantity.' And there was more. Behind the court, two twelve-storey buildings house the Procura where the investigating magistrates and prosecutors work, a massive grille of steel bars keeping people out and at a distance.

Garbage was scaling a high wall on the other side of the road when I called to talk with Roberti, and was still there when I went back to meet Gianni Melillo, an anti-Mafia magistrate to whom I had been introduced several years before in Rome. Dapper and limping slightly, he walked with a cane as he moved to greet me when I entered his office on the tenth floor. Vesuvius visible from the window, the view showed clearly how buildings have crept up the slope towards the mouth of the sleeping volcano, their inhabitants living on hope and hostages to the mountain's humour.

What Melillo told me about the Camorra cast new light on the clans in Campania, the region where Naples is the capital, a Mafia that threatens and erodes society as much as Cosa Nostra in Sicily and Calabria's 'Ndrangheta, Italy's best-known criminal organisations. 'The Camorra is the most evolved form of Italian organised crime. It works as a network, is structured to fit into the modern economy and thus the hardest to fight.' The Camorra changes its shape, is flexible, works in temporary consortia, and talks and deals with accountants, lawyers and members of the other professions needed for doing business in the world today.

'They have little need for clandestine meetings as they work their ways of corrupting civil society. Few people speak about this Camorra that silently elects mayors, that's protected by priests and quietly gets on with its work. It is extremely hard to deal with such infiltration of the economy, of the professions, of society.' As for the region's refuse crisis, the magistrate had few words. 'Garbage equals gold. The Casalesi saw this twenty years ago,' he said, referring to the camorra clan in and around the town of Casal di Principe, the Casalesi's stronghold some fifteen miles north of Naples.

I had spoken in Rome with Raffaele Cantone, a magistrate who had recently left the anti-Mafia group in Naples to take up an appointment as a supreme-court judge, and who had been involved for many years in investigations into the activities of the Casalesi, about whom I would later learn more. 'The Casalesi invented the refuse question, started it off with the traffic of waste from the north of Italy. They've got the background, the experience of involving politicians and of setting up business consortia,' he told me as we sat in the cafe of the supreme court, the vast Palazzaccio that neighbours the Sant'Angelo castle and overlooks the Tiber.

As the Neapolitan crisis turned garbage into even bigger business, so Camorra clans in Naples and elsewhere in the province were drawn in. According to Cantone, the Camorra helped the authorities to find sites where the accumulating rubbish could be taken. 'Investigators need to look closely at the firms that have been brought in to tackle the problem. Many are linked to the Camorra.'

The Camorra offers services, Roberti had told me, and in waste collection and disposal it discovered a service that, initially at least, would attract the attention of magistrates and the police less than its usual illicit activities. The Camorra did not plan its entry into waste management but seized the opportunity smartly when it arose. Its involvement in the garbage business began in the late 1980s, the result of the construction of a system of major roads that loop east to west across the plain north of Naples, from Acerra to Qualiano and from Nola to near the coast, a road that passes close to Casal di Principe.

Constructing about sixty miles of roads was profitable, and made more so because they run above the plain, either as viaducts on concrete pillars or on dyke-like embankments, and allowed the contractors to earn much more than by building them level with the plain itself. And this opened a vast new business because excavations left holes in the ground that could be profitably filled.

Urban waste was trucked in from towns and cities in the centre and north of Italy and with the refuse came bags, bins, barrels and drums full of industrial waste that were dumped untreated into the holes that dotted the path of the new roads and into quarries in the area. Northern businessmen, perhaps unwittingly, certainly through the Camorra's intermediaries, found an easy solution to their problems of waste disposal as toxic materials from industries as diverse as metalworking, tanning, textiles, chemicals, paper and pharmaceuticals were carried south to be buried under and around the plain north of Naples. About seven million tonnes of industrial waste are unaccounted for every year in Italy and the Campania region probably receives more than its share.

Replying to questions, a *camorrista* who had decided to cooperate with the authorities told magistrates how the burial of drums of toxic waste from Verona had yielded two hundred million lire, about eighty thousand pounds. Another *camorrista* who had broken with his past revealed how he had been asked to dispose of twenty-four drums of waste in an illegal tip in Mondragone, a town by the sea. He refused, turning down a deal that would have earned his clan one hundred million lire for every drum, a figure that pointed strongly to contents that were highly toxic. Almost certainly another *camorrista* took the business on, perhaps burying the drums in the land of an unknowing farmer in the area.

It is impossible to say how much industrial waste is buried in that area of about three hundred square miles near Naples, how dangerous that waste is or when or how its effects might be felt. But it was less the problem of illegal dumping than the matter of the refuse from the city's one million inhabitants that was taxing the authorities when I walked into the offices of the Campania region in Via Santa Lucia near the royal palace.

In theory, each commune is responsible for the day-to-day job of waste management, although the regional authorities have the job of planning and ensuring that the region has the facilities it needs. In practice, however, special commissioners, appointed by the government in Rome to tackle an emergency, had been in charge in Campania since 1994, turning the garbage emergency about which so many people were talking and the media reporting into business as normal.

I met Isaia Sales, economics counsellor to Antonio Bassolino, the president of the Campania region and a former mayor of Naples who was, not surprisingly, the target of vitriolic attacks. The regional authorities had an ambitious plan that aimed at building seven plants for treating refuse and a waste-to-energy plant that would burn the treated waste to produce electricity, but this ran into stubborn resistance. 'The plan was fiercely opposed by an alliance of the radicals, greens, far right, extreme left and the church,' Sales complained bitterly. 'And the Camorra had an interest in ensuring that the refuse problem was not resolved.'

There was a refuse tip in most communes in the region before the long-running emergency began. They were privately owned, Sales told me, but following the arrival of the special commissioner in 1994 they were taken into public ownership in a move that cut into the space in which the Camorra operates. 'There was never once a demonstration against a privately owned tip. We have been up against the refusal of people to deal collectively with a collective problem. There's little sense of the public good here.'

As photographs and film of the heaps of rotting garbage made their way into newspapers and onto television screens around the world so the image of Naples, never among the cleanest, plummeted. However, there was no noticeable impact of the crisis in the smart heart of the city or in places in the region that tourists visit, like Amalfi, Pompeii and Sorrento. I had seen something of the emergency but it had mainly affected the Neapolitan outskirts and some towns in the region, as well as many country roads that were turned into improvised tips.

Isaia Sales told me that those photographs had caused a sharp drop in the number of tourists visiting Naples, and I arranged to meet the recently appointed head of tourism, Claudio Velardi, returning to the regional authorities' offices to do so. Describing the centre of Naples as 'sufficiently clean' and the perception of the emergency as 'greater than reality', he pointed to damage that its lack of civic conscience or awareness does to Naples. 'Here you find the very worst but also the best in the world,' he added. The number of tourists was lower, he said, although figures were not reliable. Indeed figures that I later obtained showed that the number of foreign visitors had held up well in 2007 and was only slightly down on the previous year and better than any since 2001.

Even so, hotel owners were worried by the prospect that the refuse crisis would bring a steep fall in the number of guests. And that was not their only worry. Managers in luxury hotels along the Santa Lucia esplanade, near the small yacht harbour at the Castel dell'Ovo, were also concerned about how the stories of bag- and watch-snatching affect their business. 'This kind of crime creates a very poor picture of the city and hurts us. So do mafia wars, even though murders happen in districts that tourists don't visit,' the deputy manager of the elegant Grand Hotel Santa Lucia told me. The hotel advises guests to leave their watches in the hotel when they go out.

For Velardi, however, the real problems are those of prices and costs, which in Italy are uncompetitive with other holiday destinations, a weak dollar that deters Americans, and an image of Italy as old, introspective and no longer chic. 'Tourists travelling to Rio de Janeiro don't worry about gang wars in its suburbs. Turf wars between the Camorra's clans are not a good advertisement, but I don't think they put off foreign visitors.'

While in Naples I ate in various pizzerias, including Brandi in a narrow street leading towards the Quartieri Spagnoli from Via Chiaia, a pedestrian-only road that starts near the royal palace. This claims to be where the pizza margherita, adorned with mozzarella and tomato, was first made, a special pizza for the queen of Italy at the time that took her name. Four young American women were also eating there, so I asked what had brought them to the city. They were studying in Barcelona and would have preferred to have gone directly to Rome or Florence, but the cheapest flight to Italy was to Naples and they were staying for one night before heading north. They knew about the refuse crisis, but every city has problems, they said. 'Oh, and I heard that Naples is run by the Mafia,' one added with a laugh.

That is not true, although Naples, the surrounding province of which it is the capital and the neighbouring province of Caserta are darkened by what the authorities aptly describe as *alta densità mafiosa* – high mafia density. I had asked the home affairs ministry in Rome to give me the details of Italian communes whose councils had been dissolved because of mafia infiltration and found that the city of Naples is not among them. However, the ministry's list shows that seventy-five of the one hundred and seventy decrees issued between 1991 and 2006 to dissolve local administrations hit communes in the Campania region, in the provinces of Naples and Caserta above all.

Certainly Cosa Nostra in Sicily and the 'Ndrangheta in Calabria have been able to knit themselves tightly into the political fabric and local government where they are powerful, but the provinces in those two regions have received far fewer decrees dissolving town councils than the province of Naples, where forty-one were sent packing over the period for which the ministry had given me details. Twenty-three communes were dissolved in the province of Palermo and the same number in the province of Reggio Calabria, one more than in the province of Caserta.

But what I found striking as I read the list was the size of some towns in the province of Naples where the Camorra had taken a grip on local administration, or threatened to. While there are communes with less than a thousand inhabitants in the province of Reggio Calabria whose councils have been dissolved, and others not much larger, mafia infiltration around Naples has concerned some big towns: Torre del Greco with ninety-one thousand inhabitants, Casoria with eighty-two thousand, Portici with seventy thousand, Ercolano with sixty-one thousand and Afragòla with sixty thousand. Swinging a twenty-mile arc around the north of Naples encompasses several places on the ministry's list that I thought I might visit: Casal di Principe, San Cipriano di Aversa, Grazzanise, Villa di Briano, Frignano, Melito and Castel Volturno. I also had Mondragone, further up the coast, on my itinerary.

What has happened over recent years is simply the continuation of the Camorra's long history of successfully insinuating itself into the institutions of government, and of doing so in an urban context. Although a provincial Camorra developed around the end of the nineteenth century, unlike Cosa Nostra and the 'Ndrangheta, whose roots are rural, Campania's Mafia began in the city. In his book *La Camorra*, Gigi Di Fiore suggests that the word *camorra* was brought from Spain, which ruled the south of Italy from the sixteenth century for more than two hundred years, as a viceroyalty with Naples as its capital. According to Fiore, *camorra* in Sicilian means arrogance or oppressiveness, and all Neapolitans know that *fare la camorra* means to coerce.

Tommaso Astarita, a professor of history at Georgetown university in America who was born and grew up in Naples, writes in *Between Salt Water and Holy Water*, his colourful history of southern Italy, that *camorra* was the word for an illegal gaming den and first appeared at the turn of the eighteenth century. But by the mid-sixteenth century groups of criminals were banding together in Naples, the predecessors of the *camorristi* who would follow. A clan calling itself the Bella Società Riformata, with written rules and a hierarchy of grades with the *camorrista* at the top, was apparently operating early in the nineteenth century and Camorra would be used to describe the organisation of the criminals who operated in the city.

With about one million inhabitants, Naples is big, although not so remarkably big as it was in the past. In 1600, when its population was around three hundred thousand, it ranked with London and Paris as a European metropolis. Three hundred years later its inhabitants would number five hundred and fifty thousand and the city would continue to be the largest in reunified Italy for a further twenty years. Big certainly, and densely populated as its people squeeze into the city's limited space, but Naples is also vibrant, noisy, chaotic, attractive, repellent, dirty, superstitious, religious, sacrilegious, gloomy, sunny, and inhabited by the miserably poor and the very rich. And even if the Mafia does not run it, Naples is a city troubled by crime, where the growth and entrenchment of a criminal class owes much to how it was and is governed.

Accounts of Naples in the nineteenth century tell of policemen and officials abusing their power for personal gain, perhaps leading an oppressed lower class to view the Camorra as a bulwark against the despotic Bourbon monarchy. There had been major revolts in the eighteenth century and the prospect of riots was a constant concern, but when the throne was toppling in 1860, with public order under threat, even worse happened and the head of police and internal affairs minister of the kingdom sought the Camorra's help. The criminal records of *camorristi* were expunged and some of its members who had been behind the threat to public order were recruited by the state and put into police uniforms. The authorities had sold out to crime.

Stripped of its role as capital when the Bourbons departed, the city's standing declined, ministries were closed and jobs vanished. And with the arrival of the Savoy monarchy came its ideas of public order, a round-up of *camorristi*, sweeps against brigands in the countryside, special laws and the despatch of real and suspected criminals away from Naples to obligatory sojourn on islands such as Ponza and Ventotene. Even so the Camorra thrived. It expanded in rural areas by controlling markets and agricultural trade, and grew stronger in the city, where it showed its capacity to weave relations with politicians, providing them with electoral support and receiving favours in return.

The beginning of the twentieth century brought a show trial of *camorristi* that the authorities probably rigged and the emigration to America of Neapolitan *mafiosi* who saw better opportunities there than under fascism at home. That changed when the Allied forces entered Naples in October 1943, opening the possibilities for the illicit gains that the confusion, misery and shortages of war bring. A new generation of delinquents grew up working in the black market and the worlds of theft, sex for sale, corruption and contraband. The Camorra was back in strength and turf wars took over from wars run by generals and fought by their armies.

The vegetable and fruit market, supplied from the countryside around Giugliano to the northwest of Naples, Nola to the northeast and Nocera to the southeast, was the focus of one conflict. Go-betweens were the key figures in the price setting and buying and selling that was done along the Corso Novara by the railway station and into which I had turned after leaving my hotel to walk to the court. Members of clans headed by Pasquale Simonetti, a rising star, and Alfredo Maisto of Giugliano had fought a gun battle on the Melito road in 1952, but the turf war did not finish there. A smouldering row between Simonetti and Antonio Esposito led to Simonetti's murder in Corso Novara in July 1955.

Simonetti's young wife Pupetta Maresca, from the powerful Maresca family of Castellamare di Stabia, on the coast near Pompeii where the Gulf of Naples turns west towards Sorrento, took her revenge by shooting the man she held responsible for her husband's murder, the man who had sent the killer. Eighty days after Simonetti was shot, Pupetta Maresca, expecting a child, widowed three months after marrying, killed Esposito in Corso Novara, events that three years later would be the subject of *La Sfida* (the challenge), the first film directed solely by Francesco Rosi, whom I would meet and who would tell me about the films he made in and about the Mezzogiorno when I returned to Rome.

While control of the fruit and vegetable market led to a bloody struggle between clans in Giugliano and towns nearby until the mid 1970s, arguably the war that *camorristi* waged in the late 1970s and early 1980s is the one most clearly remembered. On one side there was the Nuova Camorra Organizzata, a centralised, pyramidal criminal structure led by Raffaele Cutolo who modelled the organisation on Calabria's 'Ndrangheta, and on the other the Nuova Famiglia, a temporary alliance that brought together the old camorra families who found their positions threatened. Cutolo had recruited young tearaways in prison who wanted the serious criminal careers, sense of identity and status that Cutolo promised. From sixty-two murders in 1978 the number soared to two hundred and thirty-five in 1981 and two hundred and sixty-five in 1982.

Eventually, the bloodshed drew a response from the authorities, who executed arrest warrants against hundreds of suspected *camorristi* in June 1983 and again the following year. One Neapolitan writer estimates that around one thousand five hundred people died in this war. And to many of those who survived the courts handed down long prison sentences. It had been a war with many losers, civil society certainly, but Cutolo as well, and his Nuova Camorra Organizzata which had failed in its attempt to conquer Campania.

That war rumbled on for years, as I learnt when I was shown around the Quartieri Spagnoli. 'It's no good talking only to magistrates. You ought to talk to Marco Rossi-Doria,' Gianni Melillo had told me over a pizza in a simple pizzeria of bare tables and hard chairs near the court, giving me the telephone number that I should call. So I telephoned Rossi-Doria and we arranged to meet at Gambrinus, a cafe on the corner between Via Chiaia and the vast square in front of the royal palace, and across the road from the San Carlo opera house. This is one of the smart places to have a coffee in Naples, or an *aperitivo* before dinner or *digestivo* afterwards. Yet it is also very close to the tight and crowded streets of the Quartieri Spagnoli, where order finishes and disorder begins.

Rossi-Doria had told me to look out for somebody carrying a black backpack and I picked him out at once when he arrived at the Gambrinus; blue cord trousers, a dark North Face jacket, a round bespectacled face with a salt-and-pepper beard appearing above it. His father, jailed by the fascist regime in 1930, had been a leading figure in the movement behind southern development after the war, his mother an American of Hungarian Jewish origins. Although born in Naples, he had spent much of his childhood in America.

'There was another war here after Cutolo was beaten, between the Mariano family and the Di Biase family, two years of murders that began in 1990,' said Rossi-Doria, who had moved into an apartment in the district in 1991 when it was an urban battleground. As in the other camorra wars, the opposing clans in the Quartieri Spagnoli were fighting for control of the various criminal businesses around which the local economy turns: drugs dealing, gambling, prostitution and extortion.

What marked this lethal struggle for dominance as something out of the ordinary, even for Naples, was that it took place in the very centre of the city, a few hundred yards from Via Chiaia and the Municipio (city hall), the heart of the administration where the mayor's offices are located. One of the killings in 1990 happened in a favourite nightspot of American servicemen near the city hall itself. But the bloodiest event was the following year, on the evening of Good Friday, when three youngsters who had broken away from the Mariano clan were shot dead in the street. And on the following day an off-duty policeman was murdered while trying to protect his daughter.

There were no camorra murders in this part of Naples while I was in the city, although there were signs that the authorities were expecting something. 'You don't usually see this number of the Carabinieri's cars patrolling here,' Rossi-Doria remarked. And when he took me to meet Anna, a social worker who runs an advice centre in one of the *bassi* whose rooms open straight onto the street, she mentioned that a rumour was going round that a killing was planned and that somebody in the district was the target. 'Palermo is far safer. This is a bad, bad area that you should avoid, especially on Friday and Saturday nights,' Rossi-Doria warned me. I mentioned that I had earlier walked by the Pellegrini hospital, not far away. 'You couldn't find a better place if you get shot or stabbed. Its doctors are experts in treating gunshot and knife wounds.'

Having an important father, Marco Rossi-Doria decided to make a career away from the corridors of power, in the classrooms of elementary schools in the poorest parts of Naples. 'I've become an expert in drop-outs. Kids who don't go to school are strange animals. They don't necessarily work for the clans but they are definitely at risk,' he said, adding that the fewer the years that an adolescent spends at a classroom desk, the higher the probability that he will turn to crime. 'Like poor and restless youngsters everywhere, the youth here responds to cultural authorities, and some are criminal. The Camorra treats them as adults and they respond.' The drop-out rate from school in Italy is about twenty-two per cent overall and among the worst in Europe. Naples shows badly in Italy and the Quartieri Spagnoli badly in Naples.

As we walked through the narrow streets near his home, Rossi-Doria told me how the blocks, laid out on a grid, had been built in the sixteenth century to quarter Spanish troops but were then taken over by the poor of Naples. 'It's always been a place with crime, where whores ply their trade. American soldiers came here for their black-market dealings after the war.' The population fell steeply following the earthquake in 1980 but it remains one of the most densely populated places in Europe, and a place where the unemployment rate stands at around fifty per cent.

'Ciao, professore,' shouted two lads on a motor scooter as they drew up and stopped. Neither was wearing a helmet, despite the law's requirements that they should do so, and Rossi-Doria ruffled their hair as he chatted with them. Just turned twenty, they had recently finished jail sentences for robbery and were trying to go straight by running a hot-dog stall in a busy street nearby.

Rossi-Doria had advised me to keep my small camera out of sight as taking photos can make people nervous. But I used it in the Prigiobbo brothers' pizzeria, the camera capturing a pizza as the *pizzaiolo* drew it on his paddle from the oven in the corner, where the bright red-yellow flames from the burning wood inside contrasted with the cool white and green mosaic whose pattern on the curved outside recalled the 1960s. While we ate Rossi-Doria told me of his mixed feelings for his city, of how nothing worked and how hard it is to live there. 'In Palermo there are rules but here there are none. A person's word is worthless here. Sicily's *mafiosi* are serious but *camorristi* aren't. This city is pure theatre but I like it, and the same things that I like, I dislike also,' he said with a certain resignation as we said goodbye.

I had walked past the San Carlo opera house, saw that there was a performance in the evening, a double bill of Bartók's *Bluebeard's Castle* and a little-performed opera by Ravel, and bought a ticket. A glorious theatre, built in 1737 with six tiers and one hundred and eighty-four boxes, it is the oldest working theatre in Europe, forty-one years older than Milan's La Scala. Gioachino Rossini was the San Carlo's house composer from 1815 to 1822 – the Palazzo di Domenico Barbaja where he lived, across Via Toledo from the Quartieri Spagnoli, has a plaque outside – and he was followed by Gaetano Donizetti who stayed for sixteen years.

After saying good evening to the other occupant of the box where I would sit, a season-ticket holder, I asked if the curtain would go up punctually. 'Certainly,' she replied, 'they close the doors and dim the house lights spot on time. It's the only thing in Naples that you can rely on.' Jeffrey Tate, a leading English conductor, drew fine singing from the casts and lovely playing from the orchestra which an Italian critic described as being 'in a state of grace'. Tate had been appointed music director at the San Carlo in 2005 after the death of Gary Bertini and, wondering why he had taken this on and how he found Naples, I asked to meet him.

His experience of working in Italy began in 1994 when he conducted the orchestra of the Accademia di Santa Cecilia in Rome. 'The first rehearsal was at ten o'clock and shortly before that the orchestral porter arrived at the door and said that the orchestra was ready. And literally at ten o'clock on the dot, the oboe played his A and off we went. It's been like that ever since. In that sense Naples is not an exception. Strictness is the rule of the day. There's no southern laxness.'

However, planning is another matter. Opera houses in the north of Europe usually decide their programmes four or five years ahead, because singers' engagements are set that far in the future. 'I've discovered that in Italy they're quite prepared to piece an opera together nine months before its opening night. The amazing thing is that this often works,' the conductor said with a smile. He had conducted the theatre's first performances of Leonard Bernstein's *Candide* in January 2007, less than a year after money problems had caused the planned producer to pull out, and with a new producer and sets designed in-house the opera was a great success.

He was facing a similar challenge when we met. A special commissioner, appointed by the government in August 2007 following a financial crisis at the theatre, had decided that vital renovation work should be done, causing the theatre to be shut from August 2008 until late December, after the 2008/2009 season's planned opening with Verdi's *Don Carlos*.

The singers' contracts elsewhere meant the dates for *Don Carlos* could not be altered and when its cancellation was decided in November 2007, Tate and the artistic director had to think of another opera to open the season. They hit on *Peter Grimes* by Benjamin Britten. 'I thought it would be wonderful to do a twentieth-century English masterpiece. It's a great chorus opera and one likes to begin the season with a big chorus work which shows the theatre off. And we've actually done it and put together a cast that would look very good on the stage of Covent Garden. This ability to do everything at the last minute is very Italian – it's not improvisation because they know what they are doing.'

What lured Tate south was the chance of doing, early in 2002, Humperdinck's little-known *Königskinder*, 'a rarely done piece of great beauty', which turned out to be a very successful sally to the San Carlo for the conductor to whom the prospect of working in Naples had been rather frightening. 'It was an extremely happy experience here. I loved the old theatre. It has an atmosphere of its own, very special, and everyone backstage was wonderfully human and nice to deal with. The feeling of the theatre reminded me very much of my first days at Covent Garden, an old theatre run by people who love it.'

During six years of working regularly in Naples, Tate had come to appreciate the artistry and commitment of the musicians. 'It's noticeable that the young Italians are very serious about their work. They realise they're privileged to be in this rather strange job in an otherwise unyielding and cruel world. To be able to make music and earn your living making music is an amazing thought and I think that the young musicians sense that.'

Committed to spending around four months every year in Naples, Tate had decided to rent an apartment and from its windows he could look across the Piazza dei Martiri, just beyond the other end of Via Chiaia from the Gambrinus cafe where I had met Rossi-Doria. Settled in the corner of a large sofa, Tate told me about his experience of making the city his home. He had had the opportunity of taking up the appointment of music director at La Fenice, the opera house in Venice, at the same time as he was offered the post at the San Carlo, but Venice, 'incomparably beautiful as it is', was for him simply a dead city with no real life of its own.

Tate, who was preparing for performances of Wagner's *Die Walküre* when Bertini died, and already had *Königskinder* and a Christmas concert under his Neapolitan belt, knew what he would be taking on if he took the post at the San Carlo. Without that earlier experience, he probably would not have accepted the appointment. 'It's the people. Naples is the most human place. People from all walks of life, the richest and the poorest, are all so generous with themselves, with their time. One of the most pleasant aspects of putting down roots here has been the way I've made so many friends, so quickly,' he said.

'It's a grand, fantastic city with great energy, where there's a generosity of spirit. Naples lives and breathes because of its people. They can be irritating and negligent but that doesn't really matter because the fundamentals of life keep this city going; otherwise, with the problems it has, it would have packed up long ago,' Tate mused, probably expressing the feelings of many northern European intellectuals and artists who have come under the city's spell and been enraptured by warm Neapolitan qualities. But it was easy to understand why Neapolitans had taken to Jeffrey Tate, and I was glad he had spoken to me because he had talked about the ways of Naples and its people that show the best of a city whose worst sides are those that are usually talked about.

The short string of elegant shops – Gucci, Prada, Louis Vuitton and Damiani, a high-class jeweller – leading from Piazza dei Martiri to the seafront, the Villa Comunale public gardens and the tram stop in Piazza Vittoria is only a fifteen-minute trip from my hotel, but far from it in almost every other respect. But so also are the smart apartment blocks of Posillipo and the solid middle-class streets of Vomero above the centre of the old city. I planned to visit parts of Naples that are culturally, socially and economically even further away.

Die Walküre had been well received on its opening night at the San Carlo in March 2005. When Jeffrey Tate put down his baton at the end of the opera's third performance on the evening of 30 March and the audience began applauding, Davide Chiarolanza had less than twenty-four hours to live. Twenty-three years old, Chiarolanza was murdered on the last day of March in Melito, a charmless town just north of Naples, about six miles from the city's centre. It was one pulsation in the bloodletting accompanying a turf war that, at its bloodiest, produced a dreadful wave of killings in the autumn of 2004.

The turf under dispute is about four miles by six and includes Secondigliano, Scampia and Miano, neighbouring suburbs that fall within the city's boundaries, and towns like Arzano, Giugliano, Marano and Melito whose roads and buildings melt imperceptibly into one another and into suburban Naples. The local government in Marano had been dissolved twice, in 1991 and 2004, because of the Mafia's presence and a similar end came to Melito's authorities in 2005. Councils in most of the neighbouring towns, like Casandrino, Casoria, Frattamaggiore and Sant'Antimo, have

195

also been dissolved for the same reason. With such mafia penetration in these communities north of Naples, turf wars simply go with the territory.

The gory catalogue began in April 2003 with the murder in Secondigliano of Francesco Giannino and the wounding of two companions, all friends of the sons of Paolo Di Lauro, the boss of Secondigliano and Scampia, and the murder of Giuseppe Marra, who was linked to the Di Lauro clan. Calm then reigned until the early hours of 7 October when Massimo Mele, a killer of the Di Lauro clan, was himself killed. Anti-Mafia magistrates and police working with the homicide squad in Naples had to wait until January 2004 for their next call to the scene of murder involving criminals in that area, a double homicide in Mugnano, a foretaste of the busy year that would follow.

There was an attempted murder and a wounding in February 2004, a murder in Secondigliano in March, two murders in April, another murder in Secondigliano in August and an explosion of violence in September when the area around Secondigliano was bloodied by three murders and two woundings. But that was little more than a rehearsal. According to an arrest warrant for sixty-four men and one woman from Naples signed by five prosecutors and issued on 6 December, 'The date of 28 October 2004 marked the definitive and complete rupture of equilibrium and the beginning of the violent feud.'

At about ten past five in the afternoon that day police were called to Via Cupa Vicinale Comunale d'Arco, the capital of Di Lauro's territory and close to Corso Secondigliano, the main road that runs straight as a die for about a mile and a half through the heart of the suburb. They found two men on the ground, dead from gunshot wounds, and fourteen 9mm cartridge cases nearby. Both men had lengthy criminal records; one had managed drugs dealing in various parts of the district for the Di Lauro clan and the other had managed the revenues that came from that dealing.

Two days later the Di Lauros struck back, attacking a man who later died from the wounds he received. On 1 November the police were alerted that a man related to the Di Lauro family had gone missing, and four days later monitored a conversation suggesting that the missing man had been kidnapped and killed. Police were called to the hospital in Giugliano in the afternoon of 2 November following the admission of a man who had been shot in Mugnano and would soon die; a brother of the victim had ties to the opponents of the Di Lauro clan. Di Lauro's killers were in operation again two days later, wounding a man who was related to members of the other side.

And so the murders continued throughout the month: one in the evening of 6 November in Via Labriola in Scampia, the district where the bodies of three men had been found in a car earlier that day; a drive-by murder committed by four men on two motorcycles in Mugnano on 20 November and the murder later in the day of the brother of one of those killers; a double homicide at a quarter past ten in the morning of the next day in Melito, and another murder fifty minutes later in Secondigliano; and there were five further murders before the end of the month. More killings followed, albeit less frequently, even after the magistrates had issued their arrest warrant and the sweep had taken sixty-five people into custody.

Behind the bloodshed was a struggle for the control of the flourishing drugs business in and around Scampia, which has a name as Italy's drugs supermarket where every kind of narcotic is available twenty-four hours a day, as well as of the other profitable criminal businesses in that brutal part of the Neapolitan hinterland. The clan earned enormous amounts of money under the leadership of Paolo Di Lauro, enabling it and various allied gangs to keep large payrolls, support the families of members in prison and pay the lawyers of those on trial, and thereby ensure the loyalty of subordinates and allies. In November 2004, eavesdropping on a conversation between the boss of Melito, who was in custody in Poggioreale prison, and members of his family, magistrates heard that one sales area was producing only fifteen thousand euros a day from its drug dealing, business having been badly affected by the violence; daily revenues had previously been between two and three hundred thousand euros.

Magistrates learnt that the scene had been set for the murderous clash of clans in September 2002 when Paolo Di Lauro went into hiding, passing the leadership to his son Vincenzo, who would be arrested in April 2004. His brothers Cosimo, Nunzio, Marco and Ciro then took charge, but their clan's solid structure had already begun to crumble with the flight to Spain of one of its leading members accused of cheating the organisation. Some members went with him, causing a schism that would lead to them being called either *scissionisti* or *spagnoli*. Other members, discontented with how the Di Lauro sons were managing the business, also split off and the turf war exploded.

Gianni Melillo had introduced me to two mid-ranking magistrates, Marco Del Gaudio and Simona Di Monte, who were among the five who had signed the arrest warrant in December 2004, and I later telephoned Di Monte to arrange a meeting. An attractive woman with long light-brown hair, glasses and an easy smile, she had just finished a court hearing when she invited me into her office. 'Scampia is the ante-chamber of hell,' she told me. However, most of the outskirts of Naples are best avoided.

'The turf war was really a kind of ethnic cleansing. People were murdered simply because they were related to members of the clans involved, not because they themselves were members. Their only blame was that of a blood relationship. The clans' aim was to frighten people into leaving their homes,' Di Monte said. The killing of Gelsomina Verde was particularly significant. She merely had a sentimental tie to one of the targets in a turf war and his enemies thought she could lead them to him. Verde was shot and the small car she was in was set on fire. Alongside her charred remains carabinieri found two cartridge cases and a fuel container when they arrived at the scene at half past midnight on 22 November 2004.

'Did the killings take the anti-Mafia team by surprise?' I asked. 'That there were murders did not surprise us at all because there had been warnings in the spring. The surprise came from the turf war's rapid escalation,' Di Monte told me. Coordinating the investigations and preparing an arrest warrant of three hundred and fifty pages had been a huge task for magistrates, under pressure to act to prevent the violence from escalating further. 'The challenge generated a great team spirit.'

There would be more murders in the future, she thought, because the members of the clans who had fought their war would not forget what happened during it. Innocent people would continue to die because they are brothers or cousins of clan members. 'Bloodshed is reciprocated here,' said Di Monte. Ten years would be insufficient to exhaust the desire for revenge, probably not even twenty years would be enough. The turf war had produced no winner and there would be losers in the future.

I wondered what Di Monte's background was and what had attracted her to the magistracy and to anti-Mafia work. She had graduated in law at Naples university in 1991, become a magistrate in 1995 and joined the anti-Mafia team in January 2003. 'What is this cancer that gnaws into our society, that blocks progress? I wanted to understand the Camorra. You can't see it in Vomero where I live, but it's there all the same, in extortion, in money laundering. It's everywhere.'

I asked her about her first murder case. It had happened on 30 June 1995 when she was doing her pupillage and the magistrate to whom she had been attached was on duty and had been called to a murder scene. 'Nowadays it's different. I take charge of investigations, give instructions, make sure that procedures are followed. Then I was an observer. I'd seen dead people before, on their beds, objects of prayer. That day the person who was dead had been running from killers and had suddenly been cut down, his body lying sprawled across the pavement.'

For her that first experience of murder was unreal. 'There was a morbid curiosity, everyone was standing on their balconies and looking down. It was like a festival in a town square. Even small children were gazing at the blood on the pavement. I'd never known this Naples before,' the magistrate admitted. I asked where the murder had taken place. It had happened in the long main street at Secondigliano, the Corso Secondigliano where I planned to go that afternoon. 'You're going alone?' she asked. 'Journalists are usually accompanied by the police.'

After talking to Simona Di Monte I went back to my hotel, leaving everything except a few coins, a small notebook and a pen before taking a bus for Teverola, a town as close to Caserta as Naples. Passing police head-quarters that seemed deserted, a long-abandoned station from where trains once left for Piedimonte Matese, a town at the foot of the Apennines about forty miles to the north, and the enormous Albergo dei Poveri that Carlo III founded in 1751 for the elderly and orphans of his kingdom, the bus then began to climb above the eastern part of the city. And as it climbed higher, a vast panorama opened up, the tall offices of the Centro Direzionale below to the right, and beyond them Vesuvius and the wide curve of the Gulf of Naples sweeping round far into the distance.

Turning left at the top of the hill, the bus headed towards Secondigliano and the Neapolitan hinterland. A long wall on the right hid Capodichino airport where Lucky Luciano, one time *capo dei capi* in America, died in January 1962, apparently of a heart attack although suspicions persist that his death came from poisoning. I got off the bus where the airport's wall ends, just before a large piazza from which Corso Secondigliano stretches straight ahead. This is the grim and grimy road where Simona Di Monte saw her first murder victim and a place that journalists visit in cars and with policemen.

Despite its unsavoury reputation, Secondigliano is mentioned in the Italian Touring Club's guide to Naples, which suggests that visitors should look for the former customs house near the piazza and the nineteenth- and early twentieth-century palaces and villas that dot the long main road. It was from their balconies with their wrought-iron railings, and from the newer buildings between, that people gazed down at the dead man lying on the pavement on that last day of June in 1995, and whose morbid interest Di Monte remembered.

I thought that I might get an idea of Secondigliano by asking in cafes where I stopped. 'It's fine,' replied a friendly woman, probably in her mid-thirties and of Slav origins from her accent, who put a newspaper in front of me as I ate an ice cream. Its headlines read, 'Carabinieri raid in the stronghold of the *scissionisti* – drugs and arms in Scampia, three arrests'. An Italian came through a door behind the counter, perhaps the owner, and spoke sharply to the woman, and I wondered if she was being warned not to talk to strangers.

My next stop was further along the Corso, at an attractive cafe with colourful displays of pastries and chocolates where I was served a coffee by a pretty girl with a troubled face who did not want to talk and simply nodded her head, frightened when I asked about life in Secondigliano. On my way I had been passed by carabinieri in two Land Rovers, anti-riot grilles over their windows, and heard a man telling his wife, as she was about to drive away, to make sure that the car's doors were locked. At every junction one or two young men seated on mopeds or motor-scooters watched passers-by and passing traffic, and occasionally zipped up or down or across the road. These were the clan's lookouts about whom Di Monte had warned me, and as I walked I heard the whistles as they signalled to each other. Near the Corso's end, where Secondigliano runs into Scampia, the place that Di Monte had described as the ante-chamber of hell, I caught a local bus back into the centre of Naples.

Scampia was also on my list of places to visit, though I would call twice more at the court to talk with investigating magistrates who deal with crime in the province of Caserta, the northern part of Campania, and the lower part of Lazio, the region of which Rome is the capital. 'Scampia!' exclaimed Francesco Curcio with surprise when I told him where I would go the following day.

Before going to Scampia, I met the secretary of the CGIL trade union for the Campania region, whose offices are in a side street near my hotel. 'There is no industry and little work in Secondigliano, and Scampia is just a place where people live, in social housing and privately owned cooperative apartments built during the 1960s and 1970s,' Michele Gravano told me. Lack of jobs is not their only problem. Home to around forty-five thousand people, Scampia was born without services, with no police station and with poor public transport, factors that fed the social degradation in which the Camorra has thrived. 'Something needs to be put there, like the university that is talked about but which academics oppose.'

Gravano gave me the name and telephone number of the trade union's local secretary in Scampia whom I contacted. Unsure of where its offices were, I took a taxi from near the station in Naples and told the driver the address, Distretto Sanitario 48, the local health service in Scampia. But he left me outside the unit that deals with mental health instead of the main clinic, and the taxi had gone when I discovered the driver's mistake.

Was I concerned? Only that I might not arrive at the CGIL's office before it closed at noon. Should I have been concerned? Perhaps, but I was near a bus terminus and soon discovered which bus to catch. Route C74 took me past roads whose names I recognised at once. They appear often in the arrest warrant that Marco Del Gaudio and Simona Di Monte had signed: Via Labriola, Via Monte Rosa, Via Fratelli Cervi and Via Ghisleri, crossing and running into and out of each other along the bus's route around Scampia, had each been the scene of at least one murder. After getting off the bus and asking a guard outside the main clinic for directions, I walked towards a neighbouring block.

'What do you want?' asked one of two young men standing on a balcony and watching the car park by the building, alert eyes in expressionless faces. The offices of the CGIL were just a few yards ahead. Thankfully they were still open, although Alfredo Erpete, the local secretary had gone to the bus terminus to meet me but he soon returned. Who were the two young men who had asked what I wanted? 'Those two, they were taking the sun,'

Erpete told me with a resigned and knowing shrug. As in Secondigliano, so in Scampia.

A retired technician who had worked for forty years in a large engineering company in Naples, Erpete had represented the Communist Party in parliament in Rome in 1979, had been a city councillor in Naples from 1993 until 1997 and had lived in Secondigliano since 1969. 'We want to lift this place out of the social and cultural abyss into which it has fallen,' he said. Stocky, bearded and with short grey hair, Erpete is part of a small group committed to nurturing civic values in a civic desert. Scampia is the district in Naples with the youngest average age, but with unemployment over thirty per cent the prospects for its young people are bleak. 'There is a terrible fear that youngsters have no future and certainly if we don't turn things around ...' Erpete paused. '... But we just have to say that they do have a future.'

When the CGIL's office, its windows well protected with heavy metal grilles, opened at the end of the 1990s it had run into opposition from those who consider Scampia to be their territory. 'After we close at midday another life begins around here,' Erpete said, adding that they did not want to put people at risk by staying open longer. Antonio Veroni, a colleague of Erpete, locked the two massive steel doors behind us and said that he would accompany me by car to the underground railway station. The weather was fine and I had seen from the bus that to walk would take no more than fifteen minutes, but Veroni insisted. And when we reached the station he came through the arch with me and waited until I began climbing the stairs to the ticket hall. As the train started the journey back into Naples I saw again the infamous Vele, the three of the original seven fourteen-storey white blocks that still await demolition, the most visited part of Italy's supermarket for drugs.

I left the city in the afternoon, driving past Capodichino and along the Corso Secondigliano that I had visited on foot, past the junction where Secondigliano becomes Scampia on the left and where a large recently built prison, probably the biggest employer in the district, rises behind fences and walls on the right. More blood would soon be shed nearby.

Blazed across the front page of the following morning's *Cronache di Napoli* were headlines that read 'Scissionista boss killed'. At around four o'clock in the afternoon, about an hour after I had driven past, Salvatore

Cipolletta, thirty-seven years old and a rising figure in local crime with ambitions to be the boss in Mugnano, was murdered in what police thought was a settling of accounts within the clan that opposed the Di Lauros. Cipolletta was walking in Via Labriola when his killers shot him in the back and then three times in the head after he had fallen to the ground.

There may be signs welcoming visitors to Melito, but I did not see them and was not even aware that I had passed into the town as I drove along the Via Roma. For the anti-Mafia magistrates in Naples, Melito was at the very centre of the killings and woundings that they were investigating. One of the leading figures of the turf war was shot and wounded on the town's main road in September 2004, a prelude to the escalation of bloodshed in the autumn that followed.

Melito adjoins the Di Lauro's stronghold in Secondigliano, is their dependency and their man in the town was Federico Bizzarro until the clan decided to support a group of his subordinates in a murderous coup. The rebels failed in February 2004 when Bizzarro escaped an attempt on his life in which his nephew was shot and wounded. They thought there would be an opportunity at the beginning of April after Bizzarro's mother died, but the police were at the funeral in force and, in any case, Bizzarro stayed away. However, his former partners in crime would be successful later in the month.

On the morning of 26 April Bizzarro asked an associate to book a room in a hotel for that same day. 'Because the Hotel Mediterraneo was full, the choice fell on the Hotel Giulia,' wrote the investigating magistrates. The camorra boss had been used to meeting a lover on Mondays or Tuesdays in one of the hotels along the Naples outer ring road. He arrived at the Hotel Giulia at around three o'clock in the afternoon, left an identity document with the receptionist and went up to a third-floor room, where his lover joined him about an hour later. Within two hours he would be dead.

Just before six o'clock a group of at least six men, wearing dark glasses, berets and slipovers with the word Polizia across them, burst into the hotel, held up a waiter and the receptionist and ordered a copy to be coded of the electronic key to room 308. Four of the hit squad went to the third floor but the key failed to work. Calling out that they were the police, the killers ordered Bizzarro to open the door, began firing as he approached it, blasted the door open and broke in. Their shots hit Bizzarro several times and they delivered a coup de grâce to the head at close range, a horrific scene to which his lover, who had been in 'a state of intimacy', was witness.

After losing my way in Melito and Giugliano, I eventually found myself on the busy outer ring road, heading west towards Qualiano, taking the slip road alongside overhead carriageways and driving past numerous car-dealers and hotels, the Saint Louis, the Ginepro and the Green, before pulling in to the Giulia.

I parked behind the hotel, underneath a white canvas awning strung near pine trees and palms, and walked into the reception area. Its location beside the ring road is ugly but the hotel itself is smart. I left my passport at the desk and was given an electronic key to room 302. Taking the lift to the third floor, I stepped out onto a tastefully decorated landing – room 308 a few paces along, through an arch and across the corridor – and opened the door to my room.

This was quite the nicest room in which I stayed during the whole of my journey through the South: a splendid bathroom, large, well-lit with sand-coloured marble on the floor and walls, and an airy, spacious bedroom with a pleasant, unaggressive mix of light yellow walls and deep red bedspread. From a small terrace I could see, beyond the pines and palms, men working on a swimming pool. And I dined well too, served by courteous staff. The following morning, when problems with telephone lines prevented credit-card settlement of the bill and the manager suggested paying by bank draft when I got back to Rome, Jeffrey Tate's words about Neapolitan hospitality came to mind.

12

CASAL DI PRINCIPE

Mafia System

LEAVING MY BAG in the hotel room in Qualiano, I had set off late in the afternoon for Mondragone, where *camorristi* had run a tip for toxic waste and where, heading south along the Appian Way, ancient Romans had turned inland from the sea. About five miles from Qualiano I reached the coast and turned north along the line of another Roman road, the Via Domiziana, named after Domitian, a tough and unpopular emperor keen on gladiatorial contests who met a violent end, his stabbing plotted by a cabal of high-ranking Romans. The senate decreed that his name should be erased from public records but this road, from Naples to Pozzuoli, Cuma and Mondragone still bears it.

As far as I could see, Castel Volturno, a seaside town of about twenty thousand inhabitants half-way to Mondragone, has no redeeming features. It is a town about which good words are few and passing travellers soon see why, the main road a market for sex, pavements and pull-ins the patches where black prostitutes ply their trade. Its run-down buildings now homes for the migrant poor, Castel Volturno may have been pretty some fifty years ago, then one-fifth the size it is today, but any prettiness, if once there was, has gone.

Castel Volturno's main road is no place to stop for tea and I pressed on five miles past large dumps of rubbish into Mondragone, a dreary town with a smart cafe. Driving up the coast I got a sense of this northern part of

Campania, a fertile plain called the Terra di Lavoro, the land of work that stretches flat inland fifteen miles to Caserta where hills begin at the city's back, and runs twenty miles from south to north to halt abruptly at Mount Crestegallo behind Mondragone.

Bounded to the north and east by high land, to the west by the sea and to the south by towns that edge the Neapolitan conurbation, the Terra di Lavoro is where the Camorra discovered waste disposal and where the Casalesi about whom anti-Mafia magistrates had spoken to me are the local power. I returned to my hotel in Qualiano by a different route, driving inland and entering a neighbouring commune, Cancello Arnone, about five miles from the coast. This village would briefly make news a month after I passed through, a murder bloodying a farm in the countryside nearby.

For sixty-nine-year-old Umberto Bidognetti, the dawn that day in early May of 2008, was like any other dawn, the start of a daily routine that tending a herd of buffalo brings, work like any other day. But as Bidognetti was getting ready for his day, killers were preparing his death. From the still of the fields, broken by birdsong and the lowing of the herd, two gunmen suddenly appeared, fired a volley of shots, and delivered a final round to Bidognetti's head to make sure that he was dead, an execution carried out as *mafiosi* do when settling their accounts. Bidognetti's son Domenico had started cooperating with the authorities several months before his father's murder and had described *camorristi* as cowards, clowns and rabbits, insults to which the bosses thought they must respond. While Umberto Bidognetti had had nothing to do with the world of crime, the Bidognetti family is one of four that counts in this part of Campania and its boss, Francesco Bidognetti, had been caught, put on trial, found guilty and faced life in jail for murder. The killing of Umberto would serve as a warning to potential defectors that they should stay silent or their families would be punished.

Domenico would not have been the only problem on Bidognetti's mind when he set off for work on the day that he was murdered. The garbage crisis in Naples had done more than deter tourists from visiting the city and the region. Agriculture had also been badly hit. Shoppers had shunned produce grown in the intensively cultivated smallholdings in the plain behind Vesuvius, around towns like Sarno and Pomigliano. Photographs and film of country roads filled with waste had made people wonder what was in or on the salads, tomatoes and other vegetables grown in surrounding fields. However, farmers in the Terra di Lavoro had suffered more, dairy farmers with buffalo herds hurt most and with them the dairies that turn buffalo milk into mozzarella cheese. Faced with collapsing sales, a crisis that deepened when dioxin was discovered in small quantities in buffalo milk and cheese made from it, farmers and dairies will not soon forget the start to 2008 and what Campania's waste emergency and the Camorra's toxic dumps had done to them.

Worried about the presence of this highly toxic compound in the cheese and a risk to public health, China, Japan, Singapore and South Korea blocked imports of buffalo mozzarella from Italy while America, France and Germany threatened to do the same. And as well as commercial pressure from export markets there was bureaucratic pressure from the European Union in Brussels, which asked the government in Rome to check the farms and dairies involved in making mozzarella. Meanwhile, carabinieri and magistrates had acted, blocking sales from about a hundred farms and dairies in Campania, and checks later showed that about three per cent of milk samples fell short of laid-down standards.

Campania's mozzarella crisis was a bitter example of how a healthy business can quickly sicken. 'You know, buffalo mozzarella was one of the region's few great successes,' said Gennaro Testa, the head of promotion at the consortium whose job is to protect the cheese's name and ensure that those who make it conform to the regulations governing the product. From thirty thousand tonnes in 2000, the production of buffalo mozzarella increased by more than half to reach around fifty thousand tonnes in 2007, of which one-sixth was sold abroad. Some people thought that sales were halved during the opening months of 2008, others said that the impact of the scandal was less and that sales had fallen by only a quarter.

Whatever the real figure, many of the two thousand farms with buffalo herds and the one hundred and thirty dairies attached to the consortium were badly hit by the crisis. 'The media exaggerated, blowing up the problem of dioxin out of all proportion. Buffalo don't feed in rubbish tips,' Testa told me. Even so, the consortium faced a massive problem of limiting the damage and restoring the image of what had been the only strong farming and food business in which the region can claim to be unique.

Testa had given me the name of one of the oldest farms, a family concern founded in 1919 called Campania Felix, fortunate or happy Campania, in the countryside near a small town called Grazzanise. I stopped there to talk to Enrico Parente, the owner of the business whose family had begun the buffalo farm and whose dairy now produces around three-quarters of a tonne of mozzarella every day. When the crisis blew up in 2008 the firm was lucky and, although ninety-nine per cent of its production goes abroad, mainly to Britain and America, its sales did not suffer badly, probably because Parente had reacted quickly and had ordered checks immediately the scandal exploded. Being a farm with eight hundred head of buffalo, medium to large on the scale of farms in the area, also helped. Farms with small herds suffered most.

Parente was furious all the same. 'The media behaved irresponsibly, aggressively and criminally, scaring consumers for no reason whatever. I wonder which multinational group was behind this wicked campaign. Reputations are very easy to destroy, but so hard to rebuild.'

'What distinguishes a buffalo mozzarella from mozzarella made with cows' milk?' I asked. He relaxed and his expression softened. 'Its aroma is absolutely special, intense, recalling the concentrated scent of cyclamens and fresh grass. It's important to eat it fresh when it's elastic and gummy – it becomes creamier as it ages.'

'Does the Camorra cause you problems?' I had asked Parente's wife, and she had shaken her head defensively and said that it did not. Yet the farm and its dairy lie near the heart of the Casalesi's territory and driving there from Qualiano I had again passed Cancello Arnone where Umberto Bidognetti would be gunned down on his buffalo farm a few weeks later. The Parentes' dairy is two miles or so from there and about mid-way between it and Grazzanise, where the council was dissolved twice during the 1990s because of mafia infiltration.

About five miles from Grazzanise as the crow flies, and around three times that distance from the centre of Naples, Casal di Principe, capital of the Casalesi clan, is the largest of a cluster of towns and has around twenty thousand inhabitants. Like Grazzanise, it also lost its council twice in the 1990s because of mafia infiltration. And so the story has been repeated in that five-mile strip of Campania in which six towns lie: San Cipriano d'Aversa, council dissolved in 1992; Casapesenna, council dissolved in 1991 and 1996; Villa di Briano, council dissolved in 1992 and 1998; Frignano, council dissolved in 1993; and Casaluce, council dissolved in 2006.

About sixty-five thousand people live in that small part of the Terra di Lavoro under the Camorra's thumb, but the Camorra has controlled all the Terra di Lavoro for many years.

The mayor of Casal di Principe had agreed to meet me at midday in the town hall. I stopped on the outskirts of the town to ask a shopkeeper the way. 'Just carry straight down the Corso Umberto.' And so I did, following the main street, asking again when I saw a *vigile urbano*, town policeman, and learning that I had arrived. Leaving the car outside the Chicco d'Oro cafe I walked into a side street and across a small piazza to Via Alfieri, where the town hall stands.

Cipriano Cristiano is a doctor. He had turned forty-nine a few months before I met him, been in local politics for seven years, first as a town councillor and then as a councillor in Caserta's provincial government from 2002 to 2004, and was elected mayor in 2007, standing in the ranks of Forza Italia, Silvio Berlusconi's party. Cristiano was not there when I reached the town hall but was expected soon. Berlusconi had just won parliamentary elections and had been returned to power that day, so I was not surprised that the mayor was busy.

But the wait was short and the gatekeeper nodded his head when a dark blue Mercedes estate car turned into the town hall's courtyard a few minutes later. I walked over to Cristiano and introduced myself. Genial, round-faced, smoothly shaven, elegantly dressed in a dark blue suit, dark blue shirt, a blue tie with an unobtrusive pattern and well-polished black shoes, he was a match for the suavest Harley Street consultant. He smiled, offered me his hand and led me into the town hall and up to his office. Testa at the mozzarella consortium and Parente at Campania Felix had told me how the garbage crisis was affecting business. Cristiano now added his anger, particularly about the sensational way that the press and television had treated the news, and how they had created the impression that dioxin was an ingredient in every buffalo mozzarella that left Campania's dairies.

Most of the commune is farmland, buffalo and dairies are important for the town's economy and the crisis had shaken people there. 'I don't blame all doctors because one is found to be bad,' said Cristiano. The scandal of mozzarella contaminated with dioxin had done enormous damage, not only to farmers and dairies but to many others also, the service firms and suppliers whose livelihoods depend on how the farms and dairies fare.

However, Casal di Principe is less dependent on buffaloes and their mozzarella than other towns in the Terra di Lavoro. It has a flourishing building industry as well. Franco Roberti, the anti-Mafia magistrate in Naples, had told me how the Casalesi camorra clan is expert in winning and working on public-sector contracts and I had spoken at length with Marco Del Gaudio, an anti-Mafia magistrate to whom Gianni Melillo had introduced me and whom he had described as a *giovane lupo* (young wolf), a sharp anti-Mafia man, keen on hunting down *camorristi* and bringing them to trial. As I would later learn, he was assigned the hard job of investigating the murder of Umberto Bidognetti in Cancello Arnone.

'There is an unusually large number of building firms in Casal di Principe and they enjoy great advantages when bidding for contracts. The Casalesi are the strongest and the best, and they use the same system that Angelo Siino thought up for Cosa Nostra in the 1980s, rigging bids carefully so that the Mafia's own choice of firms wins the contracts,' Del Gaudio told me. The Casalesi had moved into eastern Europe ahead of the crowd, understanding how markets were changing before the competition did. And they had expanded at home, into Emilia Romagna, the region that lies between Tuscany and Lombardy. When Del Gaudio spoke about the Casalesi, he meant the Camorra's clan, not the people from the town.

'Our construction workers are the most skilled in Europe,' Casal di Principe's mayor bragged, adding that the town exports manpower, weekly commuters who work on sites in Tuscany and Emilia Romagna. 'People here are very hard working.'

As Cristiano's office filled with local politicians, councillors and members of the town's executive committee keen to get down to work following Berlusconi's victory, this was not the best time to be talking to the mayor. But he introduced me to them as they crowded in, among them a farmer who complained vociferously about the crisis that was hurting buffalo mozzarella and an impeccably dressed, good-looking, tough-talking woman who grumbled about the difficulties that the town's name creates, reminding me of what Dino Paternostro, the trade union leader in Corleone, had said about the drawbacks of having that as his birthplace on his passport. 'Our young people are penalised when they are interviewed for jobs. Casal di Principe says Camorra to outsiders.'

A slim man in early middle age with an angular impassive face sat near me while I asked my questions and his companions spoke. He did not speak but simply eyed me closely.

Cristiano knows what many outsiders think of his town and would like its other, better features to be recognised too. 'Many people here live within the law. There is so much denigration but there are positive as well as negative sides.' Yet the positive sides struggle to make themselves seen. About two and a half years before I met Casal di Principe's mayor, the court in Santa Maria Capua Vetere, a town under the hills near Caserta, had passed sentences on members of the Casalesi clan found guilty of crimes that ranged from mafia association to murder. More than fifty of the one hundred and thirty defendants who were on trial had been born in Casal di Principe, and over thirty were born in San Cipriano d'Aversa, the neighbouring town.

Angry about how the town's mozzarella had suffered at the hands of journalists, the mayor was irritated by the picture of Casal di Principe that a recent book had painted. Published in 2006, Roberto Saviano's *Gomorra* describes the awful brutality of the *camorristi* who consider the town, its neighbours, the Terra di Lavoro and much more to be their turf, and the degradation and the fear that their dominance brings. 'The book dealt a sharp shock to the area,' he remarked.

'Saviano's book certainly made people aware of the problem of the Camorra and anybody who encourages the fight against it is welcome, but it is biased. It doesn't show the town's good points.' The mayor was annoyed that the book gave the idea that all Casalesi are *camorristi*. 'We need a more vigilant state and less fiction,' Cristiano complained.

Spartacus is a name that stirs the imagination and it is the name given to the trial of the Casalesi clan. Thinking up names for trials, arrest warrants and court orders allows flights of fantasy that investigating crimes and prosecuting criminals does not. The warrant for the arrest of forty-five people in Caltanissetta province signed by judge Giovanbattista Tona in November 2005, three hundred and fifty-nine pages long, is called Odessa. A warrant issued in Reggio Calabria for the arrest of a group of thirty-five people in Locri was given the name Primavera. Anaconda, Olimpia, Armonia and Para Rei are others in my files.

I wondered about the connection between Spartacus, Casal di Principe and the Casalesi clan and asked Marco Del Gaudio, but he could not add to what I already knew. The leader of the uprising of slaves against the Romans in 73BC had local links. Perhaps the area's best-known historical figure, Spartacus was trained in a gladiators' school in Capua, a few miles from the court where the Casalesi stood trial, and it was from there he escaped to build an army of former slaves, tens of thousands who took on the Roman legions. Defeated two years later, thousands of Spartacus' followers were crucified along the Appian Way and their bodies left for years, gruesome reminders of Roman ruthlessness.

This was the story of Spartacus that Stanley Kubrick turned into a film with Kirk Douglas and Laurence Olivier as its stars, more than three hours of epic Hollywood. Although it lacked stars, with a cast of hundreds that played a long-running courtroom drama the Spartacus trial in Santa Maria Capua Vetere was also epic. The first hearing before a presiding judge, Catello Marano, supported by a second magistrate, Raffaello Magi, and six *giudici popolari*, members of a jury, was on 1 July 1998. More than seven years later, on 15 September 2005, Marano read out the verdicts and nine months would pass before well over three thousand pages of judgement would be written and lodged. Fifty hearings, from February to July 2004, were needed for the prosecution to wind up its case, followed by a further hundred and eight hearings for defending lawyers who completed their cases a year later.

Gladiators, weapons, armies, battles and blood. Such was the ancient world in which Spartacus made his name and the modern world in which the Casalesi made theirs is similar. The Casalesi had, for years, escaped the spotlight of attention. No longer.

The judgement needed more than fifty pages merely to list the events about which evidence was heard, events that happened far back in time. A murder committed in April 1982 headed the criminal catalogue, and more than twenty-three years would pass before that September day in 2005 when the court retired to consider its verdict, gazing into a past in which the most recent crimes had been committed ten years before. People grow old and die over such a span, young people lose their youth. And so they did during the trial, ten of the accused dying before the sentences were announced. Sixty-five years old when the trial began, Nicola Alfiero was seventy-two when it ended, the oldest defendant, convicted for mafia association and sentenced to five years in prison. Just twenty-five at the trial's opening, Salvatore Venosa, the youngest accused, already in prison for other matters, had turned thirty-two by its end when he also was found guilty of mafia association.

'The story of the trial,' wrote the magistrate Raffaello Magi in the judgement, 'could be told as the story of a ready-mix concrete works in the commune of Santa Maria La Fossa, established in the distant year of 1983 and transferred, in connection with the crimes investigated here, from Antonio Bardellino to Carmine Schiavone, though not without resistance and recrimination from others who also considered themselves to be the owners.' Santa Maria La Fossa, whose council was dissolved in 1992 and again in 1996, is a small town of about five thousand that adjoins Grazzanise, territory of the Casalesi clan like all the towns around there.

Alternatively, suggested Magi, the story could begin with the decision on 27 May 1988 of a leading camorra figure called Luigi Basile to turn himself in at a Carabinieri station in Naples. Armed with a pistol whose serial number had been erased, his surrender to the authorities was a sign that something dramatic had happened or was about to happen. A respected figure in criminal circles, Basile was a close associate of Bardellino, the undisputed boss of the Terra di Lavoro, a *camorrista* tied to Cosa Nostra and one of the Nuova Famiglia that had defeated Raffaele Cutolo's Nuova Camorra Organizzata. Bardellino, who had been behind a killing in Castel Volturno in January that year, had been murdered in Brazil two days before Basile's surprise arrival at the Carabinieri station, and a nephew of Bardellino was murdered in Casal di Principe on the day after his uncle died.

Neither the body of Bardellino nor that of his nephew would ever be found, but their deaths set off a ferocious war for control of the area that would leave many dead. There was a double murder in San Cipriano d'Aversa on 10 July and another murder there two days later. Pasquale Piccolo was killed on 21 July, on the Via Flacca coastal road between Gaeta and Sperlonga in the southern part of the Lazio region, south of Rome, and Pasquale Santagata in Castel Volturno on the following day. A week before Christmas another member of Bardellino's family died, gunned down with a second victim in a gambling den in Casapesenna, a violent shoot-out in which a large armoury was deployed. From the cartridges that police found at the scene, weapons experts thought that four semi-automatic 12-gauge shotguns and eight pistols and revolvers had been used.

There were five murders in Casal di Principe in April 1989. One was a quadruple killing in the centre, in Via Alfieri, the street that runs beside the town hall. Three of the dead men lived in the town, the fourth was from San Cipriano. All were armed and the oldest was just thirty. The war between the factions that sought to succeed Bardellino brought two more murders that year. And the catalogue of bloodshed continued: nine dead in 1990, seventeen dead in 1991, including five on 15 April in two separate incidents and three in Castel Volturno on 7 July, and eleven dead in 1992.

Two of the incidents in 1992 were double murders. Giuseppe De Falco, whose brother Vincenzo had been shot dead in Casal di Principe in February of the year before, died in one of them. The car in which he was travelling that April was ambushed on the highway between the town and Castel Volturno and his companion, Caterina Mancini, died with him under devastating gunfire from a 12-gauge shotgun, a pistol and two automatic weapons. There had been a short chase along the dual carriageway and the killers made sure that their victims were dead. This was the first occasion that a woman had died in the war for control of the Terra di Lavoro and that in itself contained a message for De Falco's wife to stay silent about everything she knew.

As the Spartacus trial showed, in the evidence of homicides and shootings and police searches, members of the Casalesi clan were heavily armed. At three o'clock in the morning of 5 January 1985 a car carrying four men was stopped in Casal di Principe and found to be carrying twenty-four sticks of dynamite and three pistols. In the years that followed the authorities would find sawn-off 12-gauge shotguns, semi-automatic 7.65 calibre Brownings, Kalashnikovs, Uzis, Smith & Wessons, Heckler & Kochs, automatics, semi-automatics, sub-machine guns, pump-action shotguns and the munitions to go with them. Buying arms was not a problem. In August 1990 an American servicewoman in Naples had sold Francesco Schiavone three .357 Magnum pistols. Combatants in the Terra di Lavoro could call on every type of murderous weapon and various sources of supply. And, as with *mafiosi* everywhere, the large armouries and military action served to protect and expand their economic interests.

Eventually a new leader emerged from the violence around Casal di Principe, Francesco Schiavone known as Sandokan. Yet while the Casalesi threatened, wounded and killed each other, the businesses from which they made their money continued much as usual, with rich pickings from the large-scale public works of the 1980s and 1990s.

Bardellino had made sure that a good part of the money that went to the region after the 1980 earthquake southeast of Naples went to his clan. Then, in October 1985, the chairman of the Campania regional government approved the construction of the highway that runs from the Rome-to-Naples autostrada, from a junction between Naples and Caserta, past Casal di Principe and Villa Literno to join the road along the coast. The cost was initially put at seventy billion lire, but as work progressed so the cost escalated, soaring to two hundred and forty billion lire by the time the road was finished in 1990, a huge sum even today.

Bardellino was still alive when an even bigger project began, the rebuilding of a thirty-mile drainage channel called the Regi Lagni from near Caserta across the plain to the coast about four miles south of Castel Volturno. Work began in June 1987, was completed in 1992 at a cost of four hundred and eighty billion lire and was another bonanza for the Casalesi clan, whose own construction companies and ready-mix concrete firms provided them with a direct flow of income while they made more money by extorting other firms involved. Squeezing the firms that built a prison at Santa Maria Capua Vetere in the early 1990s also helped swell the wealth of the Casalesi clan.

And the opportunities for enrichment did not stop. Indeed, public spending on construction in the Terra di Lavoro seemed planned with the clan in mind. No sooner did one major project come to end than another began. Early in 1999 I went to two construction sites in the province of Caserta to talk to engineers who were managing the building of the high-speed railway line from Rome to Naples on which work had started in 1995. The first train should have run in April of the year that I visited the sites but there had been lengthy delays and the line would eventually open six years late. Red tape had contributed to the slippage but so had the Camorra, said the senior engineer with whom I spoke. Reading the judgement of the Spartacus trial, and about the intimidation that the Casalesi had brought to bear to win sub-contracts for their firms and jobs for their friends, I recalled that wet and muddy day I had spent unknowingly in the territory of the clan asking about the high-speed railway line.

'The Casalesi are experts at creating and exploiting political connections.

The Camorra in the city has more difficulty in influencing politicians than the Casalesi do in the small towns where they operate,' said Marco Del Gaudio. Provincial towns are places where many folk are family, brothers, cousins, great-uncles or family of their spouses, across the street or down the road, and where a person putting up for public office can count on kin and more for votes.

And another big difference concerns drugs. Whereas city clans make money selling drugs through networks of pushers, the Casalesi clan made an iron rule that there would be no pushing of drugs in their town; family pressures perhaps account for this. The figures are eloquent. In fifteen years there were fewer than ten drug-related arrests in Casal di Principe, while in Castel Volturno drugs crime brought well over three thousand arrests during that same period.

'Tell me about yourself. Why did you become a magistrate?' I asked Del Gaudio. A Neapolitan, born in 1966, he had considered an academic career when he finished his degree in law. However, academic life in Italy often entails years of being someone else's bag-carrier, whereas the magistracy offers early responsibility and autonomy. He had investigated the violence of police towards No-Global demonstrators in Naples in the run-up to the G8 meeting in Genoa in July 2001, a very sensitive case.

A slight figure with thinning brown hair and a shy smile, it was difficult to imagine Del Gaudio taking on the Casalesi. He had been a magistrate for eleven years when he transferred to the anti-Mafia team in 2005. He was drawn to the work partly by the sense of urgency that goes with it. 'Every investigation, every trial is a priority.' And with crime seemingly behind many things in Naples and around the city, and the Camorra behind the crime, being a member of the anti-Mafia team takes a magistrate to the heart of the issue.

Thanks to the efforts of investigators and magistrates, the courts had put the heads of two families of the Casalesi clan, the Bidognetti and Schiavone (of whom thirteen with this name were among the accused in the Spartacus trial), into prison and Del Gaudio and a colleague, Antonello Ardituro, to whom he introduced me, headed the search for the other two bosses, Antonio Iovine and Michele Zagaria. The judge in Santa Maria Capua Vetere had sentenced both to life in prison for murder.

'Extremely dangerous, special search programme', are the words above a set of thirty mug-shots on the Most Wanted List issued by the home affairs ministry in Rome. These are the criminals that the authorities most want to see behind bars and among the photographs are those of Antonio Iovine and Michele Zagaria. 'It's an old picture of Iovine and you can see why he's called the *bambinello*,' said Del Gaudio.

Antonio Iovine was born in San Cipriano d'Aversa in 1964 but his photograph, perhaps taken after his arrest following a shoot-out in April 1991, shows what seems to be the nice boy-next-door, soft faced, doe eyed, with a kind of Beatles haircut. He was released from prison at the end of February 1995 and was on the run when the arrest warrants that were precursors to the Spartacus trial were issued in December that year. Like Iovine, Zagaria was also born in San Cipriano, although six years before the *bambinello*. He had been arrested in Casapesenna in September 1988 when found carrying a pistol and had been granted house arrest in March 1989, although he went on the run after seven months. He would be arrested again in April 1991 and released two years later. Rearrested in October 1993, Zagaria was placed under house arrest in October 1995 but released from this the following month and he managed to avoid the net when the Spartacus sweep rounded up the clan one week later.

Del Gaudio believes that they are hiding in the area where they were born and where they have always operated. 'But how have they been able to avoid capture?' I asked, thinking that years of saturation coverage by the police would surely have led to them being caught. One reason this has not happened may be due to the police forces themselves, where some members may be willing to tip off *camorristi* when sweeps are planned. I had learnt of such betrayal in Palermo. In an impermeable society, defended by tight, impenetrable networks, Iovine and Zagaria are safer in Casal di Principe or San Cipriano than anywhere else.

'They were born into a very particular world and learnt its rules when they were young. The towns are strongholds for the clan's families,' said Del Gaudio, who is sure that the two criminals are not only protected by their families but also enjoy high-level cover from people above suspicion. 'Criminals on the run need two things. Contacts with their families and contacts with their businesses, and for these they need to hide near home. When Iovine and Zagaria are caught they will be caught near home.' Provenzano's capture in Sicily, near the town where he was born, was evidence for this.

'You can feel the 'Ndrangheta's presence, touch it with your hands,' Emilio Sirianni, a Calabrian magistrate, had told me when describing the area south of Locri. 'It's in the air you breathe,' said Del Gaudio about the Camorra's pervasive presence in the area that the Casalesi consider their own. Carabinieri move with obvious visibility, using members of the force who are known. 'They don't go in unmarked cars. They try to avoid setting off alarms unnecessarily.'

Outsiders are people to be suspected, their questions go unanswered. 'Locals simply clam up,' Del Gaudio warned me before I went there. On my return to Rome I saw a television documentary about Casal di Principe and its camorra clan and wondered, for a while, how the journalists and cameramen had been able to move so freely, meet locals and ask their questions. Then, as the camera swung round, a police car and two policemen came into view, only a few steps away.

After talking with the mayor I walked in the centre for a while, past the Carabinieri station and then back to the car. I had surely been noticed and my progress followed, but I did not feel the oppressiveness I had felt in the outskirts of Naples, in Secondigliano and Scampia. Turning left into Via Veticale, past the Carabinieri station again and past houses with high walls and video cameras that monitor what is happening and who is around, I drove to the Asse di Supporto, as the highway between Caserta and the coast is known, and headed inland. From the road above the plain the Terra di Lavoro spread away to the left, the flat land dotted occasionally by farm buildings, often the sheds where buffalo are kept.

Soon a slip-road offered an exit to Frignano. There, on 28 April 1991, Antonio Iovine had waited with four other killers to ambush Sebastiano Caterino and his nephew Vincenzo Maisto who were in a car that had just turned off the autostrada at Caserta. The hit squad had been told that Caterino and Maisto had left Modena in the north of Italy and had placed a lookout at the autostrada's exit, but the would-be victims changed their route and the murderers' plan was foiled. However, there was shooting at that junction at Frignano, between carabinieri and the killers, that left Iovine wounded and in custody. The carabinieri found that the *camorristi* were carrying two 12-gauge shotguns, an Uzi sub-machine gun, two pistols and a .38 Special revolver.

One of Caterino's group would be murdered in Frignano in August that year and an opponent of Caterino would die in a nearby town later that same day. Arrested in October 1991, Caterino remained in prison for almost three years but by then his nephew had been killed, gunned down in San Cipriano, with another victim of the violence dead beside him. Caterino would stand accused of association with the Mafia in the Spartacus trial but would not live to see the trial end. Not yet forty-eight years old, Caterino was murdered in Santa Maria Capua Vetere in October 2003, more than twelve years after he brushed close to death on the highway near Frignano.

I drove by the spot where the ambush failed, past a large parking area beyond which a dirty white concrete wall with solid green gates blocked the view of what lay behind. But in front of it a refuse mountain of tyres, mattresses, large plastic drums and household waste was visible to all who passed. Further down, an elderly man was sweeping the road outside his home, trying to gather together the plastic bags, sheets of paper and cardboard and cans and other rubbish the wind had blown that way. And he was still sweeping when I passed there again, after losing myself in the town.

Closed and claustrophobic, the grid of narrow streets was confusing, streets wide enough for one car only, many one-way with arrows pointing the direction in which I had to go. It is a town of low buildings, grey homes outwardly and drably alike, and no signs where streets cross to help the lost. Unknowing, I had passed from Frignano into Villa di Briano, then on joining a wide road I found myself in Casal di Principe, and turned again into Via Veticale, passing the Carabinieri station once more. I remembered Del Gaudio's words. 'It's impossible to arrive there and not be noticed.'

Caserta, the provincial capital, was my next stop but before that I would spend the last evening of my journey through the South in an anonymous hotel near the autostrada, a place where truckers stop to eat and sleep.

Italy's answer to Versailles, a grand statement of eighteenth-century architecture, the Reggia royal palace in Caserta was designed by Luigi Vanvitelli and built between 1752 and 1774. I had been there before, many years ago, and wanted to visit it again. Approaching along the broad carriageway from Naples, called the Viale Carlo III after the Bourbon king who had put the palace's work in hand, it looms enormous in the distance. But as I got closer I saw that railway lines run across the road, blocking the way to the vast piazza which the palace overlooks, and that a railway station takes one corner. I had forgotten this oddity of Caserta, this strange choice of where to lay tracks and build a station.

More than two hundred and fifty yards wide and two hundred yards deep, the Reggia, with its twelve hundred rooms and vast gardens to the rear, is a magnificent building. I arrived when an exhibition of works by Jacob Philipp Hackert, a painter from Prenzlau in Brandenburg, had just ended. Hackert had been appointed court painter in 1786 and would paint a series of works depicting the ports of the Bourbon kingdom that are part of the Reggia's permanent collection.

The collection has paintings of hunting scenes and military manoeuvres by Hackert but it was the ports, painted between 1787 and 1793, that caught my attention. Hackert had travelled in Puglia in 1788 and in Calabria and Sicily in 1790. I paused in front of each as I walked through the rooms of the palace where they are hung, paintings of some of the places that I had visited on my way north: Palermo, Messina, Reggio Calabria, Pizzo, Taranto, Otranto, Brindisi and Naples, with ships and boats and jetties where people were walking, talking and doing business.

Gaetano Treppiccione is a criminal lawyer whose chambers are in Capua and whose work takes him mainly to the court in Santa Maria Capua Vetere, about five miles west of Caserta. He had sat across the table from me at dinner in Capua one evening towards the end of 2005 and I had been interested in what he said then about crime in the area. So I telephoned him and we arranged to meet outside Caserta's railway station and from there went to a nearby cafe where he told me more.

'There are good people in Casal di Principe but they are under great pressure to conform to what the Camorra wants. And local politics are not completely free.' One of the roots of the problem of organised crime is a generalised disregard for rules and the tolerance of the authorities towards this. 'People don't obey the law and the police don't enforce it. Yet repression can be successful only if those who break the law are a small part of society,' was Treppiccione's depressing assessment. It is in a social framework in which people feel they belong only to their blood family, and have no duty to a wider community, that the Mafia and clans like the Casalesi prosper.

As I had learnt from Michele Gravano, the trade union leader in Naples, there is some industry in Marcianise, just south of Caserta, but not much, and agriculture continues to be important for the economy in the province. 'There are strong ties to the land and its ownership carries prestige,' Treppiccione explained.

I asked how the Camorra got involved. 'Many dairies belong to the Camorra and others yield to extortion and pay the *pizzo*,' he replied. The situation is better in towns where businessmen and tradesmen, in shops and offices and workshops that are often near each other, can join together and say no when *camorristi* call. And when I spoke with Treppiccione, some people in Santa Maria Capua Vetere were doing just that and forming an anti-racket group. But the reality is far different in the countryside, where isolation makes fighting back much harder and it is easier to pay the clan or accept the men it chooses as watchmen and herdsmen.

Avvocato Aldo Scalzone had been murdered in San Cipriano d'Aversa in October 1991. There was evidence in the Spartacus trial that he had been close to Vincenzo De Falco, murdered earlier that year, and I wondered if being a criminal lawyer might carry risks. 'If lawyers behave professionally they shouldn't be in danger. Lawyers put themselves at risk when they share certain interests with their criminal clients and are expected to get results, when they think that certain methods will produce those results and they fail to do so. That's when clients ask them to explain why cases have been lost.'

In forty years of practice, Treppiccione's path would almost certainly have crossed that of Francesco Curcio, the magistrate in Naples who was surprised that I had decided to visit Scampia. Curcio's first post was in the court in Santa Maria Capua Vetere, where he worked from 1989 until 1995 and where he was one of the team involved in the Spartacus case. It was a part of the country dense with criminal activity and yet for years the authorities had done little. A lack of resources contributed to their inaction. 'There were only six investigating magistrates in the court at the end of the 1980s. It was a golden period for the Camorra. Now there are twenty-five magistrates,' Curcio told me.

And it was a golden period for public works in the Terra di Lavoro, when the firms that did the work were owned by *camorristi*, or their brothers or their cousins, and when, even if large northern Italian companies won the contracts, work went to local firms. 'The high-speed train line is nearing completion in this area and the seemingly inexhaustible flow of money from public works is coming to an end, so the Casalesi have turned to other businesses,' said Curcio. The Casalesi adapt to change and have dug themselves deeply into the economy.

Into extortion, definitely. And construction, certainly, and ballast, concrete, plant hire and earthmoving, and the tertiary sector, waste management, hotels and catering, and buffalo farming and dairies, and food processing on an industrial scale. 'They cornered the market in whey, collecting it from dairies throughout Campania and selling it to companies in France that made butter for the food industry. They were generating revenues of three hundred billion lire a year in the late 1990s.' Even so, Curcio added, the Casalesi are not always as sharp as they think they are. 'They have a real passion for owning land and buffalo farms, which is rather stupid because these are assets that we can easily seize.'

A member of the anti-Mafia team in Naples, Curcio now spends a large amount of time in Rome helping to deal with the Camorra's expansion into Lazio, the region of which Rome is the capital. 'The danger has been underestimated in the lower part of Lazio, the southern provinces of Latina, along the coast, and Frosinone that are far from Rome and far from Naples and tend to be forgotten,' he said. 'The cultural climate in lower Lazio is similar to that in Campania in which there is a weakness that allows criminals to infiltrate. Businessmen are willing to be complicit. The Casalesi have made alliances in lower Lazio, made investments and bought land. There is no shooting but the economy is at risk.'

And Lazio and Rome were where I headed now, following the Via Appia for a while and then the Via Casilina, another consular road that radiated from ancient Rome. Just north of Capua I stopped at the Due Pine dairy in Pastorano, where Gennaro Testa of the buffalo mozzarella consortium had arranged for me to pick up some freshly made cheese, a taste of Campania at its best. And from there I made a small diversion towards Teano, but not to visit. A few miles beyond the town, along a country road, over the autostrada and around a bend, I slowed, pulled to the side and stopped at the reason for this unusual choice of route.

One evening, some time before I set out on my journey north from Sicily, I had sat on the terrace of the family home of Antonio Ingroia, a magistrate friend in Palermo. And from the terrace I had looked across a valley, over clumps of prickly pears, at a monument on a hilltop some way off. There, on that hill near Calatifimi in southwest Sicily, on 15 May 1860, Giuseppe Garibaldi, who had landed with a thousand men at Marsala four days before, won his first battle against Bourbon troops and began the march that would end with Italy once again united. At the roadside near Teano stands another monument, much smaller, easy to miss, poorly tended behind its iron railings. There, deep in the countryside in the north of Campania, on 26 October 1860, Garibaldi and his men met Victor Emmanuel, the king from Piedmont whose army had been heading south. 'Saluto il Re d'Italia – I salute the King of Italy,' said Garibaldi, launching the South into the unknown, an adventure into which it would carry its wealth of history, art and culture, and its baggage of backwardness, problems and the Mafia.

13

―――――

ROME

Church and State

THE PIEDMONTESE MONARCHY and its troops did not take democracy to the South. Attempts to elect an assembly in Naples to draw up a constitution were blocked, only a small part of the adult population was allowed to vote in a referendum held in October 1860, discussion was limited and uninformed, opponents of the unitary state were dissuaded from making known their views and the ballot was probably rigged. The northern rulers moved rapidly to impose their laws and ways of governing, and the South had been conquered rather than liberated.

Taxes were increased to reduce the public debt with which Piedmont had saddled itself and a tax on the milling of wheat, that was particularly detested, was introduced. The government also raised revenues by appropriating common land and land belonging to religious bodies, and this badly hurt southerners. Landless peasants resented the sale of land that they believed was theirs, and the closure of religious bodies was a double blow as these had provided jobs for their wider communities and played a charitable role in helping the poor.

And the state's appropriation of the property of religious bodies continues to be remembered and still rankles. One Sunday morning Giuseppe Camilleri, an energetic and cultured Sicilian from Naro, took me to Palma di Montechiaro, the town of the Tomasis and seat of 'The Leopard' in Giuseppe Tomasi di Lampedusa's book *Il Gattopardo* and Visconti's film of the same name. He showed me the Benedictine nunnery in whose lobby a rotating hatch allows the enclosed order of nuns to communicate with the world outside, and outsiders to buy the almond biscuits for which the nunnery is famous. 'The prince,' wrote Giuseppe Tomasi di Lampedusa in his novel that caught the period when the Bourbon kingdom died, 'liked the almond cakes which the nuns made up from an ancient recipe.' As we went down the steep, broad curve of pale stone steps outside the nunnery, Camilleri told me sadly about what the confiscation of the assets of religious bodies had meant for people in that far part of Sicily.

Conscription was another hated measure that the Piedmontese took south. The wealthy and well connected escaped the call to arms, while poor young men, on whose labour their families depended, were caught. Many took off and swelled the bands of outlaws hiding in the countryside. The Piedmontese responded to lawlessness with sweeps to capture men dodging military service and with repression, holding villages under siege and shooting suspected brigands. To maintain order, the government kept a large standing army in the South, and when it withdrew troops from Sicily following war with Austria in 1866, an uprising briefly won Palermo for the insurgents.

That there was a southern question in the newly reunified Italy became clear to some northern thinkers and politicians. Ten years after that revolt in Palermo, Leopoldo Franchetti and Sidney Sonnino, two Tuscan intellectuals, went to Sicily to investigate the island's administration and the Mafia. Carabinieri and troops were in evidence everywhere, wrote Franchetti after their journey, but despite shows of force the government made little progress in imposing public order. 'Here government administration has camped in the midst of a society whose rules are based on the presumption that public authority does not exist ... The powers and influences that the law seeks to combat are more effective than the organisation that seeks to enforce the law.'

Treated by the government as an uncivilised land apart, the South's reaction to annexation reinforced that view. Certainly the policy of sending the worst policemen and the worst civil servants there helped neither the government's reputation nor the South's administration. Franchetti thought that Sicily, with its tradition of relying on the Mafia for enforcing rules, needed the best policemen rather than the worst. Some sixteen different prefects, the government's representatives in the provinces, held office in Palermo during the fifteen years following reunification. A change of minister in Rome, or sign of efficiency that would upset local notables, usually led to a prefect's transfer elsewhere. According to Franchetti, instead of facing up to the responsibilities of government, and sacrificing party and other interests, ministers of every colour sought agreements with the powerful locals in Sicily whom they should have sought to destroy.

Once diffident and distrustful of Bourbon authority and the government in Naples, southerners had reason to dislike and distrust the House of Savoy and the government in Rome. How the new rulers governed was an encouragement to law-breaking. And whereas the Bourbons had been paternalistic towards the poorer parts of society and suspicious of the nobility, members of the new parliament left local affairs to local bigwigs. Italy's reunification helped to reshape relationships and alter the balance of power in the South, changes that helped the Mafia consolidate its role as an intermediary between subjects and the state and between workers and their employers.

Progress passed the South by in the closing decades of the nineteenth century and the opening decades of the twentieth. Before the March on Rome that brought the fascists to power in 1922, Benito Mussolini said that he would solve the southern problem. That was an empty boast. Measures like the colonisation of Italy's possessions abroad, the policy of autarchy and agricultural improvement schemes eased conditions, but there was no land reform that might have had an impact in the South. The Mafia comfortably survived the fascist *ventennio* with its corrupt and inefficient government.

The Allies had been in southern Italy for almost two years when fascism eventually fell in April 1945. The role of Cosa Nostra in helping American forces in their push across western Sicily is legendary, and so is the Allies' appointment of *mafiosi* as mayors in numerous Sicilian towns. Unlike northern Italy, the South did not produce a resistance movement to oppose the Nazi–Fascist axis and there was no cleansing or moral renewal when the fighting ceased. Landowners, the middle class and the Mafia, who had formed the ruling order for more than half a century, continued to do so after Mussolini and his movement were beaten, supported by the church and conservative politicians frightened of a communist advance.

The Mezzogiorno's problem, wrote Paolo Sylos Labini, an eminent southern intellectual, was one of civic and cultural development and the South's economic troubles and weakness were essentially a consequence of civic backwardness, which in turn was the result of history. Much needed to be changed in institutions that affected civic development like schools, health services, the justice system and public administration, said Sylos Labini. He thought that the influence of political parties and the bureaucracy, their ability to demand bribes and their power of patronage, needed to be drastically reduced.

Indeed, one reason politicians did not make a priority of changing southern thinking, of cultural advance, of encouraging a sense of civic duty, was that they owed their positions to a modern feudalism. This was the *sottobosco* (undergrowth) of government and power, the patronage that allowed politicians to decide appointments, give jobs and award promotions in a very large number of companies, institutions and organisations, to approve grants or loans, and to decide where factories should be built. The levers of power were in the big public-sector banks, the state holding corporations and their many subsidiaries, and the large state boards. Political barons willingly connived in encouraging a condition of dependency among voters.

The *sottobosco* provided a network of relations within which the Christian Democrat Party built its dominant position in the south. Giulio Andreotti in Sicily, Antonio and Silvio Gava in Naples, Aldo Moro in Puglia and Emilio Colombo in Basilicata were among the party's notables who, between 1960 and 1990, were enormously powerful in their political strongholds and influential in Rome. Although the *sottobosco* has been trimmed back, even now politicians have the corrupting tools of patronage in their hands: the power to arrange allowances for the unentitled, push public works as favours, and fix jobs in local governments, in the bodies and companies they control, and in the private firms to which they contract work.

From the Bourbons to the House of Savoy, fascism, the hegemonic Christian Democrats of Italy's post-war republic and the fragmentation that followed *tangentopoli* in 1992, the Mezzogiorno has experienced a century and a half of upheaval in its governing class. Yet even as the political and institutional framework in southern Italy changed radically, so backwardness, maladministration, the Mafia and the Roman Catholic church have remained among the constants.

'I'm convinced that the church's teaching is not enough to cure the South of its terrible sickness – the sickness with which Cosa Nostra, the 'Ndrangheta, the Camorra and the Sacra Corona Unita infect the South. It's an old sickness with no cure, or so it seems. The sickness continues despite the church's work and the work of schools and institutions,' Giovanni Marra, the elderly archbishop of Messina, told me pessimistically, without passion, almost in resignation, when I sat before him one evening trying to learn how the church tackles that particular southern problem.

People must be taught to obey the law. 'We have a role in this, teaching God's law above all, but man's as well, the law that regulates society. Alas, our work can only have a small effect because the society in which people live and the families in which children grow up are the main influences. Parish priests teach that laws should be obeyed, even in the smallest matters, but respect for the law is simply not found in daily life. The man in the street doesn't think laws are important.' And as the visitor to southern Italy, or to Rome or cities and towns in northern Italy, quickly sees, disregarding rules seems a national trait.

Indeed, Italy itself is a pathological rule-breaker. Figures from the European Court of Justice show that the Bel Paese is the European Union's most delinquent member. In 2007 the court issued twenty-three judgements against Italy for failure to fulfil its obligations. The next worst offender had committed thirteen infringements, while Britain was guilty of just two. The court would later rule that a tax amnesty enacted in 2002, covering value added tax that should have been part of the EU's revenues, broke EU law. And in the spring of 2008, in a blatant breach of European rules, Alitalia, the bankrupt national airline, was kept flying with illegal state aid. Although Italy is a founder member of the Community, its governments have little compunction about cheating their European partners.

Several people with whom I spoke as I travelled through the South said that a policy of zero tolerance was needed on minor offences and that a start must be made in enforcing laws. I wondered about this when I walked around Naples, about where and how zero tolerance might begin in a city where breaking rules seems as normal as keeping to them. Every few steps are marked by one illegality or another: pedestrian crossings blocked by cars; pedestrian areas seized by shopkeepers; parking on corners, at bus stops, on pavements and two abreast; buildings altered without permits;

traffic lights ignored; and contraband and pirated goods sold widely and openly on the streets.

'Copying CDs or computer programs or video games just isn't seen as crime; neither is selling contraband cigarettes or fake fashion items,' Marco Rossi-Doria had told me as we walked through the narrow streets of the Quartieri Spagnoli. 'And those who do it think they are doing honest work.'

'Repression is needed but, like teaching, alone it's not enough. Society has to change, to offer youngsters regular and legal work. And if they don't find jobs, some will take the wrong path whatever they've been taught. To deal with the Mafia, the South needs the teaching of schools and the church, and it needs the police and the courts, the institutions for fighting crime, but it also needs a healthy economy,' Archbishop Marra emphasised. But how can business be attracted to where rule breaking seems the rule?

'Repent! God's judgement will come some day!' were the words that Pope John Paul II addressed to the Mafia when he held an open-air Mass in the Valley of the Temples in Agrigento in May 1993. 'In the wake of so much suffering, you have the right to live in peace. Those who are guilty of disturbing this peace have many human victims on their conscience. They must understand that killing innocent human beings cannot be allowed,' the pope told the faithful gathered there. Less than three weeks after he delivered this message, Cosa Nostra planted a bomb in Florence that killed five people and two months later its bombs badly damaged San Giovanni in Laterano, the cathedral of Rome, and another of the capital's churches.

Then, on 15 September 1993, a killer shot Padre Pino Puglisi, the parish priest of Brancaccio, the eastern suburb of Palermo where I had gone to meet his successor. The day of his death was Padre Puglisi's fifty-fifth birthday and two weeks later he would have celebrated three years in the difficult parish where he was born and where he had tried to bring hope to the young people, for most of whom the future offered little. When the two-man hit team stopped him near his home he had smiled and said, 'I was expecting this.' Less than six months later, early one morning in March 1994, Don Giuseppe Diana, the parish priest of Casal di Principe, would be gunned down as he was preparing to say Mass.

'The attacks on the churches in Rome and the murder of Padre Puglisi were Cosa Nostra's reply to the pope's speech in Agrigento,' Alessandra

Dino, a professor of sociology at Palermo university, told me. She described the church's position on the Mafia as contradictory and ambiguous, and said that churchmen were too often more interested in saving sinners' souls than in caring for the sinners' victims. 'By ignoring the gravity of crimes, they show an inexplicable indulgence bordering on complicity. Priests queue up to visit Provenzano.'

And in giving sinners the chance of salvation and release from blame without the need for earthly judgement, she noted, the church effectively offers itself as an alternative to the state. Moreover, the contempt some churchmen express for *mafiosi* who cooperate with the authorities does not help the fight against organised crime. 'They speak of *pentiti* as traitors, point to Judas and suggest that betrayal is a crime like murder.'

The church could have done much more when its teaching was closely followed by most Italians, thirty, forty or fifty years ago before television took a hold and before Italy had drifted towards the secular society that it is today. It could probably still do more, but as I travelled through the South bishops and priests told me they do not ignore or minimise the Mafia's evil hold and that many members of the church actively work to break that grip. 'I don't have to absolve a person who confesses. If a *mafioso* says in the confessional that he repents, then he must publicly admit his crimes and accept punishment for them,' Archbishop Marra told me.

Even so, an event early in 2004 seems emblematic of the church's failure to give a moral lead. In celebration of Giulio Andreotti's eighty-fifth birthday on 14 January that year, the Pontificia Università Lateranense awarded him an *honoris causa* degree in civil and canon law. The entire Roman Curia and the diplomatic corps in Rome were invited to the ceremony which was televised worldwide. It was a major event for the university, which dates from the time of Pope Clement XIV in the eighteenth century, and the pope had personally approved the award to Andreotti, a person 'always inspired by Christian values'.

Yet in July 2003 the appeal court in Palermo had lodged a judgement that raised questions about his values. The judgement acquitted the veteran politician on a charge of complicity with the Mafia, a crime that entered the criminal code in 1982, but upheld the prosecution's case that the former prime minister had been engaged in criminal association until the spring of 1980, although the statute of limitations had become effective for that crime. 'The authentic, stable and friendly openness towards *mafiosi* did not continue beyond the spring of 1980,' said the court. Andreotti's faction of his party in Sicily had been backed by important mafia figures and Andreotti himself had been grateful for electoral support from *mafiosi*.

The court recognised that the final adminstrations headed by Andreotti had promoted measures against the Mafia and thought that this showed 'a kind of intention to make up for past errors'. Yet what had gone before was damning. The court found that 'Senator Andreotti knew full well that his Sicilian associates had friendly relations with some mafia bosses; he in turn cultivated friendly relations with those bosses; he showed willingness to be at their disposal that was not simply a pretence, though it was not necessarily followed by concrete, consistent helpful actions; he asked them for favours; he met them; he interacted with them; he suggested to them how they should deal with the delicate Mattarella question, but without success in getting his suggestions followed; he induced them to trust him and to speak to him about extremely grave facts (like the assassination of President Mattarella) in the certain knowledge that they ran no risk of being reported; he failed to report them, in particular with regard to the murder of President Mattarella, even though he would have been able to provide very useful evidence.'

What was the Vatican's message in awarding an *honoris causa* degree in canon and civil law to such a man who had been involved in a criminal association and been friendly with *mafiosi*? Dino described the church as ambiguous, a word that also fits Andreotti, sometimes called the *divo* (god or star) or *Zio Giulio* (Uncle Julius) by *mafiosi*, and who acquired the label *Belzebù* in the decades that he manoeuvred and manipulated silently and slipperily in the murky corridors of Italian power. 'Power wears out those who lack it,' he once said. In many decades in politics, power was something that the devout and churchgoing Andreotti rarely lacked.

'Powerful people are often ambiguous,' Francesco Rosi, the eminent film director, told me. Born in Naples in 1922, Rosi has worked often in the South. *La Sfida* (The Challenge), made in 1958, his first film as a solo director and the first to be made about the Camorra, was triggered by the murder in Naples in 1955 of Pasquale Simonetti and his widow's revenge. Rosi followed *La Sfida* with a series of groundbreaking films about the South: *I Magliari* (The Weavers) in 1959, *Salvatore Giuliano* in 1961 and

Le Mani sulla Città (Hands over the City) in 1963, as well as later works like *Il Caso Mattei* (The Mattei Affair, 1971), much of which was filmed in Sicily, *Lucky Luciano* (1973) and *Cristo si è Fermato a Eboli* (Christ Stopped at Eboli, 1979).

'These films show Italy realistically, allowing people who didn't live then to see the problems, the conditions and the ways of life of those who did. *La Sfida* is a film about the camorra system from within. And it's a film about Naples, with all its contradictions and characteristics, from its cruelty and ferocity to its kindness and sentimentality. I tried to show the city as it was, without the picturesque and folklore,' Rosi explained. Wearing brown corduroy trousers, a blue cardigan and open-necked shirt, Rosi relaxed in one of those comfortable lounge chairs that looked modern when he was making his first films. Beyond the book-laden table in the middle of the room I could see a terrace with small citrus trees and views across the cupolas of the churches in Rome's historic centre, a world away from the grit and poverty of Naples.

Rosi told me how he conceived and made that first film, how he learnt about the market for tomatoes and the difficulties of the smallholders who grew them, and about how the Camorra exploited the smallholders and how the smallholders tried to resist that exploitation but always had to submit. The film's plot revolves around an ambitious young *camorrista* who challenges the boss. 'At the end he is killed. And in a certain sense this is the logic of the Camorra, that its rules must be respected.'

La Sfida was made on location, as were Rosi's other films about the South. 'Did you have difficulties with the Mafia?' I asked, thinking of how the Mafia controls its turf. He told me that he had not, that he had been able to move freely, without worry, and that he had never faced obstruction or been put under pressure. 'I've tried in all my films to provide a testimony to the events that I portrayed, using non-professional actors who actually experienced those events. In *Salvatore Giuliano*, I used people who were at that ghastly massacre at Portella della Ginestra in 1947. And I've used the places where events happened as locations, so I filmed *Cristo si è Fermato a Eboli* in Aliano, in the very house where Carlo Levi lived while he was there. This approach to cinema is realistic and provides an emotional charge,' said Rosi. But he has always rejected the use of gratuitous violence for effect, preferring reason to what he describes as 'the perverse fascination of violence'.

Noting that people were much more submissive in the past, he pointed to recent public demonstrations against the Mafia in Sicily, Calabria and Campania as signs of hope for the future. Rosi thinks that the fight may eventually be won. 'We must be optimistic, and we must act optimistically even if our thoughts are pessimistic.'

Corrado Stajano, a writer, holds a darker view. Like Rosi's films, a good part of his work also looks at the South and at the Mafia. 'The lack of progress is a huge disappointment. At one time it seemed that the Mafia could be beaten and that people wanted it beaten. Then the desire for change ebbed, outrage softened and the enemy became the magistrates, not the Mafia.' Stajano is half Sicilian, so perhaps his bleak assessment is also a matter of regional character, I thought, remembering Marco Rossi-Doria's words as we walked around the Quartieri Spagnoli in Naples, about the seriousness of Sicilians and the Neapolitan lack of it.

Un Eroe Borghese (A Middle-Class Hero), Stajano's fine but desolate account of the work and murder in July 1979 of Giorgio Ambrosoli, the state-appointed liquidator of the financial empire of Michele Sindona, tells how Ambrosoli threatened the interests of the powerful and paid with his life. Ambrosoli's murder in Milan was the betrayal of a good man by Italian politicians and a corrupt and cynical class of bankers and businessmen, but it was perhaps the inevitable outcome of his unequal struggle against a mafia banker with influential friends in Rome and a Mafia closely tied to finance far from Sicily.

But Stajano had been writing about the South for many years before the publication of Un Eroe Borghese in 1991, at first about those mysteries, those strangenesses of Sicily that intrigue outsiders, 'about princes and dukes and the shadow of The Leopard'. Then in the mid 1970s he wrote Africo, a book about the 'Ndrangheta in a town in southern Calabria, on the Ionian coast not far from San Luca. 'I began writing obsessively about the Mafia, travelling often to Palermo from the late 1970s. It was then Falcone told me that some of his colleagues said that the Mafia didn't exist,' Stajano remembered, while he prepared coffee in the kitchen of his apartment in the centre of Milan.

He was in Palermo for much of the bloody summer of 1982 that began with the killing of Pio La Torre, the leader of the Communist Party, and climaxed with the murder of the prefect Carlo Alberto dalla Chiesa in

September. And his journeys south continued through the 1980s, when he got to know the other magistrates who formed the anti-Mafia team; Antonino Caponnetto, Paolo Borsellino, Giuseppe Di Lello and Leonardo Guarnotta. 'I was there for those terribly distressing funerals in 1992 but have been back little since then. You need to be careful in Palermo, about the person on your right, and the one on your left.' Stajano wrote about the suspicions, concerns and anguish that events in Sicily had caused him in *Palermo Felicissima* (Most Fortunate Palermo). His mother was from Cremona on the River Po but his father was from Noto in Sicily's south-eastern corner and he had spent his summers there in the 1930s. 'I had heard the word Mafia as a boy and instinctively it scared me, conjuring up a web of threat and horror.'

He would get close to mafia matters again in the mid-1990s when, as a senator, he served on parliament's anti-Mafia commission. He was able, during one of its hearings, to take Silvio Berlusconi, then prime minister, to task for minimising the presence of the Mafia and for complaining how films about the Mafia showed Italy in bad light. 'It's the Mafia, Prime Minister, that harms the image of Italian governments abroad. The Mafia is the enemy, not films about the Mafia,' Stajano rebuked Berlusconi. And from his seat in the senate Stajano watched with a sense of shame as fellow senators, from right to left of the political spectrum, would approach Giulio Andreotti, senator for life, to shake his hand and express esteem. 'It was disgraceful. Such deference to a man who had been a friend of *mafiosi*!'

That several ugly facts from Andreotti's past were brought into the open was due to the determination of Gian Carlo Caselli, the chief prosecutor in Palermo from the beginning of 1993 for almost seven years, and of his team of magistrates. Because of Andreotti's position, the *mafiosi* with whom he was friendly considered themselves 'protected at the highest level of legal power', said the court. It is hardly surprising that the court found that Andreotti had helped to strengthen Cosa Nostra. Yet, in a shocking media campaign of disinformation, distortion and downright lies, the supreme court's judgement in October 2004 that he had been guilty of criminal association was widely reported as the politician's definitive acquittal and innocence.

When Gian Carlo Caselli spoke to me in Palermo in the autumn of 1998, it was the first time I had met a member of the anti-Mafia service and, although we had spoken and met in the years between, I wanted to talk with him again after finishing my journey through the South and had flown to Turin to do so. Before going to the court I walked through the city that was once Piedmont's capital and the seat of the House of Savoy, passing the red-brick Palazzo Carignano where Italy's first parliament had met in 1861, the Cambio restaurant frequented by Cavour across the square. And as I looked at the well-preserved palaces and churches and the trim squares, and thought of the money that was spent to keep the city smart, Naples and Palermo came to mind, poor and run-down places, once the capitals of the southern kingdom.

I took the lift to the seventh floor of the city's new court that I had visited five years before when Caselli had just been appointed prosecutor-general. The years had passed but had left no trace of their passing upon him, his energy and enthusiasm were undimmed, his concern for justice undiminished. I asked him about the strange way in which the judgement in the Andreotti case had been reported. 'Evidently the fact that the supreme court found proven that Italy's most important post-war politician, seven times prime minister, colluded with the Mafia until 1980 does not interest people.'

Caselli was not surprised that the speaker of the senate, a member of Berlusconi's party who held Italy's second highest office of state, had congratulated Andreotti on the end of 'a long Calvary'. The speaker of the lower house, Italy's third highest office of state, had declared his delight, 'as a friend, a Christian Democrat and speaker of the lower house', adding that what Andreotti had been subjected to had been 'absolutely improper and had amounted, at times, to persecution'.

'There's a tendency to deny the truth. The fact is that the truth and a certain sector of politics are incompatible and this sector of politics tends always to acquit itself, even when court judgements confirm the gravest facts. Perhaps they don't carry the guilt of crime but they ought to trigger heavy political and moral penalties. Instead the moral question has vanished and prosecutors are the villains,' said Caselli. Indeed, prosecutors on mafia cases involving politicians have often been viciously attacked, called assassins, terrorists, perverts, liars, criminals, torturers and other terms of abuse.

Caselli himself was punished for exposing the awkward truth about politicians and their relations with the Mafia. Arguably no magistrate was better equipped to head the national anti-Mafia agency in 2005 when the post fell vacant, but from desire for revenge and to show other magistrates that investigating politicians was unwise, the Berlusconi government then in office passed a special law that excluded Caselli from the job.

'You know,' Caselli reminded me as we said goodbye, 'the new court is named after Bruno Caccia, a magistrate that the 'Ndrangheta murdered here in Piedmont in 1983.' Calabrian, Sicilian or Neapolitan, Italy's Mafias have long spread beyond their southern strongholds, into places where they do not seem a threat.

Azienda Agricola Suvignano rings less sweetly to the ear than the names of other Tuscan villas. It is not the Star of Chianti, The Granary or The Little Fountain, simply Suvignano Farm, a collection of buildings set in an enormous spread of about two thousand acres at Monteroni d'Arbia in the Crete Senesi, an area with round, greyish clay hills recorded in works by Duccio and Lorenzetti. About ten miles south of Siena, near the small river that Dante wrote of as being tinged red with blood, the Azienda Agricola Suvignano is a recent addition to the list of the region's holiday homes.

In February 1995, when a court in Palermo seized the assets of Vincenzo Piazza, Agricola Suvignano was on the long list of properties, firms, bank accounts and securities portfolios covered by the largest seizure ever ordered. Confiscation followed two and a half years later and was confirmed by the supreme court in March 2007. Born in Palermo seventy-six years earlier, Piazza was more than a *uomo d'onore* (man of honour) a leading member of the Uditore family; he was a *consigliere* (counsellor) because of his connections with the world outside Cosa Nostra and because he was one of his family's wisest members. Piazza had laundered money from businesses like drugs trafficking and extortion, 'supplying the criminal brotherhood with a contribution of vital importance and securing considerable personal benefit for himself'.

The spacious sixteenth-century house at the centre of the Suvignano estate sleeps twenty-two, attracting parties of Americans and Britons who pay around five thousand euros a week in rent, and more to hire cooks for the authentic Tuscan taste that self-catering cannot give. Those foreign visitors may know about the region's history and culture but probably know little of the recent past of the Sienese villa where they are guests.

Its rolling hills splashed by vineyards and olive groves, its skylines marked here and there by lines of cypress and pine, placid Tuscany seems so distant from the world of organised crime, but other mafia properties have been found there and probably more will be discovered. As time passes, however, finding and seizing assets grows harder. In Tuscany and other regions and countries far from the Italian South, by employing the ablest lawyers and accountants to conjure up schemes, and using associates in banks and financial institutions, the Mafia seeks safe hiding places for its wealth. 'Milan and Palermo were tightly linked in the 1970s and 1980s, when huge sums of money from drugs flowed north,' Gioacchino Natoli, a senior magistrate, told me one evening over dinner in the Sicilian capital. Almost certainly some Italian businessmen used mafia money to build their businesses. The Mafia sends funds across borders, into and out of tax havens and soft jurisdictions where few questions are asked, uses fronts and cut-outs, and holds its illicit gains in many types of asset. The trail eventually runs dry, even for the sharpest and most diligent investigators and prosecutors, and those assets are effectively then clean.

With their huge wealth and great power, can Italy's Mafias ever be beaten? Has any Italian government really been committed to winning the battle, had the energy to persevere against the difficulties and found the resources that were needed? Can the battle now be won?

'There was an opportunity to beat the Mafia after the murders on the highway at Capaci and outside the apartment block in Via D'Amelio,' Antonio Ingroia reflected in January 2002. That opportunity had arrived with the surge of public outrage at the murders of Falcone and Borsellino but had been let slip. And despite the arrests of *mafiosi* and the convictions that prosecutors have gained in courts since Ingroia spoke to me that time, victory seems as illusory now, as vain a hope as it was then.

One hot and humid Wednesday early in July 2008, I travelled again to Palermo. On this occasion I went to chair a panel that was presenting a new book, *Il Ritorno del Principe* (The Return of the Prince), a bleak analysis by Roberto Scarpinato, a senior anti-Mafia magistrate and one of the prosecutors of Giulio Andreotti, of the deep roots of corruption and the Mafia. The publisher had booked a room for me at the Jolly hotel on the seafront, the same hotel where Bernardo Provenzano had celebrated his return from France in 2003, although the staff whom I asked did not remember that notorious guest. Late in the afternoon I walked through the

Kalsa district immediately behind the hotel, passing the stone that marks where Giovanni Falcone's birthplace stood and the nearby house where Paolo Borsellino was born. A few days before he was murdered, Borsellino had last spoken publicly in the courtyard of the Casa Professa and it was in this place, charged with such memories, that *Il Ritorno del Principe* was presented. There was, Scarpinato told a packed courtyard, systematic collusion between the Mafia and politics that involves all parties in 'the criminality of power, a system of corrupt and rapacious power'. Italy's dark sickness is the 'criminality of its governing class'.

During the five years that followed Silvio Berlusconi's victory in the election of April 2001, the Mafia's clans were helped by the malevolent attacks that rightwing politicians delivered against the magistracy, in a campaign of vilification and mendacity that delegitimised its work. 'These judges are mad twice over. First, because they are politically that way, and second, because they are mad anyway. To do that that job you need to be mentally disturbed, you need psychic disturbances,' said Berlusconi, then prime minister, to a journalist in 2003. Five years later he returned to the attack. 'Prosecutors should have periodic check-ups on their mental health,' suggested Berlusconi, soon to be prime minister again, unconcerned that such comments undermine the efforts of those whose jobs take them day after day to murder scenes, onto the cheerless streets of southern towns and cities to question witnesses and the victims of extortion, into prisons, and into the courts to tackle the Mafia.

Words damage and so do actions. Legislation and financial restrictions that weaken the magistracy and the justice system, and laws to protect his own interests and those of friends, are features of Berlusconi's time in power. Prime minister again in April 2008, Berlusconi made a priority of introducing stringent limits on the use of telephone taps, despite their value in tackling crime. Travelling through the South, I learnt that justice is understaffed and poorly equipped, and back in Rome Fiorella Pilato, a member of the Consiglio Superiore della Magistratura, the magistracy's governing body, added to the sad picture of the daily struggle that magistrates face. 'The system is unmanageable,' she told me. Deprived of funds, lacking structures and the usual tools that courts need to do their work, Italian justice staggers into a future that looks worse even than its past.

And the problems that courts face are greater in the Mezzogiorno than elsewhere. 'There's little satisfaction for magistrates in those southern, frontier courts where work is delicate, difficult and dangerous,' said Pilato. As head of a commission responsible for transferring and appointing magistrates, she was trying to deal with an avalanche of requests for transfers from southern courts and the reluctance of magistrates to go to them. Many posts, particularly those of investigating and prosecuting magistrate, remained unfilled.

The difficulties concerning investigating and prosecuting magistrates arose from a law passed by Berlusconi's administration and poorly amended by the centre-left government that followed him in 2006. In fact, having made laws that hindered rather than helped the system, the centre-left administrations that governed from 1996 to 2001 carry some of the blame for the shaky state of Italian criminal justice. They increased formal guarantees, compromising the need for justice to be quicker and hitting the rights of the victims of crime, and what they so arrogantly called the *giusto processo* (fair trial) law of 1999 was nothing of the kind. It was a bad law that has done nothing to ensure that trials are fair.

Responding to particularly violent events, when public opinion demanded action, governments have sent the army south. Giuliano Amato's administration despatched thousands of soldiers to take over routine police duties in Sicily after Paolo Borsellino was murdered in 1992; called Operation Vespri Siciliani, it lasted until 1998. And under the orders of institutional and centre-left governments in the mid-1990s, soldiers would also become policemen in Calabria, Puglia and Naples. Then, in September 2008, the Berlusconi government ordered five hundred soldiers to the Casalesi's stronghold soon after the murder of six Africans and an Italian in Castel Volturno. Yet soldiers are more a token than the solution. Beating the Mafia calls for prolonged political commitment, the provision of appropriate resources and profound change in society and culture, but usually Italy's politicians just mouth their opposition to the Mafia and slide shamelessly from the task.

Yet I wonder if matters could be different. After meeting Francesco Rosi I had walked down the Spanish Steps, past the house where the poet John Keats died, across the Piazza di Spagna, past Bernini's *barcaccia* fountain and through Rome's fashion streets to Palazzo Chigi, where the prime minister has his offices. Antonio Ingroia had gone there in November 2002 with colleagues from Palermo to ask Berlusconi questions about his past. Ingroia was prosecuting Marcello Dell'Utri, the prime minister's friend and close associate, on charges of complicity with the Mafia and wanted to question Berlusconi, a witness in the case. A *mafioso* had told the authorities that the Mafia had put money into Berlusconi's business empire, and Ingroia's investigations could not identify the origins of all the capital it received in the late 1970s and first half of the 1980s. The anti-Mafia team was also interested in Berlusconi's employment of Vittorio Mangano, a *mafioso*, at his villa near Milan in the 1970s.

However, the journey to Rome of Ingroia and his colleagues was in vain. Berlusconi had been advised not to answer questions and had availed himself of the right to silence. In other advanced democracies such a refusal to answer magistrates' questions would disqualify a man from public office, but not in Italy. This was an important mafia case. People had a right to know, not just Italians, Italy's European partners too, but Berlusconi stayed silent.

Sentenced to ten years' imprisonment in the 1980s for trafficking in drugs, a further fifteen years for the same crime in 1999, fifteen years for extortion in 2000 and to life in prison for murder three days before he died later that year, Mangano was a major criminal with a lengthy record. This was the *mafioso* whom Dell'Utri called a hero in April 2008, a view with which Berlusconi said that he agreed. Yet three days later he would win elections that would take him back to power. Berlusconi had interesting companions during his ascent in business and his descent into politics. Cesare Previti, a close friend, lawyer and business associate from the mid-1970s, defence minister in his first government, would be found guilty of bribing judges and given a heavy prison sentence.

I strolled through Rome's historic centre, the heart of the Eternal City, past the Palazzo Chigi and Montecitorio, home of parliament's lower house, and then cut left through the Piazza della Rotonda, where the Pantheon stands, to reach Palazzo Madama, the building where the senate meets.

Salvatore Cuffaro sits here, elected for a small centre-right party in April 2008 just two months after the court in Palermo had found him guilty of helping *mafiosi* and sentenced him to five years in jail. And Dell'Utri is a senator also, elected in Forza Italia's party list in 2006 and 2008, although found guilty of complicity with the Mafia. While on trial in Palermo he had stood in elections in May 2001 for the Lombardy I constituency and his seventy thousand votes had easily won the seat. Did those voters care that they were voting for a candidate with mafia ties? Do links with the Mafia count for nothing among wealthy, bourgeois Milanese, citizens of a city once described as Italy's moral capital? Is the Mafia unimportant?

And the senate is, of course, where Giulio Andreotti has sat since 1991, senator for life because he had 'brought honour to his motherland in the social, scientific, artistic and literary fields'. General Carlo Alberto dalla Chiesa, the prefect of Palermo, found something very different during the four months of the summer of 1982 that he was in the Sicilian capital before mafia killers gunned him down, confiding to his diary that Andreotti's faction was 'in it up to the neck'. And the general had written to the prime minister in Rome that Andreotti's faction was 'the most polluted political family in the place'. Brought honour to his motherland?

Why is Andreotti lauded as a statesman, invited to television talk shows and his opinion eagerly sought by journalists? Why is he so admired? Why do politicians hold him in such esteem? I asked Nando dalla Chiesa, the murdered general's son, a professor of economic sociology in Milan who had served two terms in parliament's lower house and one term in the senate.

'It's the moral arrogance of a political caste that admits no blame and has no shame. They want to believe, must believe, that Andreotti committed no crime. They don't want to read the court's judgement, have decided that he is innocent and was acquitted, and nothing more need be said. And they want to forget that they too are responsible.'

And why do parties put up candidates with mafia ties and Italians vote for them? 'Simply because these candidates win votes, and because the Mafia controls votes across the South,' he explained. And what of Milan, the capital of the North, where Dell'Utri was elected? That is a matter of moral decline. 'Milan lost its civic sense many years ago when it became the capital of easy money and lax morality. It's a city that can make no claim to moral leadership,' dalla Chiesa stated bluntly about his home town. Milan is, of course, the city that won the name of *tangentopoli* (bribesville), the place where the huge corruption scandal erupted in 1992.

During August 2007 lengthy investigations by Italy's business newspaper looked closely at the Italian lack of civic sense, the disregard for the public good and the acceptance of broken laws and rules. And at the beginning of 2008, as though *tangentopoli* had never happened, the court of accounts whose job is to check where public money goes, launched a warning that corruption was widely spread. Italy wanders without a moral compass and many Italians are happy at this drift, but with no moral compass the Mafia's evil presence will continue to blot the South.

Nando dalla Chiesa believes that taking a moral stand can win votes, that Italians can acquire a civic sense, that good can be nurtured and spread, that the future is not completely black and that the Mafia can be beaten. But is that so? I had travelled from the farthest part of Sicily to Rome, seen some of the wonders that enrich the South, enjoyed its beauty, its heritage of art and culture, and met many good people who share dalla Chiesa's hopes. I had also touched the reality of the South, felt the fears and concerns, seen the ugliness, read of the violence and the brutal events that impact daily on people's lives, listened while people told me of them, experienced doubts and suspicions, seen how the church and politicians work, and I ask how hope survives.

AUTHOR'S NOTE

FOREIGNERS HAVE LONG MADE JOURNEYS in southern Italy and written about them in books, something of which I was made aware well before embarking on my own journey through the South. One Christmas some years ago, probably during the late 1980s or early 1990s, the Bank of Italy sent me elegantly bound copies of Mendelssohn's *Lettere dall'Italia* and Mommsen's *Viaggio in Italia*, the records of nineteenth-century travellers. And at another Christmas, a splendid edition of Hélène Tuzet's *Viaggiatori stranieri in Sicilia nel XVIII secolo* arrived. The first two books are fascinating personal accounts while Tuzet's work brings together the experiences of mainly French and German travellers and describes what they found in Sicily when they visited.

I always try to find time to browse in bookshops when away from Rome, and I made an even bigger effort to do so during the many weeks that I spent in the South. It was during one such pause, in either Messina or Reggio Calabria, that I bought three books published by Rubbettino, a local publisher, that showed that even Calabria was on the itineraries of northern European travellers two centuries ago and more. Friedrich von Stolberg wrote about his experiences when he was there in 1792 and so did the Frenchman Duret de Tavel, an officer in the Napoleonic army in Calabria between 1807 and 1810.

Not surprisingly, Englishmen were also drawn to the South and Rubbettino recently published a book by a young Calabrese about English travellers in Calabria in the eighteenth and nineteenth century. In the bookshop of the airport in Reggio Calabria I found Edward Lear's diary of his journey on foot around the southern part of Calabria in 1847, published in Italian by Laruffa, a publisher in the city. And in Locri I spoke with a young student who had been involved in anti-Mafia demonstrations, meeting her in the offices of her father's small publishing house. Franco Pancallo Editore had just published, in Italian, Henry Swinburne's *Viaggio in Calabria 1777–1778* and I was grateful to Franco Pancallo for his kind gift of a copy. George Gissing, Norman Douglas and D. H. Lawrence also travelled and wrote about the South. And one day after I had completed my journey, exploring the loft of my parents' house I came across H. V. Morton's *A Traveller in Southern Italy* that my mother had bought in 1976, seven years after it was published.

And there are, of course, many books about Italy, its people and the South. I found the *Breve Storia della Sicilia*, the Italian edition of the work by Moses Finley, Denis Mack Smith and Christopher Duggan, helpful in understanding the island's past, and Duggan's *Concise History of Italy* and Paul Ginsborg's two books *A History of Contemporary Italy: Society and Politics 1943–1988* and *Italy and its Discontents: Family, Civil Society, State 1980–2001* placed the South in a national context. Tommaso Astarita's highly readable book *Between Salt Water and Holy Water: A History of Southern Italy* is an excellent way to begin understanding the South. And so is *Naples '44*, Norman Lewis's diary of his experiences as an intelligence officer with the Allied forces in Naples. Carlo Levi's *Christ Stopped at Eboli* had been on my bookshelves for many years and I have enjoyed returning to it. *Fields of Fire: A Life of Sir William Hamilton* by David Constantine was another of the works that I read before, during and after travelling in the South.

However, learning and writing about the Mafia were the reasons that I travelled through the South and I found some excellent books in English on the subject, beginning with Norman Lewis's *The Honoured Society* of 1964. Claire Sterling's *The Mafia*, published in 1990, Alexander Stille's *Excellent Cadavers* (1995), Peter Robb's *Midnight in Sicily* (1996), Clare Longrigg's *Mafia Women* (1997), and John Dickie's *Cosa Nostra* (2004), are all informative and good to read, and I particularly enjoyed the works of Robb and Dickie which, like the others, focus on Sicily. Sterling's book also deals at length with Cosa Nostra in America.

There is no shortage of books in Italian on the Mafia and, like those in English, they are mostly about Sicily and its Mafia. Three books were published on Provenzano within two years of his capture, for example. The first was about the search for Italy's most wanted man, with a blow-by-blow account of his capture, while the second looked at how the *capo dei capi* communicated with the rest of the organisation and the third at the network of cover and political complicity that had allowed Provenzano to stay free.

There are numerous books about Giovanni Falcone, Paolo Borsellino and their killers and about the maxi-trial in the 1980s. And there are books about politics, business and the Mafia, the church and the Mafia, health services and the Mafia, and about the *lotta contadina*, the agricultural workers' struggle for land reform. A browser among the shelves of bookshops in Palermo finds plenty of books on the Mafia, but perhaps the place to start is *La Sicilia nel 1876*, the report of the famous investigation by Leopoldo Franchetti and Sidney Sonnino.

While I found some books on the Camorra, they were many fewer than those on Cosa Nostra, although Roberto Saviano's splendidly vivid and violent *Gomorra* has probably sold more copies than all the books on Cosa Nostra put together. Even fewer are books dealing with the 'Ndrangheta, while the Apulian Mafia, as far as I could see, has yet to attract writers.

Books were, however, only a part of the source material that served me in reporting my journey through the South. In every region through which I travelled I bought the local newspapers and found them a rich source of information. And like the English writers on the Mafia, and Italians, I also acquired and have used various court documents, judgements, arrest warrants and seizure orders. But I relied heavily on meeting people, asking questions and writing down their answers, filling fifteen hundred-page notebooks in the process. I also taped several hours of interviews and transcribed them. Memory was jogged by referring to the hundreds of photographs that I took using a small digital camera, a device that has largely done away with the need to jot down observations.

Work commitments and the impossibility of arranging meetings one after the other meant that I undertook my journey in steps rather than continuously. It would have been too much to have expected the various bishops, prosecutors, businessmen, mayors, trade unionists and other people with whom I spoke to have been available precisely when I was in their town or city. And, of course, I had other matters to research and write about while doing the legwork for the book. However, my journey through the South was as I have told it, beginning in Gela, on Sicily's southern coast, and ending at Teano, between Naples and Rome. It began in the autumn of 2005 when I met Rosario Crocetta, Gela's mayor, and ended in the spring of 2008 with the stop I made at the memorial that marks Garibaldi's meeting with King Victor Emmanuel.

I owe thanks to the many people who gave me their time while I was travelling through the South, who are mostly mentioned in the book. And far from the Mezzogiorno, I was greatly helped by Peter Carson at Profile Books, who pointed me in the right direction by suggesting that I should write a personal account rather than a journalist's report, although he was unable to divert me to Sardinia which, as I told him, was a kingdom ruled from Turin by the House of Savoy. I would like to thank my friend David Walker who, hearing of my journey through southern Italy, recalled how much he had enjoyed working at the Teatro Massimo in Palermo and suggested that I should read John Berendt's *The City of Fallen Angels*. I am very grateful to Anne Engel, my agent, for her encouragement and close attention to what I wrote, and to my barrister brother, Michael, who also read the typescript, making helpful legal points and telling me that my choice of words sometimes betrayed the years I have lived in Italy.

I have returned to various places about which I have written and in some I found changes, sometimes for the better. The hotel where I stayed in Gela has been renovated, for example, and presents a far nicer face than it did before. And throughout the South the fight against the Mafia has led to numerous arrests, including the capture of leading mafia bosses and increasing resistance by businessmen to extortion. Whether this progress will be maintained remains to be seen. Certainly, late one evening in July 2008 when I sat in the piazza outside the Focacceria San Francesco in Palermo, a restaurant guarded twenty-four hours a day by carabinieri because its owner refused to pay dues to Cosa Nostra, the magistrates Gian Carlo Caselli on my right, Roberto Scarpinato beyond him and Gioacchino Natoli across the table, a platoon of their armed bodyguards manning the piazza, I was reminded yet again of the Mafia's terrible threat and the abnormality of life in southern Italy.

INDEX